Supplement to volume 48 (2018) of the
Proceedings of the Seminar for Arabian Studies

Languages, scripts and their uses in ancient North Arabia

Papers from the Special Session of the Seminar for Arabian Studies held on 5 August 2017

edited by
M.C.A. Macdonald

Seminar for Arabian Studies

Archaeopress
Oxford

2018

This Supplement is available with volume 48 of the *Proceedings of the Seminar for Arabian Studies* and orders should be sent to
Archaeopress Publishing Ltd, Summertown Pavilion, 18–24 Middle Way, Oxford OX2 7LG, UK.
Tel +44(0)1865-311914 Fax +44(0)1865-512231
e-mail info@archaeopress.com
http://www.archaeopress.com
For the availability of back issues see The British Foundation for the Study of Arabia's website:
http://www.thebfsa.org/content/seminar-proceedings

Seminar for Arabian Studies
c/o the Department of the Middle East, The British Museum
London, WC1B 3DG, United Kingdom
e-mail psas@thebfsa.org
The British Foundation for the Study of Arabia: www.thebfsa.org

The Steering Committee of the Seminar for Arabian Studies is currently made up of twelve academic members. The Editorial Committee of the *Proceedings of the Seminar for Arabian Studies* includes eight additional members as follows:

STEERING COMMITTEE

Dr Derek Kennet (Chair)
Dr Robert Wilson (Treasurer)
Dr Janet Starkey (Editor of PSAS)
Dr Tim Power (Assistant Editor)
Dr Julian Jansen van Rensburg (Assistant Editor)
Dr Harry Munt (Assistant Editor)
Prof. Rob Carter
Dr Nadia Durrani
Dr Orhan Elmaz
Mr Michael C.A. Macdonald
Dr St John Simpson
Dr Lucy Wadeson

EDITORIAL COMMITTEE: ADDITIONAL MEMBERS

Professor Alessandra Avanzini
Professor Soumyen Bandyopadhyay
Dr Ricardo Eichmann
Professor Clive Holes
Professor Khalil Al-Muaikel
Professor Daniel T. Potts
Professor Christian J. Robin
Professor Lloyd Weeks

Opinions expressed in papers published in the *Supplement* are those of the authors and are not necessarily shared by the Editorial Committee.

The *Supplement* is produced in the Times Semitic New font, which was designed by Paul Bibire for the Seminar for Arabian Studies.

© 2018 Archaeopress Publishing, Oxford, UK.
All rights reserved. No part of this publication may be reproduced, stored in a retrieval system, or transmitted, in any form or by any means, electronic, mechanical, photocopying, recording, or otherwise, without the prior permission of the publisher.
ISSN 0308-8421
ISBN 978-1-78491-899-6
ISBN 978-1-78491-900-9 (e-pdf)

The Steering Committee of the Seminar for Arabian Studies is most grateful to the
MBI Al Jaber Foundation
for its continued generosity in making a substantial grant towards the running costs of the Seminar and the editorial expenses of producing the *Proceedings*.

Contents

Guidelines and Transliteration i

Introduction iii
Michael C.A. Macdonald

The use of languages and scripts in settled areas

Towards a re-assessment of the Ancient North Arabian alphabets used in the oasis of al-ʿUlā 1
Michael C.A. Macdonald

Scribal practices in contact: two Minaic/Dadanitic mixed texts 21
Fokelien Kootstra

'Literacy in literate societies': the scribe in Nabataean and other Aramaic contexts 31
John F. Healey

The role of Aramaic on the Arabian Peninsula in the second half of the first millennium BC 39
Peter Stein

The use of languages and scripts among nomads

New research on the 'Thamudic' graffiti from the region of Ḥimā (Najrān, Saudi Arabia) 53
Alessia Prioletta with a note by Christian J. Robin

A survey of the Ancient North Arabian inscriptions from the Dūmat al-Jandal area (Saudi Arabia) 71
Jérôme Norris

A preliminary investigation of an Ancient North Arabian invocation from the Madaba region of central Jordan 95
Hani Hayajneh

Understanding Safaitic inscriptions in their topographical context 101
Ali Al-Manaser

The earliest attestation of *laysa* and the implications for its etymology 111
Ahmad Al-Jallad

Papers read at the Special Session 121

Guidelines and Transliteration

Guidelines for Authors

For details on the submission of papers and the preparation of papers for publication, authors are requested to consult and follow the latest *Guidelines for Authors.* These are available on the British Foundation for the Study of Arabia website at www.thebfsa.org/content/psas-guidelines. Please contact the editors on PSAS@thebfsa.org for further information.

Fonts

Electronic versions of papers being submitted for publication should be submitted in Times Semitic New 12-point font if at all possible, with double-line spacing on A4-paper size and 2.45 cm margins all round. This free font set along with the recommended Greek font set, called TimesClassicGreek (tmsrr_1.ttf), can be downloaded as a zip file from the BFSA/Seminar website at www.thebfsa.org/publications/psas-guidelines/.

The BFSA System of Transliteration of Relevant Characters

Quotations, single words, and phrases from Arabic or other languages written in non-Roman alphabets, are transliterated according to the systems set out below.

We firmly encourage authors to use the correctly transliterated form of any place name, but the names used for types of pottery, archaeological periods, and cultures which have become archaeological standards should be used in that form: Umm an-Nar, Julfar ware, etc. If any place name needs to be given in a non-standard format, the correctly transliterated form should be added in the first instance in any paper (see *Guidelines for Authors* for more details).

Personal names, toponyms, and other words that have entered English or French in a particular form, should be used in that form when they occur in an English or French sentence, unless they are part of a quotation in the original language, or of a correctly transliterated name or phrase. In the latter cases, they should be correctly transliterated, even when they occur in an English or French sentence.

1. Arabic

ء	ʾ	ج	j	ذ	dh (<u>dh</u>)	ش	sh (<u>sh</u>)	ظ	ẓ	ق	q	ن	n
ب	b	ح	ḥ	ر	r	ص	ṣ	ع	ʿ	ك	k	ه	h
ت	t	خ	kh (<u>kh</u>)	ز	z	ض	ḍ	غ	gh (<u>gh</u>)	ل	l	و	w
ث	th (<u>th</u>)	د	d	س	s	ط	ṭ	ف	f	م	m	ي	y
Vowels		a i u ā ī ū		Diphthongs		aw	ay						

The underlined variants can be used to avoid any ambiguity, e.g. *lam yu<u>sh</u>ir* vs. *lam yushir.*
Initial *hamzah* is omitted.
Alif maqṣūrah is transliterated as *ā*.
The *lām* of the article is not assimilated before the ‘sun letters’, thus the form should be *al-shams* not *ash-shams*.
The *hamzat al-waṣl* of the article should be shown after vowels except after the preposition *li-*, as in the Arabic script, e.g. *wa-ʾl-wazīr*, *fī ʾl-bayt*, but *li-l-wazīr*.
Tāʾ marbūṭah (ة) should be rendered *-ah*, except in a construct: e.g. *birkah*, *zakāh*, and *birkat al-sibāḥah*, *zakāt al-fiṭr*.

2. Persian, Urdu, and Ottoman Turkish

Please transliterate these languages using the system set out for Arabic above with the additional letters transliterated according to the system in the *Encyclopaedia of Islam* (http://referenceworks.brillonline.com/entries/encyclopaedia-islamica/system-of-transliteration-of-arabic-and-persian-characters-transliteration) except that *ž* is used instead of *zh*. There is a useful table to convert Ottoman Turkish to modern Turkish characters on http://en.wikipedia.org/wiki/Ottoman_Turkish_language.

3. Ancient North and South Arabian consonants

ʾ	b	t	ṯ	g	ḥ	ḫ	d	ḏ	r	z	s^1	s^2	s^3	ṣ
ḍ	ṭ	ẓ	ʿ	ġ	f	q	k	l	m	n	h	w	y	

4. Other Semitic languages

Please use the transliteration systems outlined in the *Bulletin of the American Schools of Oriental Research* (BASOR) 262 (1986), p. 3. (www.jstor.org/stable/i258780).

M.C.A. Macdonald (ed.), *Languages, scripts and their uses in ancient North Arabia.* (Supplement to volume 48 of the Proceedings of the Seminar for Arabian Studies). Oxford: Archaeopress, 2018: iii–vi

Introduction

Michael C.A. Macdonald

Most of the papers published in this volume were presented at a Special Session of the fifty-first Seminar for Arabian Studies held at the British Museum on 5 August 2017. Its subject was 'Languages, scripts, and their uses in ancient North Arabia' and it was held to celebrate the completion in the previous March of Phase 2 of the 'Online Corpus of the Inscriptions of Ancient North Arabia' (OCIANA).

This was a project funded by the United Kingdom's Arts and Humanities Research Council and based at the Khalili Research Centre, University of Oxford. Its aim was to create a freely accessible online database of all the inscriptions from ancient Arabia north of Yemen, with up-to-date readings and translations, *apparatus criticus*, commentaries where necessary, as well as all available accurate information on provenance and context and, whenever possible, good photographs. In Phase 2 all the Safaitic, Hismaic, Dadanitic, Taymanitic, and Hasaitic inscriptions known at the time were entered (some 40,000), though inevitably more have been found since and will be added in Phase 3 when the so-called 'Thamudic' inscriptions and other corpora will also be entered. The database is accessible online and each corpus (Safaitic, Dadanitic, etc.) can be downloaded as a pdf at http://krc.orient.ox.ac.uk/ociana/index.php.

A list of the papers presented at the Special Session can be found at the end of this volume. In most cases, the paper published here is a more complete and detailed version of the one given at the Seminar. Three of the authors — Laïla Nehmé, Chiara della Puppa, and Sulayman Al-Theeb — decided not to submit their papers for publication. While I obviously regret this, I entirely understand the reasons why each of them came to this decision. In addition, Ahmad Al-Jallad decided to submit a different paper, and Christian Robin contributed a note to Alessia Prioletta's rather than his full paper.

The first paper in this volume was not given at the Special Session but was written by me some years ago and, though not published, was distributed widely in manuscript. This volume seemed an ideal place to present an updated version of it and — using editor's privilege! — I have therefore included it.

After the final paper of the Special Session Laïla Nehmé and Ahmad Al-Jallad presented me with a *Festschrift* which they had edited to celebrate my seventieth birthday (Nehmé & Al-Jallad 2018). It contains thirty-two fascinating articles on a wide range of subjects dear to my heart. The thought-provoking new material, analyses, and discussions will ensure that my old age will be anything but restful! I am extremely grateful to all those who contributed to it and especially to my very dear friends and colleagues Laïla Nehmé and Ahmad Al-Jallad, who had the idea of the *Festschrift* in the first place and who took on the enormous task of editing the volume.

Finally, I would like to thank the British Foundation for the Study of Arabia, the Seminar for Arabian Studies, the Khalili Research Centre University of Oxford, and the Seven Pillars of Wisdom Trust, for their generous grants without which the Special Session and this volume would not have been possible.

* * *

By now it is widely known that between at least the mid-first millennium BC and the fourth (?) century AD, literacy was widespread among the populations of North Arabia. A surprisingly large number of different scripts was used to express several languages and dialects, many of which are very imperfectly known.[1] The majority of the scripts belonged to the 'South Semitic script family' which also includes Ancient South Arabian (ASA) and the scripts used by some of the Ethiopic languages such as Gəʿəz and Amharic. In antiquity, the South Semitic script family was used only in Arabia and its immediate environs, but within this area large numbers of people, both settled and nomadic, used the scripts derived from it to carve graffiti.[2]

Until recently the term 'Ancient North Arabian' (ANA), which in fact describes a number of related scripts, was extended to describe the *languages* which

[1] This is particularly true of those found in the Thamudic B, C, and D inscriptions, which are generally very short, and also of the newly deciphered Himaitic texts, on which see Prioletta (this volume).

[2] See e.g. Macdonald 2010 for an overview, as well as the individual papers in this volume.

they expressed and which were also assumed to be related (e.g. Macdonald 2004). In the past five years, however, Ahmad Al-Jallad and Fokelien Kootstra have effectively shown that this is not so. Thanks to their work we now know that the language of the Safaitic inscriptions is predominantly Old Arabic (Al-Jallad 2015: 10–14), while that of the Taymanitic inscriptions is more closely related to the North-West Semitic languages than to Arabic (Kootstra 2016: 104–107). Kootstra's continuing work on Dadanitic may well show that it belongs to neither group, but we must wait for the completion of her PhD thesis for more information on this.

In addition to those writing in ANA scripts, Dadan (modern al-ᶜUlā) hosted a trading (?) colony of Minaeans. Kootstra's paper in this volume is the first step in a process of minute and careful analysis, which reveals previously unrecognized links between the scribal practices of the Minaean and the Dadanite communities — something which might be expected but has so far never been demonstrated. It should be read together with Irene Rossi's careful analysis of the differences between the language and orthography of these 'Marginal Minaic' inscriptions and those from the Minaean homeland (2014: 113–115).

Staying in Dadan, I hope that my contribution to this volume will dispel some long-established misconceptions about the palaeography of the Dadanitic inscriptions and provide a more secure basis for their study, even if this means accepting that there are things that we do not — and in some cases cannot — know.

Two papers reveal new Ancient North Arabian scripts. Jérôme Norris's excellent study of the graffiti in an area near Dūmat al-Jandal (al-Jawf) has not only increased the number of 'Dumaitic' inscriptions from three to twenty-three but has identified and analysed a large number of texts in other, previously unrecognized, ANA scripts. His paper presents a fascinating picture of this relatively small area where — either simultaneously or consecutively — individuals using a number of different script traditions lived, or passed through, leaving their mark.

Alessia Prioletta's paper reports on Christian Robin's decipherment of the graffiti in the area of Ḥimā, near Najrān (southern Saudi Arabia) and describes in detail these 'Himaitic' inscriptions which were previously known as 'Southern Thamudic'.[3] Although they had been known since 1951 and the script had been recognized as ANA it had not been completely deciphered and had therefore been placed in the 'Thamudic pending file' (Macdonald 2000: 44). This paper, along with Norris's, has enormously extended our knowledge of the Ancient North Arabian scripts in both the north and south of the Peninsula.

Two other papers, by Ali Al-Manaser and Hani Hayajneh, deal with graffiti in the better-known ANA scripts of the desert, Safaitic and Hismaic respectively. This is also a field in which many new discoveries are being made, thanks to massive new surveys recording thousands of previously unknown inscriptions,[4] and minute analyses of the texts such as those by Ahmad Al-Jallad (2014; 2015; 2016; Al-Jallad & Jaworska, forthcoming) and Chiara della Puppa. It is a pity that the latter's paper could not be published in this volume (it forms part of her doctoral thesis) since it impressed many of the participants at the Special Session and is cited in several of the papers here. Ahmad Al-Jallad, in a change of subject from his paper at the Session, has recognized the first occurrence in a Safaitic inscription of the Arabic verb *laysa* and has contributed a detailed and very interesting study on its origins.

In addition to local scripts of the South Semitic script family, it is increasingly recognized that the Aramaic script was widely used in various forms and at different periods, in oases such as Taymāᵓ and in the Gulf. Old Aramaic inscriptions have been found in Dadan[5] and on the Darb al-Bakra[6] while formal texts and graffiti in Imperial (Official) Aramaic have been found in and around Taymāᵓ and in Bahrain and the Oman peninsula. Peter Stein has contributed an excellent study of the Aramaic used in these areas, why it came to be used, and its relationship with the local languages and scripts.

We now know that when the Lihyanites occupied Taymāᵓ they used Imperial Aramaic rather than Dadanitic presumably because Aramaic was an 'international' language and was already in common use at Taymāᵓ, not only for formal inscriptions but for tombstones carved by

[3] Unfortunately, Christian Robin was unable to attend the Special Session and his paper was read on his behalf by Alessia Prioletta. Together they decided that, rather than submit for publication two papers on a very similar subject, Robin would add a note to Prioletta's paper.

[4] These are the Badia Surveys of 2015, 2017, and 2018 undertaken on the initiative of, and in 2017 and 2018 led by, Ali Al-Manaser, which are systematically recording inscriptions in the basalt desert (*ḥarrah*) of north-eastern Jordan. Approximately 10,000 inscriptions have been recorded so far, each with its precise GPS co-ordinates and they will be published in Phase 3 of OCIANA.

[5] These are as yet unpublished and I thank Prof. Sulayman Al-Dhiyīb (Al-Theeb) for showing me photographs of them.

[6] From the route between Madāᵓin Ṣāliḥ and Petra, discovered by Prof. Ali Al-Ghabbān and published in Macdonald (in press, a).

amateurs (rather than scribes) and for graffiti.[7] Indeed, in the environs of Taymāʾ, we have graffiti by two kings of Liḥyān in a local development of Imperial Aramaic.[8] Presumably, after the Achaemenid Empire ceased to maintain scribal schools in Arabia, a number of local derivatives of Imperial Aramaic developed, of which we have examples in Taymāʾ and in the Gulf (see Stein, this volume). Eventually, towards the end of the first century BC, the Nabataeans conquered north-west Arabia bringing with them their own local development of the script which replaced the local Arabian versions in the area. John Healey's study of scribes in 'literate societies' such as Nabataea is a very interesting exploration of societies in which reading and writing are essential to their functioning, but in which large numbers of the population may not be literate.

After a couple of centuries of Roman rule, and especially after the southern border of *Provincia Arabia* was moved much further north under Diocletian, north-west Arabia was more or less left to its own devices. Greek had not penetrated this area to anything like the same extent as it did in what is now Jordan and southern Syria. Arabic remained a purely spoken language and Aramaic remained the dominant written language and script. Gradually, the knowledge of the Aramaic language seems to have declined, apart from a few stock phrases, and it seems that the Nabataean script came to be used to write Arabic, particularly on portable materials (which, alas, have not survived). We know this because a script develops through its use in ink on portable materials, and therefore the changes in the script that we see in graffiti on stone are simply snapshots of a development which was continuing on papyrus, parchment, or potsherds.[9] This is how the Nabataean script developed into what *we* think of as the 'Arabic script'.[10] Laïla Nehmé concluded the Special Session with a fascinating paper on this subject, which unfortunately she did not have time to prepare for publication here, but I look forward to its publication elsewhere in due course.

I hope that the reader will find in this volume a picture of the latest research on the languages, scripts, and their uses in ancient North Arabia. It has been a pleasure editing it and I have learned a great deal from all the papers. I would like to thank all the authors for their contributions, Helen Knox for her meticulous copy-editing, Rajka Makjanic for her page setting, and all at Archaeopress for producing such a beautiful volume.

Michael C.A. Macdonald
Wolfson College
Oxford
30 April 2018.

[7] See Macdonald (in press, b) and Macdonald & Al-Najem (in press).

[8] These are *šhrw* in Al-Theeb 2014: 34 and *Msʿwdw* in Jaussen & Savignac 1909–1922, ii Nabataean 334, 335, 337 and a fourth text recently discovered by the Epigraphy and Landscape in the Hinterland of Taymāʾ project. For many years there has been uncertainty as to whether *Msʿwdw* really was a king of Liḥyān, or simply a claimant or imposter, since no inscriptions dated to his reign had been found. This uncertainty has now been resolved with the discovery in Taymāʾ of a dedication in the local Aramaic script of the oasis dated to year three of 'Msʿwdw king of Liḥyān' (TM.TAr.004, Taymāʾ Museum registration number 488, see Macdonald & Al-Najem, in press).

[9] See Macdonald 2010: 21; 2015: 13–14.

[10] On this process see the numerous works by L. Nehmé who has made a profound study of this development; e.g. Nehmé 2010; Avner, Nehmé, & Robin 2013; Nehmé 2017.

References

Avner U., Nehmé L. & Robin C.J. 2013. A rock inscription mentioning Thaʿalaba, an Arab king from Ghassan. *Arabian Epigraphic Notes* 24: 237–256.

Al-Jallad A. 2014. An ancient Arabian Zodiac. The constellations in the Safaitic inscriptions, Part I. *Arabian Archaeology and Epigraphy* 25: 214–230.

Al-Jallad A. 2015. *An outline of the grammar of the Safaitic inscriptions.* (Studies in Semitic Languages and Linguistics, 80). Leiden: Brill.

Al-Jallad A. 2016. An ancient Arabian Zodiac. The constellations in the Safaitic inscriptions, Part II. *Arabian Archaeology and Epigraphy* 27: 84–106.

Al-Jallad A. & Jaworska K. (forthcoming). *A dictionary and grammar of the Safaitic inscriptions*. (2 volumes).

Jaussen A. & Savignac M.R. 1909–1922. *Mission archéologique en Arabie*. (5 volumes). Paris: Leroux/Geuthner.

Kootstra F. 2016. The language of the Taymanitic inscriptions and its classification. *Arabian Epigraphic Notes* 2: 67–140.

Macdonald M.C.A. 2000. Reflections on the linguistic map of pre-Islamic Arabia. *Arabian Archaeology and Epigraphy* 11: 28–79. [Reprinted with addenda and corrigenda as article III in M.C.A. Macdonald, *Literacy and identity in pre-Islamic Arabia*. (Variorum Collected Studies, CS906). Farnham: Ashgate, 2009.

Macdonald M.C.A. 2004. Ancient North Arabian. Pages 488–533 in R. Woodard (ed.), *The Cambridge encylopedia of the world's ancient languages.* Cambridge: Cambridge University Press.

Macdonald M.C.A. 2010. Ancient Arabia and the written word. Pages 5–28 in M.C.A. Macdonald (ed.), *The development of Arabic as a written language*. (Supplement to the Proceedings of the Seminar for Arabian Studies, 40). Oxford: Archaeopress.

Macdonald M.C.A. 2015. On the uses of writing in ancient Arabia and the role of palaeography in studying them. *Arabian Epigraphic Notes* 1: 1–50.

Macdonald M.C.A. (in press, a). The Ancient North and South Arabian inscriptions on the Darb al-Bakra. In L. Nehmé (ed.), *Darb al-Bakra, the ancient route between Ḥegrā and Petra*. Riyadh: Saudi Commission for Tourism and National Heritage.

Macdonald M.C.A. (in press, b). *Catalogue of the inscriptions discovered in the Saudi-German excavations at Taymāʾ 2004–2015*. With contributions by A. Hausleiter, F. Imbert, H. Schaudig, P. Stein & F. Tourtet. (*Taymāʾ II*). Oxford: Archaeopress.

Macdonald M.C.A. & Al-Najem M. (in press). *Catalogue of the inscriptions in the Taymāʾ Museum*. With contributions by F. Imbert & P. Stein. (*Taymāʾ III*). Oxford: Archaeopress.

Nehmé L. 2010. A glimpse of the development of the Nabataean script into Arabic based on old and new epigraphic material. Pages 47–88 in M.C.A. Macdonald (ed.), *The development of Arabic as a written language*. (Supplement to the Proceedings of the Seminar for Arabian Studies, 40). Oxford: Archaeopress.

Nehmé L. 2017. New dated inscriptions (Nabataean and pre-Islamic Arabic) from a site near al-Jawf, ancient Dūmah, Saudi Arabia. *Arabian Epigraphic Notes* 3: 121–164.

Nehmé L. & Al-Jallad A. (eds). 2018. *To the Madbar and back again: Studies in the languages, archaeology, and cultures of Arabia dedicated to Michael C.A. Macdonald*. (Studies in Semitic Languages and Linguistics, 92). Leiden: Brill.

Prioletta A. (this volume). New research on the 'Thamudic' graffiti from the region of Ḥimā (Najrān, Saudi Arabia). With a note by Christian Robin. Pages 53–69 in M.C.A. Macdonald (ed.), *Languages, scripts, and their uses in ancient North Arabia*. (Supplement to volume 48 of the Proceedings of the Seminar for Arabian Studies). Oxford: Archaeopress, 2018.

Rossi I. 2014. The Minaeans beyond Maᶜīn. Pages 111–124 in O. Elmaz & J.C.E. Watson (eds), *Languages of southern Arabia*. (Supplement to the Proceedings of the Seminar for Arabian Studies, 44). Oxford: Archaeopress.

Stein P. (this volume). The role of Aramaic on the Arabian Peninsula in the second half of the first millennium BC. Pages 39–49 in M.C.A. Macdonald (ed.), *Languages, scripts, and their uses in ancient North Arabia*. (Supplement to volume 48 of the Proceedings of the Seminar for Arabian Studies). Oxford: Archaeopress, 2018.

Al-Theeb [Al-Dhiyīb] 2014. *Nuqūš mawqiᶜ Sarmadāʾ muḥāfaẓāt Taymāʾ*. (Silsilah ᶜilmiyah maḥkūmah taṣaddara-ha al-jamīᶜah al-saᶜūdiyyah li-l-dirāsāt al-athāriyah, 12). Riyadh: Jamiᶜat al-malik Saᶜūd.

The use of languages and scripts in settled areas

M.C.A. Macdonald (ed.), *Languages, scripts and their uses in ancient North Arabia.* (Supplement to volume 48 of the Proceedings of the Seminar for Arabian Studies). Oxford: Archaeopress, 2018: 1–19

Towards a re-assessment of the Ancient North Arabian alphabets used in the oasis of al-ᶜUlā

MICHAEL C.A. MACDONALD

Summary*

It has so far proved impossible to assign absolute dates to any of the pre-Islamic monuments in the oasis of al-ᶜUlā. Frustration at this has driven some scholars to try to establish a sequence of letter forms in the inscriptions as a means of dating. This enterprise was doomed to failure, however, since such a sequence could be no more than subjective and hypothetical if it was not itself based on dated documents. This paper tries to clear up some of the misconceptions which have plagued the subject for decades, and concentrates on research questions which the material, as it exists at present, *is* capable of answering, leaving the problem of chronology until archaeological and historical research in the oasis has provided sufficient dating evidence.

Keywords: Dadanitic script, palaeography, inscriptions, graffiti, chronology

The large oasis of al-ᶜUlā, in north-west Arabia, contains the site of ancient Dadan[1] and much else besides. It sits on one of the principal south–north trade routes of western Arabia, dominating both the shortest route from Yemen to Gaza and a relatively easy descent from the escarpment to the Red Sea, and thence to the north-east coast of Egypt (see Macdonald 1997: 334). It must have been a prosperous and cosmopolitan trading centre, and was the seat of the kingdoms of Dadan and of Liḥyān, as well as a Minaean 'colony' and possibly other polities at present unknown.

Although teams from King Saᶜūd University, Riyadh have been conducting excavations at the site of Khuraybah in al-ᶜUlā since 2003 (see e.g. Al-Saᶜīd 2011; Al-Saᶜīd & Al-Ghazī 1434–1435/2013–2014; Al-Theeb 2013; Al-Theeb et al. 2016), unfortunately so far no absolute chronology for the site has been established, let alone for the large number of inscriptions from outside the site or originating from the site but found in secondary contexts, which have been published since the 1880s. As a result, there are as yet no firmly established dates for the kingdoms of Dadan and Liḥyān or for any of their monuments.[2] It has even proved impossible to establish a *relative* chronology based on firm evidence for the history of the oasis, let alone to tie the texts and monuments into an absolute sequence. Although several of the inscriptions include dates according to the regnal years of kings of Liḥyān and other local rulers, not a single one can be securely dated in absolute terms, and all attempts to construct even a relative sequence of kings have been founded on a misuse of palaeographical method[3] and theories — usually presented as fact — based on layer upon layer of unprovable assumptions.

In desperation at the lack of dating evidence, some scholars, notably Winnett and Caskel, have turned palaeographical methodology inside out and tried to establish a relative chronology based solely on letter forms extracted from inscriptions *which are themselves entirely undated*. They and others then tried to tie these imaginary sequences into an absolute chronology by relying on some extremely dubious historical assumptions (see below).

* I first wrote this article in 2005 but for various reasons did not publish it at that time, although it has since circulated fairly widely in manuscript. Given the subject of this Supplement, it seemed a suitable place to present an updated version of it, even though it was not read at the Special Session.

[1] For this transliteration of what is almost certainly the original form of the name, instead of the traditional 'Dedan' which was taken over from the *Dədān* of the Hebrew Bible, see Sima 2000 and Macdonald 2000: 63, n. 1. For the reasons why I have reclassified as 'Dadanitic' the scripts formerly known as 'Dedanite' and 'Lihyanite', see Macdonald 2000: 33.

[2] However, for recent attempts to establish at least a rough absolute chronology for the kingdoms of Dadan and Liḥyān, reviewing all the available evidence, see Rohmer & Charloux 2015: 299–311; and Rohmer (forthcoming).

[3] Following Caskel, see most recently Farès-Drappeau 2003; 2005: 116–126. For my comments on Pirenne's much more sophisticated, but still ultimately flawed, attempt to do the same thing for the South Arabian script, see Macdonald 2015: 24–26.

An example of this is Kitchen's attempt to produce a chronology of the kings of Liḥyān (1994: 44–54, 57). He started by taking Winnett's 'palaeographical' chronology (on which see below) as a basis for creating an imaginary sequence of the kings. He then builds assumption upon assumption, making arbitrary (and all too common) identifications of individuals found in texts in widely separated places, on the basis of a single (rather common) name,[4] and assigning reigns of at least sixteen years to each king of Liḥyān on the basis that this is the average reign-length of kings in Egypt and Mesopotamia. I cannot see how this is supposed to help scholars working on pre-Islamic Arabia. We are in desperate need of *facts*, not a false sense of chronological security based on nothing more than imperfectly informed speculation. This recognition is extremely inconvenient for historians, but it seems to me better to accept our present ignorance and wait until more information becomes available than to base further study on a confection of assumptions, for which there is simply no firm evidence.[5]

This lack of a secure chronological sequence and the desire to establish one, have badly distorted the way the scripts used in the oasis have been studied. In the past, the aim of such studies has almost always been to produce a tool for dating, and in the pursuit of this elusive and illusory objective, it was quickly forgotten that palaeography is not a substitute for dating evidence but is itself dependent on it. In discussions elsewhere (Macdonald 2015: 17–18), I have drawn attention to the fact — all too often forgotten in Semitic epigraphy — that a true sequence of letter forms can only be created when one form is known, from non-palaeographical evidence, to be earlier or later than another. Moreover, for comparisons between letter forms to be valid they need to have been created in as near as possible the same conditions, that is, they should have been produced with and on similar materials and should have come from the same calligraphic tradition (as in a monastic or chancellery scriptorium), in order to eliminate, as far as possible, extraneous and ephemeral reasons for the differences. What Pirenne called 'la paléographie comparée' (1956: 91), which extracts and compares letter forms from documents on different materials, produced in different periods and often in widely separated places, can only produce confusion or, even worse, an illusion of knowledge (on this see Macdonald 2015: 18–22).

If one has a mass of undated inscriptions, even from the same site, any sequence of letter forms one creates can only be hypothetical and based on subjective assumptions about how letter forms develop. This is a perilous pursuit. There are numerous examples of shapes which, after a long and varied development, end up looking remarkably similar to their own supposed remote 'ancestor' or the 'ancestor' of another letter.[6] Even when evidence exists that letter form A in one particular context is older than letter form B in a different context, this does not permit us to say that B *must* have developed from A, or that all examples of A must be older than all examples of B. Unless one is dealing with the limited output of a strictly controlled scriptorium, there are far too many variables involved for such judgements to be of any value.

Dating is only one — relatively minor — function of palaeographical analysis. Yet, in Near Eastern studies in general, and in Arabia in particular, it has for far too long dominated the way we look at writing. The study of the letter forms in the inscriptions from al-ᶜUlā provides a particularly blatant example of this.

It is to F.V. Winnett's great credit that he was the first to recognize the difference in the inscriptions from al-ᶜUlā between (i) the *m* which was closed at the base; (ii) the *m*

[4] See e.g. the identification of *gs*^{2}*m bn s*^{2}*hr* in JSLih 349 with 'Geshem/Gashmū the Arab' in Nehemiah 2: 19; 6: 1, 2, 6 (Winnett 1937: 51; Albright 1953: 4) as well as with the father of *Qynw br Gšm* king of Qēdār in the inscription on one of the bowls from Tell al-Maskhūṭah (Rabinowitz 1956: 6), identifications maintained by Graf (1990: 139–140, and Kitchen 1994: 49–50), even though Winnett had described them as 'a moot question' twenty years before (Winnett & Reed 1970: 116–117). All this purely on the basis of the name *gs*^{2}*m/gešem/gašmū/gšm*, despite the long distance between Dadan and Jerusalem, the complete lack of evidence for a connection between Qēdār and Dadan, the uncertain date of the inscriptions, and the fact that *gs*^{2}*m* was an extremely common name in ancient north Arabia (in OCIANA, consulted 19 March 2018, there were 76 examples in Safaitic, 19 in Hismaic, 4 in Dadanitic); see Rohmer (forthcoming).

[5] For an excellent antidote to this see Rohmer & Charloux's very careful analysis of what we know and what we cannot know and the picture which they present *as a hypothesis* (2015), and Rohmer (forthcoming).

[6] To cite only a handful of examples: the form of Safaitic *alif* is closer to the early Phoenician *alep* than is any other form of this letter in the South Semitic alphabet family. Yet the texts in which it appears are generally held to date from the first century BC to the fourth century AD and in fact, of course, the Safaitic sign did not develop from the Phoenician but from the proto-*alif* of the South Semitic alphabetic tradition. Samaritan *tau* is often identical to the form in the Mesha stela. Nabataean *semkath* developed a form virtually identical to Phoenician *q* (e.g. in *CIS* i.122/1), yet no one would claim that this was anything more than chance, etc. Within the same script, letters develop similar, sometimes identical shapes and are then sometimes differentiated again. Thus, in Nabataean, *r* having started off identical to *d*, as in Imperial Aramaic, was slowly differentiated from it and instead became identical with *z*. In all these cases and many others, we have sufficient evidence to enable us to show that these similarities are the accidental outcomes of a long development. Surely, therefore, it is dangerous to draw conclusions about the relationships of letter forms drawn from unrelated, usually undated, documents, when we have little or no evidence for the processes by which each letter reached the form it has in these texts.

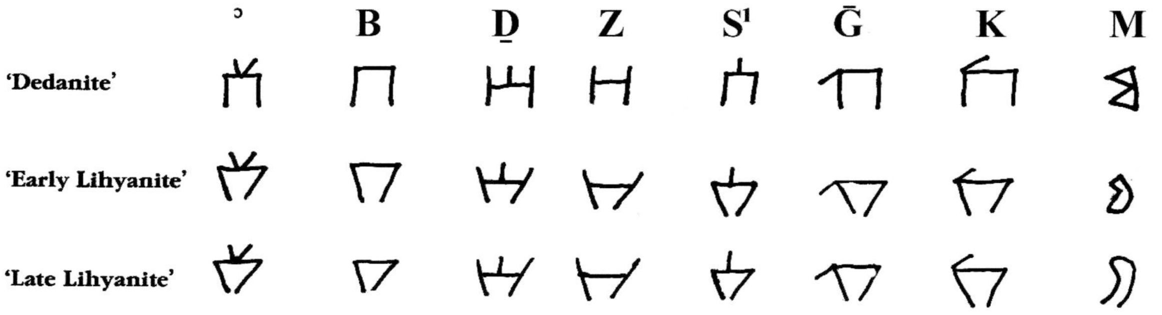

Figure 1. *An illustration of Winnett's assumed palaeographical development and his division into 'Dedanite', 'Early Lihyanite', and 'Late Lihyanite (drawing by Macdonald).*

with an open base; and (iii) the *g* (Fig. 1). It is unfortunate, however, that he then assumed that the 'open-based' *m* was later than the closed type, without citing any evidence in support of this claim.[7] From this assumption, he then went on to adapt and expand Grimme's division of the inscriptions from al-ᶜUlā into 'Dedanite' and 'Lihyanite' (Grimme 1932), and assigned to the 'Dedanite' group all those texts in which the shafts of the letters ᵓ, *b*, *d̲*, *z*, *s¹*, *ġ*, and *k* are parallel, and placed in the 'Lihyanite' group all those in which these shafts converge towards the base. Finally, he subdivided the 'Lihyanite' texts into those with a closed *m*, which he considered 'early', and those with an open *m*, which he considered 'late' (Winnett 1937: 10–11) (Fig. 1). All this is very neat and tidy, but unfortunately reality is seldom susceptible to such clear divisions. It will become obvious below that the way various forms of the same letters were used at al-ᶜUlā was far too complex to be explained simply on chronological grounds.

Seventeen years later, Caskel took Winnett's division as the basis for a much more detailed sequence of letter forms which he divided into a chronological sequence of six stages.[8] Unfortunately, he never explained the basis on which he assigned all the inscriptions from al-ᶜUlā published at that time to one or other of his stages. Instead, he described some features of some of the letter forms in each category and explained how he thought they developed from those in the previous category.[9] Given the total lack of absolute, or even secure relative, chronological data for these inscriptions, one is left with the impression that his assignment of particular texts to particular stages must have been a largely subjective process based, at best, on the reasoning 'this looks as if it could have developed out of that'. Caskel then tried to fit his stages into a reconstruction of the history of the oasis by using a series of bizarre assumptions and leaps of the imagination.[10]

Caskel's proposed sequence of letter forms is undermined by another problem. He considered the letter forms used in the rock inscriptions (and stelae) on the one hand, and those in the graffiti on the other, as *two different scripts* with parallel developments.[11] In fact Caskel's script tables themselves (Fig. 2) show that, when dealing with letter forms, the division between '(monumental) inscriptions' and 'graffiti' is an artificial one, wherever the dividing line is drawn. As can be seen

[7] Winnett 1937: 9–11; and 'the group employing the *mīm* with the open base seems to be the younger of the two' (1937: 9–10). Presumably, he assumed that the 'open-based' *m* could only be a development from the 'closed' form.

[8] Caskel 1954: 22–34. His categories are: *dedanisch*, *frühlihyanisch*, *dedanisch-lihyanisch*, *spätlihyanisch*, *früh-spätlihyanisch*, and *minäisierende Graffiti*.

[9] But he postulated a hiatus between the 'dedanische Schrift' and the 'frühlihyanische Schrift' since he regarded the latter as 'eine bewußte Neuschöpfung' (Caskel 1954: 23).

[10] For instance, 'Die Einführung einer neuen Schrift aber deutet im Alten Orient auf einen neuen religiösen und politischen Zustand' (Caskel 1954: 35); or 'Nun ist es schlechterdings ausgeschlossen, daß jemand in einem fremden Staate nach seinem heimischen König datiert' (1954: 35–36). It is on this basis that he claims a Nabataean occupation between the 'frühlihyanisch' and 'spätlihyanisch' periods and identifies the 'era' of the former as that of the Province of Syria (starting in 64 BC) and that of the latter as the era of the Provincia Arabia (starting in AD 106). His calculations of the lengths of these periods on assumed average numbers of inscriptions per year over periods of fifty years are simply breathtaking!

[11] See Caskel 1954: 23: 'Im Lihyanischen müssen wir die Graffiti von den Felsinschriften trennen, weil sie sich davon durch besondere Züge unterscheiden'. He does not specify in what ways their development is different. He also identified a 'kursiv' form (see Fig. 2), although he does not specify exactly what he means by this term. He seems to see the 'kursiv' forms as arising from those of the graffiti in the 'frühlihyanische' period (1954: 25) and then to have been 'borrowed' by the script of the 'spätlihyanische' rock inscriptions: 'außerdem entlehnt sie, auch hier wieder unregelmäßig, einige kursiv Buchstaben den Graffiti' (1954: 27).

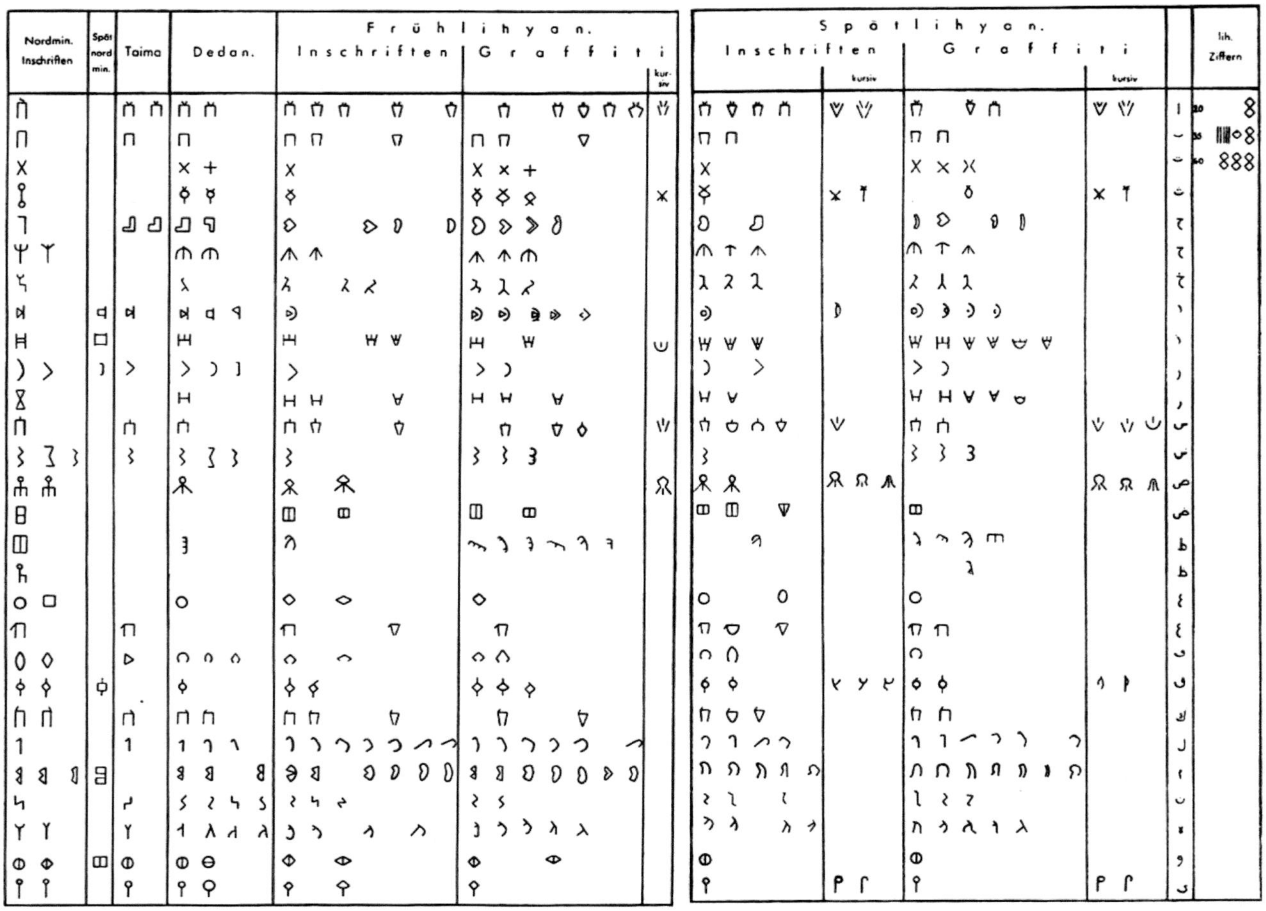

Figure 2. *Caskel's script tables (from Caskel 1954: 33–34).*

on Figure 2, the letter forms are much the same in both, and this is what one would expect, in view of Jacques Ryckmans' penetrating observation that in scripts where there is a difference between formal and informal letter forms, graffiti are usually carved (and often written) in the formal register (Ryckmans J 1984 [1985]: 79; 1993: 30) (see below). Thus, those who carve monumental inscriptions and those who carve graffiti usually have the same letter form in mind, and the results tend to be distinguished by differences in the skill of execution rather than by intention.

Caskel's reconstruction of the development of the 'Dedanite' and 'Lihyanite' scripts seems to have been based entirely on unsupported assumptions, and his account of 'Lihyanite history' is a startling example of bad historical methodology. Not for nothing did he begin his lecture *Das altarabische Königreich Lihyan* with the words 'It is certainly not easy to interpret inscriptions of which the alphabet is as yet not completely known and which can only be understood with difficulty in the light of other sources, without giving free rein to the imagination.'[12]

* * *

Recategorization

In my 'Reflections on the linguistic map of pre-Islamic Arabia' (Macdonald 2000: 33), I suggested that the old division of the inscriptions of al-ᶜUlā into 'Dedanite' and 'Lihyanite' was misconceived, and that the inscriptions from the oasis should be regarded as a single category, for which I suggested the term 'Dadanitic'. One advantage of

[12] 'Es ist freilich nicht einfach, Inschriften, deren Alphabeten noch nicht ganz erkannt und deren Verständnis kaum durch andere Quellen erhellt wird, zu erklären, ohne der Phantasie die Zügel schießen zu lassen' (Caskel 1950: 5).

this is that it allows us to take a fresh look at the differences in the forms of the script used in the oasis, free from the unsupported chronological assumptions imposed by Grimme's, Winnett's, and Caskel's divisions. For there is much that the palaeography of the Dadanitic inscriptions can tell us when we study it for its own sake, rather than trying to use it inappropriately as a tool for dating.

Formal and informal

Of all the Ancient North Arabian scripts, only that used in the oasis of al-ᶜUlā provides evidence of what might be called 'formal' and 'informal' registers.[13] Different 'registers' can be used in writing, as in speech. As in speech too, there are *degrees* of formality and informality which shade imperceptibly into each other. They can be seen in both the letter forms employed and in the layout of the text. At the 'formal' end of the scale are the more or less calligraphic types of writing used in official inscriptions and the copying of sacred texts. At the 'informal' end are those used in a personal letter, a chancery document, a contract, etc. 'Formality' and 'informality' refer not to the circumstances or the purpose of what is written, but to the type of script and layout used.[14] Thus, for instance, most graffiti are carved or written in a formal register — in the West, this normally means in capital letters — whereas most documents on parchment, papyrus, or paper, both official and private, are in an informal register — in the West, predominantly in lower case. This distinction is made even in scripts which have no upper or lower case, by the use of different versions of the script. Thus, in Arabic, public inscriptions, Qurʾān manuscripts, and even many shop signs tend to be in calligraphic forms, whereas more informal versions of the script are used for non-sacred manuscripts and documents on soft materials.

Three types of letter form

In Dadanitic the letters ʾ, *b*, *ḏ*, *z*, *s¹*, *ġ*, and *k*, which Winnett (followed by Caskel) regarded as diagnostic, can take three different types of shape: (1) a form with parallel vertical shafts (which Winnett and Caskel thought was early); (2) a form in which the shafts converge (which Winnett and Caskel thought was late); and (3) what I would call a 'dismembered' form (which Winnett did not deal with, and which Caskel called 'kursiv', see below). There are minor variations in (1) usually to do with the position and orientation of the small additional strokes on top, or to the side, of the frame. In (2) there is a wide range of variation, from a frame with one vertical and one slightly diagonal leg, to a triangle. But it is the shape (3) that raises the most interesting questions.

Informal writing on soft materials

Direction

Certain features of Dadanitic public inscriptions strongly suggest that the script had long been used to write documents in ink on soft or portable materials such as papyrus, parchment, or potsherds, or that texts were cut with a sharp point on sticks or palm-leaf stalks, etc.,[15] and that this practice continued in parallel with the carving of inscriptions (see Macdonald 2015: 3–7, 16; and cf. Macdonald 2003: 52–54). For instance, the almost invariable direction right to left, starting each line under the beginning of the previous one, is a feature normally developed by those writing in ink because the angle at which a nib is cut means that it can write easily in only one direction. This is much less likely to develop in societies that only carve on stone (such as those that produced the Safaitic, most of the Hismaic, and the so-called 'Thamudic' graffiti) (see Macdonald 1993: 386–387; 2005: 90–91). There are a few examples of short Dadanitic graffiti (one name or, at most, two) carved from left to right[16] and it is possible that these were the work of people more familiar with carving on stone than writing with ink.

An interesting parallel can be found in a number of messages written by Touareg tribesmen to Père Charles de Foucauld shortly before and during the First World War. The Touareg provide a fascinating example of an *oral* society which uses a script. This consonantal alphabet is known as the Tifinagh and is employed almost entirely for amusement. If a Touareg wants to write a practical document he will use Arabic or French, either himself if he is literate in these languages, or through the services of a scribe. I have examined this situation in some detail elsewhere (Macdonald 2005: 58–64), as it provides a very fruitful parallel with the circumstances in which I believe the Ancient North Arabian desert graffiti were produced.

---

[13] In Taymanitic, where one might expect such a development, an informal register remains to be identified. For Dumaitic we have at present only some twenty-three graffiti (see Norris, this volume).

[14] For a fuller definition of the terms 'registers', 'formal', and 'informal' styles of writing and 'public' and 'personal' texts, see Macdonald 2015: 28–30.

[15] Writing in ink and incising on soft wood or wax, however, have very different effects on the development of a script; see Macdonald 2015: 16.

[16] See e.g. JSLih 100, 102, 104, 110, etc.

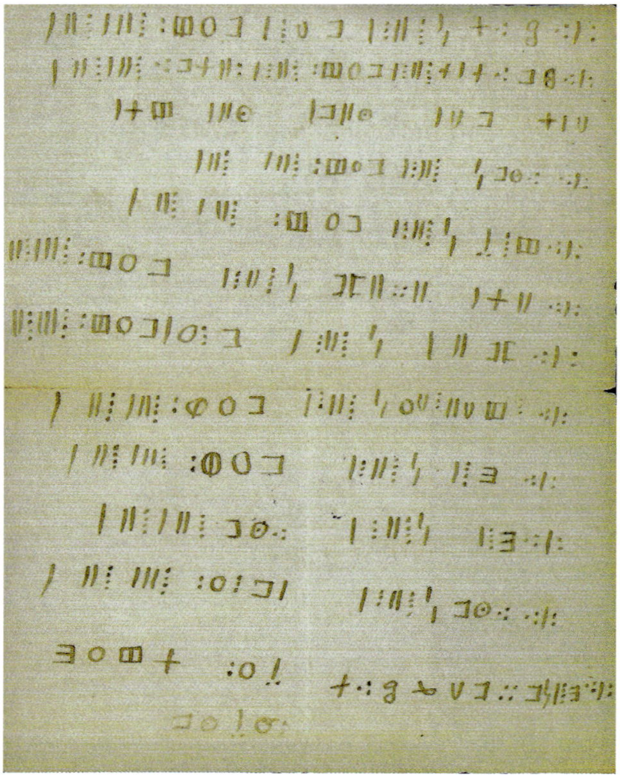

FIGURE 3. *A message in the Tifinagh written right to left in parallel lines (from Galand 1999:* Lettre *1a).*

Here, I would like to mention only the curious collection of messages sent to Père de Foucauld.

He had settled as a hermit in the desert of southern Algeria and had become very friendly with a number of Touareg of the Kel-Ahaggar. He made a deep study of the Berber language and its oral literature and was fluent in the use of the difficult Tifinagh alphabet. Over several years, some of his Touareg friends sent him occasional messages in the Tifinagh characters. These were written in ink on scraps of paper and cloth and consisted almost entirely of salutations and occasional small requests (Figs 3 & 4).[17] Like Safaitic and Hismaic, the Tifinagh is almost always carved on rocks and/or written with a finger in the sand and there is no fixed direction. It can meander, run boustrophedon, or go from bottom to top. Most of these *messages*, however, which were written in *ink*, are set out in parallel horizontal lines reading from right to left (probably imitating Arabic), as if the very act of writing with ink encouraged the use of this layout (Fig. 3). Yet, some of the same writers also occasionally wrote whole messages in vertical or horizontal boustrophedon or other arrangements (Fig. 4).[18]

[17] Such messages are described by the Tuareg as *tehult* 'salutations' rather than as 'letters'; see Casajus 1999: 97–98.

[18] In Galand 1999 compare, for instance, Lettres 1(a), 2, 3(a), and 4 (all written right to left in parallel lines) by Chikat ag Mokhammed, with Lettre 6 by the same person, which is written boustrophedon; see also the messages by Akhamouk agg Ihema, of which Lettre 10b is in horizontal boustrophedon, 15 is in vertical boustrophedon, and 16 is in parallel lines from right to left (apart from the last four characters of line 2).

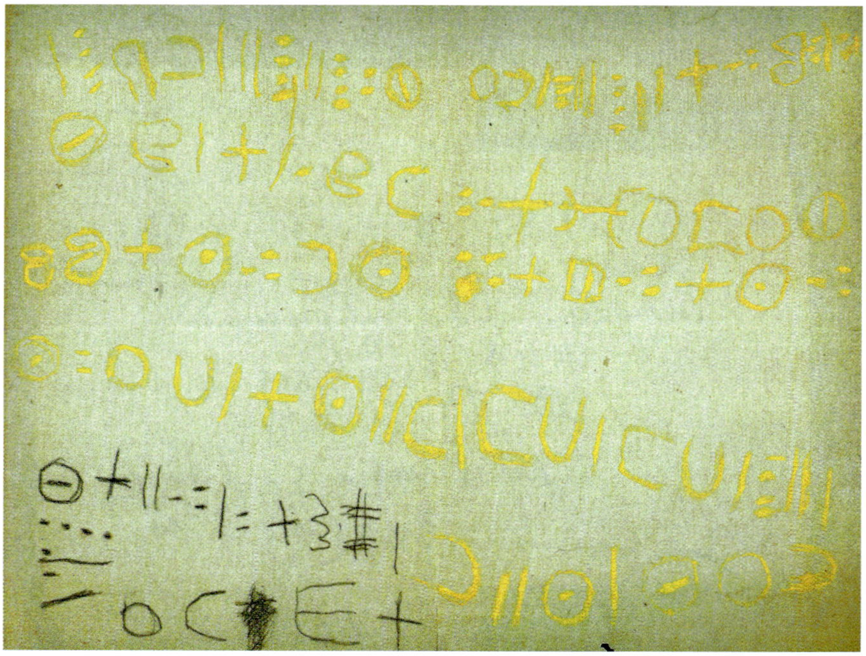

FIGURE 4. *A message in the Tifinagh written boustrophedon starting from right to left (from Galand 1999:* Lettre *6).*

Imitation of handwriting?

Thus, it is possible that the consistent direction of most of the Dadanitic texts on stone may have developed from the use of the script for writing in ink. A particularly interesting inscription in this respect is JSLih 59 (Fig. 5). This is a public inscription, *carved in relief* (see Jaussen & Savignac 1909–1922, ii: 398), yet from line 4 onwards, it gives the overall impression of a text written fast with a pen, the leftward movement of the letters giving a strong sense of flow. Even the detail of the last few letters squeezed in under the beginning of the previous line, with part of the frame cut away to accommodate them — as if they were crammed in at the bottom of a page — is suggestive of an *informal* document written in ink.

Thus, while the script of lines 4–7 is still in a formal register, the mason seems to have been trying to give the impression of the informal ductus of a handwritten document — rather like printing fonts which mimic handwriting. A text in this form cannot have been any easier to carve than one in a more conventional style and the effect here is clearly intentional. Even the 'squeezing in' of the last few letters at the end of the text is a trick, for the carver did not suddenly find himself without enough space at the end of line 6 and fitted in the remaining letters as best he could or ran onto the frame as the sculptors at Ḥegrā so often did (Fig. 6). No, he purposely reduced the size of the first three letters of the penultimate line in advance, so as to provide exactly enough room to accommodate the last five signs beneath them. The habit of cutting away part of the frame in order to squeeze in the final letters of the text is found in some other formal Dadanitic inscriptions (e.g. Fig. 7), although not in quite such a blatant form as here.

On the other hand, this inscription is exceptional and it should be emphasized that 'impressions of fluidity' and the similarity to handwriting are subjective interpretations of features which could, no doubt, be analysed quite differently.

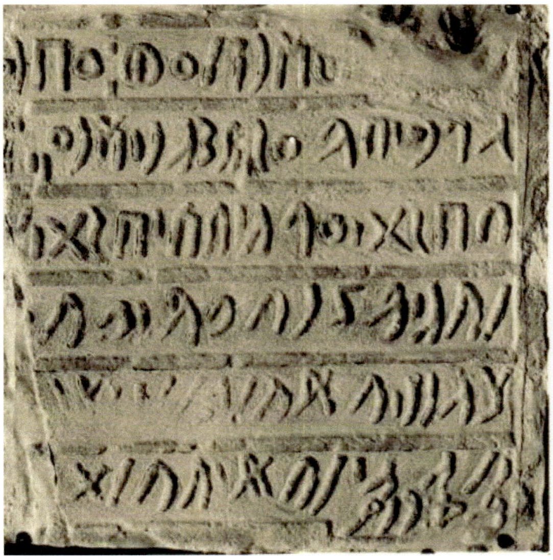

FIGURE 5. *JSLih 59.*

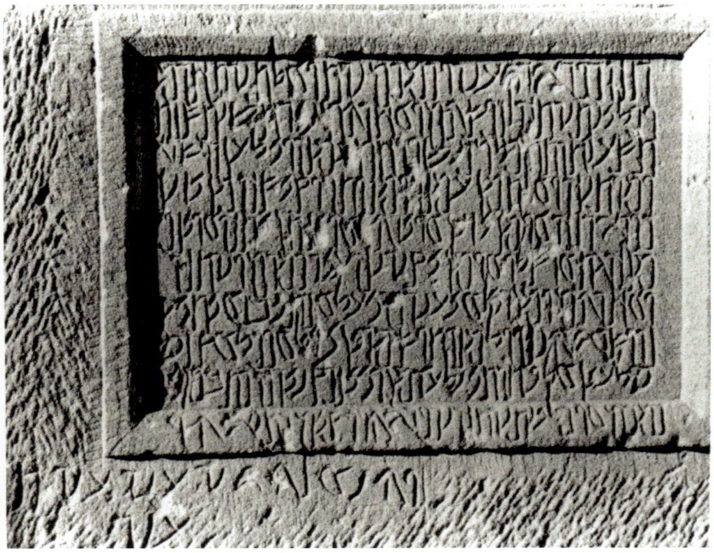

FIGURE 6. *JSNab 16. Note that the last line of the text is carved on the frame; the two lines on the rock face below are the signature of the mason.*

FIGURE 7. *The end of a Dadanitic inscription squeezed in by removing part of the frame. To judge from the surviving parts of the frame, only the tops of the letters were carved (from an unpublished Dadanitic inscription).*

Figure 8. *A Dadanitic graffito by* glḥ bn frʾh *near Madāʾin Ṣāliḥ. Note the joined letters (see Hidalgo-Chacón Diez 2018: 224–225, no. 3, and OCIANA under Ǧabal al-Ḫuraymāt 03).*

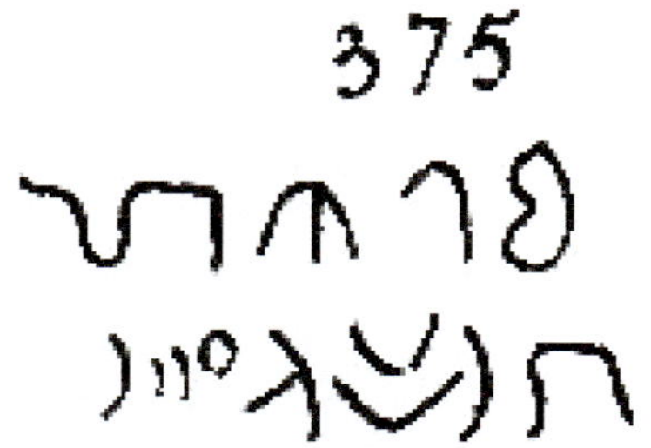

Figure 9. *JSLih 375: a Dadanitic graffito with joined letters, by the same author as the inscriptions in Figures 8 and 10.*

Figure 10. *A Dadanitic graffito by the same author at Jabal Ithlib, Madāʾin Ṣāliḥ (photograph by L. Nehmé, reproduced by kind permission of the Saudi-French mission to Madāʾin Ṣāliḥ; see Hidalgo-Chacón Diez 2018: 224–225, no. 3).*

Figure 11. *JSLih 71: photograph (from Jaussen & Savignac 1909–1922, ii: pl. LXXXVI).*

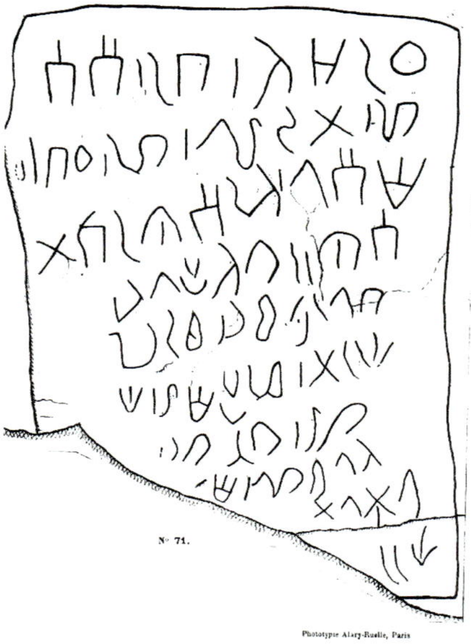

Figure 12. *JSLih 71: copy (from Jaussen & Savignac 1909–1922, ii: pl. CVIII).*

Joining

A much stronger indication of the effects of writing in ink is provided by the occasional examples of the joining of letters in Dadanitic graffiti. There is no advantage, in terms of speed or ease, in joining letters when carving on stone, so scripts which are used only on stone or in the sand (like the Tifinagh or the Ancient North Arabian desert scripts, Safaitic, Hismaic, 'Thamudic') rarely if ever develop 'joined-up writing'. The same would seem to be true of inscribing with a sharp point on wooden sticks, even when they are fresh and relatively soft. Thus, in the South Arabian minuscule the letters are not joined, despite the leftward flowing 'tails' of many of them (Fig. 13). On the other hand, when writing in ink, joining letters makes for greater speed and ease.

Examples of joins between letters which commonly occur together, either in general or in the writings of a particular author, can be seen in the joined *b-n* of *bin* and the *r-ᵓ* in the patronym on Figure 8, a feature repeated, at least in the *bn* in two other graffiti by the same author (Figs 9 & 10).[19] In this respect, JSLih 71 (Figs 11 & 12), on which see below, is unusual and revealing. There are no joins in line 1, but in both occurrences of *bn* in line 2 the letters are joined, as are the *h-n* of the definite article *hn* in line 3. Similarly, in line 5, the *r* and the word divider are joined, as are the last two letters in the line, and the *g-n* (if that is what they are) in line 6 and the *f-l* in line 8. Whether intentionally or not, this gives the impression of an engraver — who from the roughness of the work was almost certainly an amateur — more used to writing relatively quickly in ink than inscribing on rock.

[19] See JSLih 165 for another apparent example of a join, this time between the *m-n* of the name *zd-mnt*.

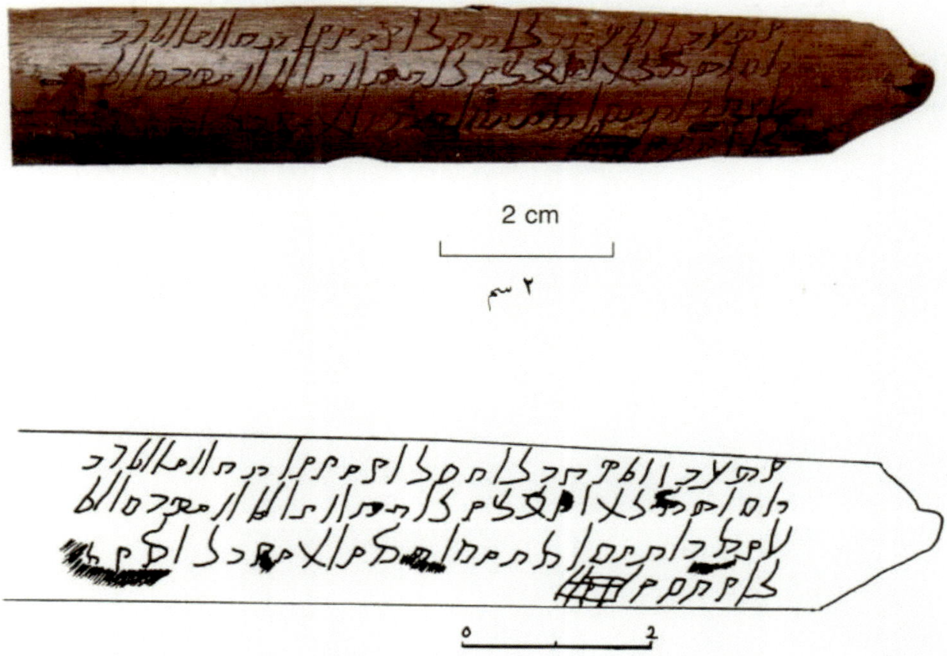

Figure 13. *An example of the* zabūr *script (from Ryckmans, Müller & Abdallah 1994: pl. 6).*

Figure 14. *U 021: an inscription in relief showing a mixture of letter forms. Note the two shapes of* d *marked by arrows.*

Figure 15. *U 048: an incised inscription showing a mixture of letter forms. Note the two shapes of* d *marked by arrows.*

Figure 16. *JSLih 383: the word* ʾfkl *in which the* k *has been formed by two cross-strokes.*

Growth of dismembered forms

It is difficult to see how the various letter forms in types (1) and (2) could have developed as the result of writing at speed on soft materials. It is probably quicker and easier to write a triangle than a frame consisting of two parallel vertical strokes and a horizontal. But the mere *convergence* of the shafts, if they do not touch, would be no quicker or easier than drawing them as parallel.

On the other hand, the 'dismembered', type (3), forms of ʾ, *ṯ*, *ḏ*, *s*^{1}, *ṣ* show a disintegration of the letter shape into separate strokes similar to that identified by J. Ryckmans in the South Arabian *zabūr* or minuscule script (1994: 241; 2001: 223–235) (Fig. 13). Indeed the 'normal Dadanitic *d*' consisting of a curve followed by a triangle or circle would seem to be the result of such a process. Nevertheless, there are examples of *d* where, instead of a curve there is a straight line. In line 3 of U 021 (Fig. 14), the third letter has this straight stem, while right next to it, the fourth sign has the 'typical' curved shape; and see also the two forms in lines 4 and 5 of U 048 (Fig. 15). Is the form with the straight line an archaism — after all it is similar to the shape in all the other South Semitic scripts — or is it a simplification of the curved form? Both explanations are possible and the juxtaposition of these two shapes provides an instructive example of the dangers of drawing chronological inferences from isolated forms, reminding us that there is no such thing as an *inevitable linear progression* in the development of letter forms outside the strictly controlled environment of a scriptorium.

It is possible that, as perhaps in the *zabūr*, the 'dismembered' forms represent shapes developed through engraving texts on soft wood with a sharp point or on wax tablets with a stylus, rather than by writing with pen and ink. In both, the dismembered forms would be quicker to produce than those with parallel or converging (but not touching) shafts. At present, this can be no more than a hypothesis and we can only hope that future excavations at al-ʿUlā will reveal a cache of everyday documents which might allow us to test it. A relatively rare example of one *process* of dismemberment can be seen in the way the letter *k* has been formed by two diagonal strokes in the word *ʾfkl* in Figure 16.

Masons

At present, we have virtually no direct evidence of the use of professional monumental masons in pre-Islamic al-ʿUlā.[20] Their existence is suggested, however, by the large number of Dadanitic formal public inscriptions which are carved in relief — a process which is far more difficult and time-consuming than inscribing, and one which must

[20] As far as I know, the only examples of the 'writer' (*h-s*^{1}*fr*) being mentioned in Dadanitic inscriptions are JSLih 82/8, an inscription carved in relief on the base of a statue ([N] *{h-ṣnʿ} w-{.}rḥ/bn//....ḍḍ/h-s*^{1}*fr...* '[N] {the sculptor} and N son of ... the writer [i.e. carver]'), and JSLih 128, which is inscribed on a rock face and reads: *l ʿḏrʾl/w-s*^{1}*fr-h/mlṭs*^{1}*/qyn{-h}* ' ʿḏrʾl and Mlṭs^1, his slave, wrote it'. Here, however, the writer (i.e. the slave) could have been a literate amateur rather than a professional mason. For my reasons for not translating the initial *lām*, see Macdonald 2006 [2008]: 294–295.

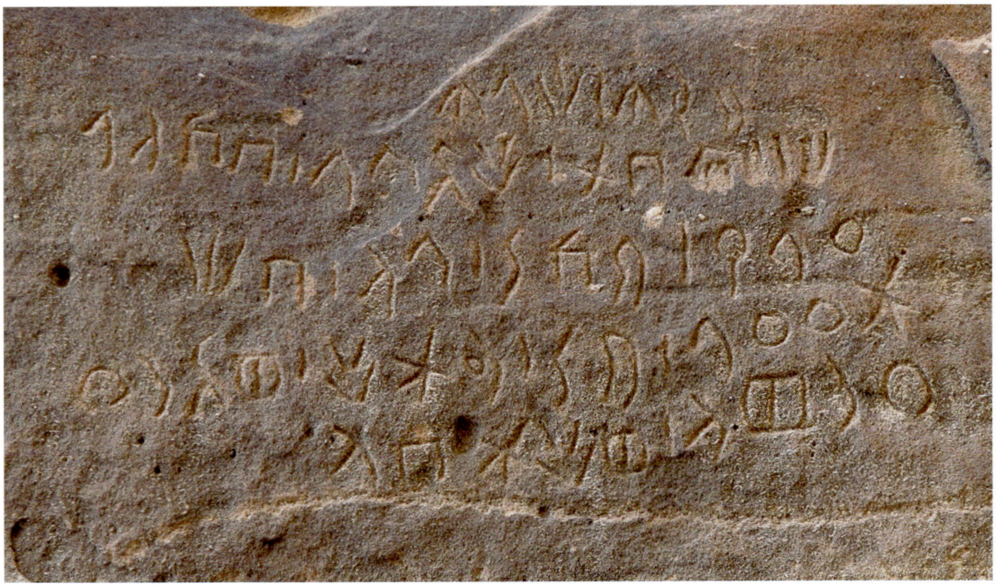

Figure 17. *U 059: an incised inscription showing a mixture of letter forms.*

Figure 18. *U 014: an inscription in relief with the last ten letters incised, showing a mixture of letter forms.*

Figure 19. *U 008: an inscription in relief showing a mixture of letter forms.*

surely have required the skill of a trained professional. These inscriptions in relief are not confined to stelae but are also common on rock faces. While an amateur might *inscribe* a public inscription in a formal register of the script, as perhaps the text on Figure 17 which records the performance of the *ẓll* ceremony, it is difficult to believe that the numerous texts in *relief* (e.g. those on Figs 18[21] and 19) were anything but the work of professionals.

[21] Note, however, that in this text the last ten characters are inscribed. See below.

In other societies, professional masons seem to have learnt the letter forms of the script from older masons or in schools, and were encouraged to maintain these shapes consistently in the inscriptions they carved to order. When fashions changed and a new style was required, this too had to be employed systematically.

Mixtures of letter forms

If we look at the formal public inscriptions at al-ᶜUlā it quickly becomes apparent that they very rarely show the sort of consistency one might expect. This can be seen in the texts on Figures 14, 18, and 19, all of which are in relief (see the analysis in the Appendix).

These have not been especially chosen for their peculiarities but are representative of the vast majority of Dadanitic formal inscriptions. This suggests that Winnett's and Caskel's division into 'early' forms with vertical shafts and 'late' ones with converging shafts is untenable. Caskel, indeed, recognized this to some extent and so created a category of 'früh-spätlihyanische Inschriften' and graffiti which, according to him, contained transitional forms. The trouble with this explanation is that the vast majority of formal Dadanitic inscriptions would seem to fall into such a category.[22]

The dismembered letters are found in both inscribed formal inscriptions and in those carved in relief. In both, they occur together with the forms with parallel and with converging uprights. Thus, for example, in U 021 (Fig. 14, see the analysis in the Appendix), which is in relief, the dismembered *alif* can be seen in lines 1 and 4, but in line 3 it has the shape with parallel shafts and in line 5 a form in which the shafts converge. The letter *ḏ* in lines 1 and 2 also has a dismembered form, but in *b* and s^1 the shafts are sometimes parallel and sometimes converging.

Another example is U 008 (Fig. 19; see the Appendix), where in line 1 *alif* has the shape with converging uprights forming a triangle, but in the rest of the text has its dismembered form. The letter *ḏ* is a triangle surmounted by three vertical strokes, and *b* and s^1 fluctuate between forms with parallel and with converging shafts. Similarly, although all three examples of *m* in this text are open at the base, their shape varies considerably. Both these inscriptions are carefully carved in relief and it is difficult to believe that this variation of letter form was due to carelessness.

It is something of a surprise to find that there is no great difference in the variation of letter forms between inscriptions in relief, which must surely have been carved by professional masons, and incised texts which could have been the work of either professionals or amateurs. Figures 15 and 17 (see the Appendix) show examples of incised formal public inscriptions, which like those in relief discussed above, record the performance of the *ẓll* ceremony. It will be seen that these two texts, which are typical of such inscriptions, display the same mixture of letter shapes as those in relief.

It seems therefore that this promiscuous use of different types of letter form in the same inscription either had a significance which is lost on us, or the monumental masons of Dadan, and their customers, considered it unimportant. The one thing we can say with certainty is that all these forms were in use at the same time and that therefore they are of no chronological significance.

JSLih 71 (Figs 11 & 12) probably contains a greater variety of letter forms than any other text in the Dadanitic script known so far. Caskel regarded it as the 'most recent Lihyanite inscription' (1954: caption to Abb. 2), but it is exceptional in a number of ways and it is therefore risky to take it as representative of a palaeographical tradition. The language of lines 4–10, which are rather crudely incised, appears to be Old Arabic rather than Dadanitic.[23] If examined in its own right, rather than as a representative stage in a palaeographical sequence, it has many interesting and revealing features.

The engraver carved the name, genealogy, and lineage group (lines 1–3) in a formal script register but expressed the rest of the text in a much more *informal* one. A similar distinction is found in some Safaitic texts, where the name, genealogy, and lineage group are carved in the so-called 'square script' (in fact, just a more calligraphic version of the Safaitic alphabet)[24] and the rest of the text in the 'everyday' forms of the letters. Thus in WH 1673 (Fig. 20), the author's name and genealogy (the lower line and the five letters on the right in the upper line) are carved in the square script, while the rest of the text (the remainder of the upper line) is in the 'normal' forms of the letters. The square script *m* of the author's name (third letter from

[22] Thus, even in JSLih 49, whose script is extremely formal and which Caskel characterized as an 'älterer lihyanische Inschrift' (1954: Abb. 1), there is a slight convergence of the verticals of *ġ* and *b* in line 9, whereas they are perfectly parallel earlier in the inscription, as are the other letters of this form.

[23] In Macdonald 2000: 52–53, I examined the possibility that lines 4–10 were in what I described as 'Dadano-Arabic'. I would now be more cautious and suggest that they *may* be in a form of Arabic, as distinct from Dadanitic, but they could also be in a form of Dadanitic; see Fokelien Kootstra's analyses of Dadanitic grammar (2018; this volume).

[24] For discussions on the nature of the so-called 'square script', see Macdonald 2006 [2008]: 291–294; 2015: 12, 30–33. Chiara della Puppa read a very interesting paper on her recent research on the subject at the Special Session but did not submit it for publication in this volume since it will form part of her doctoral thesis.

Figure 20. *WH 1673: an example of the Safaitic 'square script' and the 'normal script' in the same inscription.*

the left in the lower line) is almost immediately below the 'normal' *m* of the final word *mʿzy* (third letter from the left in the upper line).

If we return to JSLih 71, we can see that in the first three lines, giving the identity of the man described, the letters ʾ, *b*, *ḏ*, *z*, s^1, and *k* have been given formal shapes. The letters ʾ, *b*, s^1, and *k* have more or less parallel shafts, but in *z* (line 1) the shafts converge and in *ḏ* (line 3) they meet. It is noteworthy that the letter *ḏ* has this shape, even though it is part of the formal script in which the name is written. This suggests that the author felt it was a valid formal shape for this letter, and its shafts converge or meet in several other texts where most, or all, of the supposedly diagnostic letters have parallel shafts.[25]

The first word of the statement at the beginning of line 4 is still carved in the formal style, but in the rest of the text the script becomes more and more informal. Moreover, in the 'diagnostic' letters, the parallel shafts are not replaced by converging ones but by dismembered forms. Some of these forms, like those of ʾ, are very far from this letter's shape in the formal script, as is the penultimate letter in line 4, if it really is a *m*.

I would suggest that JSLih 71, which is incised not carved in relief, is probably the work of a private individual rather than of a professional mason. Indeed, it may even be the work of the subject of the inscription himself, for there is no indication in the text that he was dead, and Jaussen and Savignac found no trace of a tomb in the vicinity.[26] The inexpert and inelegant forms of all the letters (both formal and dismembered) suggest that whoever carved it was not very experienced.

While it is exceptional in a number of ways JSLih 71 is, as we have seen, by no means unusual in its mixture of letter forms, simply in the crudity of their execution. As I have said, there were clearly skilled masons at Dadan and it seems improbable that the inconsistencies in letter form within the vast majority of public inscriptions were due to carelessness. There are too many such inconsistencies and in most inscriptions the letters themselves are usually carefully cut.

Moreover, letter forms are not the only manifestation of inconsistency — or perhaps an exuberant delight in variety? — in these texts. We have already seen that in some inscriptions the final letters have been squeezed in by cutting away part of the bottom of the frame. Was this really a miscalculation on the part of the mason? These are inscriptions in relief for which the mason would surely have made a preliminary draft so that, if necessary, he could adjust the width or the spacing of the letters to accommodate the whole text. Such a practice is suggested by JSLih 48 and 57 (Figs 21 & 22), which seem to be drafts of inscriptions to be carved in relief which were never completed.[27]

Mixture of relief and incision

There are also some inscriptions carved in relief, the final lines of which are incised, sometimes because the rock face is unsuitable for relief, sometimes for reasons which are unclear. This occurs not only in rock inscriptions, for example, U 014 (Fig. 18), where the last ten letters are incised,[28] but also on stelae, for example, JSLih 52 (Fig. 23), where lines 1–7 are in relief and line 8 is incised.[29]

[25] See for example JSLih 75, U 019, and U 093.

[26] With regard to the position of JSLih 71, Jaussen and Savignac note that 'nous n'avons constaté la présence d'aucune tombe en cet endroit. Et nous savons de par ailleurs que toutes les inscriptions gravées sur les parois de Ḫereibeh n'étaient pas destinées à perpétuer le souvenir d'un défunt' (Jaussen & Savignac 1909–1922, ii: 425).

[27] At first sight, these two texts appear to provide a parallel to the type of South Arabian script used mainly on metal, known as 'l'écriture à double tracé' on which see Ryckmans J 1994: 256 and Bron 2001: 144–145. As pointed out above, however, this is probably an illusion. For examples of what 'l'écriture à double tracé' looks like carved in relief on stone, see Ryckmans G 1939: pl. IV (Ry 220 = RES 4935); and for when it is engraved on stone, see Ryckmans G 1954: pl. I (Ry 528).

[28] Note that it is not only the letters on the last line which are incised but also the s^1 at the end of the penultimate line, where the carver could easily have carved it in relief like the other letters in this line.

[29] Note that Jaussen and Savignac's photograph reproduced in Figure 18 is of a squeeze where the letters in relief appear as hollows and the incised letters appear to be raised.

Figure 21. *JSLih 48 as an example of drafting an inscription.*

Figure 22. *JSLih 57 as an example of drafting an inscription.*

Figure 23. *JSLih 52: an inscription in relief on a stele, where the last line is inscribed.*

Conclusion

What purpose is served by this appearance of miscalculation, if that is what it is? I hope that a study of all the letter forms in all the Dadanitic inscriptions for which we have photographs may throw up some solutions to these puzzles. In addition, it would be extremely valuable if a careful study could be made *in situ* of the inscriptions of al-ᶜUdhayb and Jabal ᶜIkmā as these constitute rare corpora of texts carved on the same surfaces over a period of time.

Much to the disgust of archaeologists — who are always hoping for an inscription to date their levels — most inscriptions in Arabia depend on archaeology to provide them with a chronological context. In these circumstances, I would suggest we should be patient until we have some unequivocal external evidence with which to date the inscriptions and other monuments. Then, and only then, we *may* be in a position to construct some sort of chronological sequence for the letter forms of certain classes of inscription, although I am not very hopeful. In the meantime, the construction of supposed 'palaeographical sequences' in the absence of any dated documents can only be a subjective and rather futile exercise that distracts us from all the other lines of enquiry which the inscriptions invite us to pursue. It is surely far more profitable to ask the sort of questions for which the documents *can* provide answers, than to pursue lost causes and risk imposing our own answers on the texts.

Appendix: the letter forms on Figures 14, 15, 17, 18, and 19

Fig. 14 shows U 021 in which ʾ has the dismembered form in lines 1 and 4, a form with more or less parallel shafts in line 3, and one with converging shafts in line 5. The letter *b* has parallel shafts in lines 1, 4, and 5, but they converge very slightly in the example in line 3. As noted above, *d* has a straight shaft which the circle touches in the first example in line 3, but a curved shaft which the circle does not touch in the second example in line 3 and the one in line 5. Both examples of *ḏ* are of the dismembered form (lines 1, 2). There is no example of *m*. In s^1 the shafts are parallel in line 3 but converging in line 5. Finally, in all three examples (lines 3, 4, and 5) *ṯ* has the form of a small *t* resting on a short vertical shaft, which although not technically dismembered, is clearly different from the formal shape consisting of a long vertical shaft surmounted by a circle or lozenge with 'horns'.

Fig. 15 shows U 048, an inscribed text, in which ʾ in line 1, where it is the first letter, consists of a triangle surmounted by two diagonal strokes, but almost immediately below this, in line 2, it has the form with parallel shafts, which is followed two letters later by the triangular form again. In the letters *b*, s^1, and *ġ* the verticals are always parallel, but in *ḏ* they converge. The first example of *d* (line 4) has a straight shaft, leaning backwards with the circle attached, while the second (line 5) consists of an arc with a detached circle.

Fig. 17 shows U 059, an inscribed text, in which ʾ has its dismembered form in all three examples (lines 2, 4, 5); *b* has parallel shafts in all examples (lines 2 twice, 3, 5), *ḏ* has a dismembered form which is almost three parallel vertical lines, with only a very slight slant on the outer ones (lines 2, 3); s^1 (line 1) has its dismembered form and is only distinguished from *ḏ* by the more extreme angle of its outer shafts and its slightly shorter central one; *k* (line 2) and *ġ* (line 2) have parallel shafts; the *ṯ* consists of five strokes of more or less equal length, rather than of a *t* on a short shaft, particularly the second example in line 4.

Fig. 18 shows U 014 which is in relief except for the last ten letters which are inscribed. Here, ʾ has the form with converging shafts in line 2 (twice) and a triangle in line 6 (which is inscribed rather than in relief). The shafts of *b* converge in line 1 but are parallel in both examples in line 4. The shafts converge in the single instance of *ḏ* (line 3) but are parallel in the single instance of *ġ* (line 4). The *m* (line 1) is open at the base. The single instance of s^1 (which is *inscribed* at the end of line 5, rather than in relief) is a triangle, while *ṣ*, the first letter of the text, has its dismembered form.

Fig. 19 shows U 008 where ʾ in line 1 has the form of a triangle surmounted by two diagonal strokes, but the dismembered form in lines 2, 3, and 5. In *b* (lines 1, 2 [x2], 3 [x2], and 5 [x2]) the verticals converge so slightly that they look as if they could have been intended to be parallel. In s^1 the verticals are more or less parallel in line 1 and the second example in line 5, but converge in line 4 and in the first example in line 5. The *ḏ* (line 2) is a triangle surmounted by three fingers. Although all three examples of *m* are open at the base, each is a very different shape (lines 1, 3, 4). In line 3, *y* has its formal shape (though somewhat tilted) but a more informal one in lines 1 and 5. In passing it should be noted that this better photograph shows that Sima's reading of the patronym in U 008/1 should be corrected from *nfʿ* to *nfy* (cf. the ʿ in line 4 and the *y* in line 5).

Sigla

CIS i	Phoenician inscriptions in *Corpus Inscriptionum Semiticarum. Pars I. Inscriptiones Phoenicias continens.* Paris: Reipublicae Typographeo, 1881–1962.
JSLih	Dadanitic inscriptions published in Jaussen & Savignac 1909–1922.
JSNab	Nabataean inscriptions published in Jaussen & Savignac 1909–1922.
OCIANA	Online Corpus of the Inscriptions of Ancient North Arabia http://krc.orient.ox.ac.uk/ociana/index.php
RES	Répertoire d'épigraphie sémitique. Paris: Imprimerie national, 1900–1968.

Ry Ancient South Arabian inscriptions published by G. Ryckmans.
U Dadanitic inscriptions published in Sima 1999.
WH Safaitic inscriptions published in Winnett & Harding 1978.

References

Albright W.F. 1953. Dedan. Pages 1–12 in W.F. Albright (ed.), *Geschichte und Altes Testament. Albrecht Alt zum 70. Geburtstag dargebracht.* (Beiträge zur historischen Theologie, 16). Tübingen: Mohr.

Bron F. 2001. Antiquités sudarabiques. *Semitica* 51: 141–146.

Casajus D. 1999. La vie saharienne et les 'Vies' de Charles de Foucauld. Pages 45–100 in L. Galand (ed.), *Lettres au Marabout. Messages touaregs au Père de Foucauld.* Paris: Belin.

Caskel W. 1950. *Das altarabische Königreich Lihjan.* (Festrede gehalten bei der Stiftungsfeier der Universität am 24. Mai 1950. Kölner Universitätsreden, 8). Krefeld: Scherpe.

Caskel W. 1954. *Lihyan und Lihyanisch.* (Arbeitsgemeinschaft für Forschung des Landes Nordrhein-Westfalen, Geisteswissenschaften, 4). Cologne: Westdeutscher Verlag.

Farès-Drappeau S. 2003. La chronologie des inscriptions dédanites et liḥyānites à al-ᶜUlā. État de la question. Pages 379–405 in M. Sartre (ed.). *La Syrie hellénistique.* (Topoi Supplement, 4). Lyon: Maison de l'Orient et de la Méditerranée.

Farès-Drappeau S. 2005. *Dédan et Liḥyān. Histoire des Arabes aux confins des pouvoirs perse et hellénistique (IVᵉ–IIᵉ s. avant l'ère chrétienne).* (Travaux de la Maison de l'Orient et de la Méditerranée, 42). Lyon: Maison de l'Orient et de la Méditerranée.

Galand L. (ed.). 1999. *Lettres au Marabout. Messages touaregs au Père de Foucauld.* Paris: Belin.

Graf D.F. 1990. Arabia during Achaemenid times. Pages 131–148 in H. Sancisi-Weerdenburg & A. Kuhrt (eds), *Achaemenid History IV. Centre and periphery. Proceedings of the Groningen 1986 Achaeminid History Workshop.* Leiden: Nederlands Instituut voor het Nabije Oosten.

Grimme H. 1932. Zur dedanisch-liḥjanischen Schrift. *Orientalistische Literaturzeitung* 35: 753–758.

Hidalgo-Chacón Díez M. del C. 2018. Dadanitic inscriptions from Jabal al-Khraymāt (Madāʾin Ṣāliḥ). Pages 218–237 in L. Nehmé & A. Al-Jallad (eds), *To the Madbar and back again. Studies in the languages, archaeology, and cultures of Arabia dedicated to Michael C.A. Macdonald.* (Studies in Semitic Languages and Linguistics, 92). Leiden: Brill.

Jaussen A. & Savignac M.R. 1909–1922. *Mission archéologique en Arabie.* (5 volumes). Paris: Leroux/Geuthner.

Kitchen K.A. 1994. *Documentation for Ancient Arabia. Part I: Chronological framework and historical sources.* Liverpool: Liverpool University Press.

Kootstra F. 2018. The phonemes ẓ and ṭ in the Dadanitic inscriptions. Pages 202–217 in L. Nehmé & A. Al-Jallad (eds), *To the Madbar and back again. Studies in the languages, archaeology, and cultures of Arabia dedicated to Michael C.A. Macdonald.* (Studies in Semitic Languages and Linguistics, 92). Leiden: Brill.

Kootstra F. (this volume). Scribal practices in contact: Two Minaic/Dadanitic mixed texts. Pages 21–30 in M.C.A. Macdonald (ed.), *Languages, scripts and their uses in ancient North Arabia.* (Supplement to Volume 48 of the Proceedings of the Seminar for Arabian Studies). Oxford: Archaeopress, 2018.

Macdonald M.C.A. 1993. Nomads and the Ḥawrān in the late Hellenistic and Roman periods: A reassessment of the epigraphic evidence. *Syria* 70: 303–413. [Reprinted with addenda and corrigenda as article II in Macdonald 2009].

Macdonald M.C.A. 1997. Trade routes and trade goods at the northern end of the 'Incense Road' in the first millennium B.C. Pages 333–349 in A. Avanzini (ed.), *Profumi d'Arabia. Atti del Convegno.* (Saggi di Storia Antica, 11). Rome: 'L'Erma' di Bretschneider. [Reprinted with addenda and corrigenda as article IX in Macdonald 2009].

Macdonald M.C.A. 2000. Reflections on the linguistic map of pre-Islamic Arabia. *Arabian Archaeology and Epigraphy* 11: 28–79. [Reprinted with addenda and corrigenda as article III in Macdonald 2009].

Macdonald M.C.A. 2003. Languages, scripts, and the uses of writing among the Nabataeans. Pages 36–56, 264–266 (endnotes), 274–282 (references) in G. Markoe (ed.), *Petra rediscovered: Lost city of the Nabataeans.* New York: Abrams.

Macdonald M.C.A. 2005. Literacy in an oral environment. Pages 49–118 in P. Bienkowski, C.B. Mee & E.A. Slater (eds), *Writing and ancient Near Eastern society.* Oxford: Oxford University Press. [Reprinted with addenda and corrigenda as article I in Macdonald 2009].

Macdonald M.C.A. 2006 [2008]. Burial between the desert and the sown. Cave-tombs and inscriptions near Dayr al-Kahf in Jordan. *Damaszener Mitteilungen* 15: 273–301.

Macdonald M.C.A. 2009. *Literacy and identity in pre-Islamic Arabia*. (Variorum Collected Studies, CS906). Farnham: Ashgate.

Macdonald M.C.A. 2015. On the uses of writing in ancient Arabia and the role of palaeography in studying them. *Arabian Epigraphic Notes* 1: 1–50.

Norris J. (this volume). A survey of the Ancient North Arabian inscriptions from the Dūmat al-Jandal area (Saudi Arabia). Pages 71–93 in M.C.A. Macdonald (ed.), *Languages, scripts and their uses in ancient North Arabia*. (Supplement to Volume 48 of the Proceedings of the Seminar for Arabian Studies). Oxford: Archaeopress, 2018.

Pirenne J. 1956. *Paléographie des inscriptions sud-arabes: Contribution à la chronologie et à l'histoire de l'Arabie du Sud antique*. I: *Des origines jusqu'à l'époque himyarite*. (Verhandelingen van de Koninklijke Vlaamse Academie voor Wetenschappen, Letteren en Schone Kunsten van België. Klasse der Letteren, 26). Brussels: Paleis der Academiën.

Rabinowitz I. 1956. Aramaic inscriptions of the fifth century B.C.E. from a North-Arab shrine in Egypt. *Journal of Near Eastern Studies* 15: 1–9.

Rohmer J. (forthcoming). Foreign powers and local kingdoms in Northwest Arabia: New insights into the political history of Dadan, Ḥegrā and Taymāᵓ in the later 1st millennium BC. In M. Luciani (ed.), *The Archaeology of the Arabian Peninsula 2: Connecting the evidence. Proceedings of the international workshop held in Vienna on April 25, 2016*. (OREA Series). Vienna: Austrian Academy of Sciences Press.

Rohmer J. & Charloux G. 2015. From Liḥyān to the Nabataeans: Dating the end of the Iron Age in north-west Arabia. *Proceedings of the Seminar for Arabian Studies* 45: 297–320.

Ryckmans G. 1939. Inscriptions sud-arabes, cinquième série. *Le Muséon* 52: 51–112.

Ryckmans G. 1954. Inscriptions sud-arabes, onzième série. *Le Muséon* 67: 99–119.

Ryckmans J. 1984 [1985]. Alphabets, scripts and languages in pre-Islamic Arabian epigraphical evidence. Pages 73–86 in A.T. al-Ansary, A.M. Abdalla, S. al-Sakkar & R. Mortel (eds), *Studies in the history of Arabia*. ii: *Pre-Islamic Arabia*. Riyadh: King Saud University Press.

Ryckmans J. 1993. Pétioles de palmes et bâtonnets inscrits: un type nouveau de documents du Yémen antique. *Bulletin de la classe des lettres et des sciences morales et politiques de l'Académie royale de Belgique* 4: 15–32.

Ryckmans J. 1994. Pétioles de palmes et bâtonnets sud-arabes inscrits: notes de paléographie. Pages 250–259 in N. Nebes (ed.), *Arabia Felix. Beiträge zur Sprache und Kultur des vorislamischen Arabien. Festschrift Walter W. Müller zum 60. Geburtstag*. Wiesbaden: Harrassowitz.

Ryckmans J. 2001. Origin and evolution of South Arabian minuscule writing on wood. *Arabian Archaeology and Epigraphy* 12: 223–235.

Ryckmans J., Müller W.W. & Abdallah Y.M. 1994. *Textes du Yémen antique inscrits sur bois*. (Publications de l'Institut Orientaliste de Louvain, 43). Louvain-la-Neuve: Institut Orientaliste.

Al-Saᶜīd, S.F. 2011. Dedan: Treasures of a spectacular culture. Pages 125–135 in U. Franke, A.I. Al-Ghabban, J. Gierlichs & S. Weber (eds), *Roads of Arabia. The archaeological treasures of Saudi Arabia*. Berlin: Wasmuth.

Al-Saᶜīd S.F. & Al-Ghazī ᶜA. 1434–1435/2013–2014. *Kunūz athariyyah min Dādān. Natāᵓij tanqībāt al-mawāsim as-sabaᶜah al-ᶜūlā*. Riyadh: Al-jamᶜīyah al-saᶜūdiyyah li-l-dirāsāt al-athariyyah.

Sima A. 1999. *Die lihyanischen Inschriften von al-ᶜUḏayb (Saudi-Arabien)*. (Epigraphische Forschungen auf der Arabischen Halbinsel, 1). Rahden/Westf.: Leidorf.

Sima A. 2000. Zum antiken Namen der Stadt Dedan. *Biblische Notizen* 104: 42–47.

Al-Theeb [Al-Dhiyīb] S.ᶜA. (ed.). 2013. *Al-Khuraybah (Dadan) ᶜāṣimat mamlakatay Dādān wa-Liḥyān al-taqrīr al-ūlā li-l-mawsim al-thāmin 2011m*. (Silsilat al-dirāsāt al-athariyyah al-maydāniyyah). Riyadh: Iṣdārāt al-jamīᶜah al-saᶜūdiyyah l-l-dirāsāt al-athariyyah.

Al-Theeb [Al-Dhiyīb] S.ᶜA., Mushabbī I.Ḥ., Al-Dahām S.ᶜA., Al-ᶜĀmar F.Ḥ. & Al-Dayrī J.ᶜA. 2016. *Dadan ᶜāṣimat mamlakatay Dādān wa-Liḥyān. Natāᵓij al-mawsim al-ᶜāshir 2013 m.* Riyadh: Markaz al-malik Fayṣal li-l-buḥūth wa-ᵓl-dirāsāt al-islāmiyyah.

Winnett F.V. 1937. *A study of the Liḥyanite and Thamudic inscriptions*. (University of Toronto Studies — Oriental Series, 3). Toronto: University of Toronto Press.

Winnett F.V. & Harding G.L. 1978. *Inscriptions from fifty Safaitic cairns*. (Near and Middle East Series, 9). Toronto: University of Toronto Press.

Winnett F.V. & Reed W.L. 1970. *Ancient records from North Arabia.* (Near and Middle East Series, 6). Toronto: University of Toronto Press.

Author's address

Michael C.A. Macdonald, Wolfson College, Linton Road, Oxford, OX2 6UD, UK.
e-mail michael.macdonald@orinst.ox.ac.uk

M.C.A. Macdonald (ed.), *Languages, scripts and their uses in ancient North Arabia.* (Supplement to volume 48 of the Proceedings of the Seminar for Arabian Studies). Oxford: Archaeopress, 2018: 21–30

Scribal practices in contact: two Minaic/Dadanitic mixed texts

Fokelien Kootstra

Summary

In the first millennium BC, the ancient oasis of Dadan (modern al-ᶜUlā in north-west Saudi Arabia) was one of the major halts on the incense trade route. It clearly had a vibrant literate culture since not only have some 2000 inscriptions in the local Dadanitic script been found there, but also a corpus of about sixty Minaic texts carved when the Minaeans had a trading outpost in the oasis, which is thought to be contemporaneous with the Lihyanite kingdom. This paper will investigate the possible influence the two writing traditions may have had on each other by studying in detail two inscriptions previously read as Minaic, and suggesting new readings, interpreting them as linguistically mixed Minaic/Dadanitic.

Keywords: epigraphy, orthography, scribal practice, Dadanitic, Minaic

Introduction

The ancient oasis of Dadan (modern al-ᶜUlā) can boast numerous inscriptions in different scripts. Chief among these are the Dadanitic inscriptions, carved in a local variety of the Ancient North Arabian (ANA) script family. This corpus consists of some 2000 inscriptions, about 1500 of which are informal graffiti. The formal inscriptions are for the most part highly formulaic and consist predominantly of religious, legal, funerary, and building texts. While there is not much internal dating evidence, it is commonly assumed that they were produced sometime between the sixth and first centuries BC.[1]

As well as the Dadanitic inscriptions, a corpus of a little over sixty monumental Minaic inscriptions has also been found. Even though it is difficult to establish any exact dates for the beginning and ending of the Minaean kingdom, it is roughly estimated that Minaean kings ruled in the north of modern-day Yemen between the sixth and the first centuries BC.[2] The Minaeans established a trading post in Dadan, considered to have been contemporaneous with the Lihyanite kingdom (Winnett & Reed 1970: 117–118). The Minaean presence at Dadan probably lasted from about the fourth century BC (Beeston 1979: 8) until a little before the decline of the kingdom in the south, which can probably be placed in the first century BC (Robin 1998: 184–185; Arbach 2003: § 24–25); Beeston suggested that the trading station at Dadan was abandoned around 100 BC (1979: 8).

Writing traditions in contact

There are several inscriptions that attest to the participation of Minaeans in Dadan's cultural practices as well as general contact between them. A famous example

[1] Dating evidence is extremely sparse. The presence of the word *fḥt* 'governor' has been used to suggest a date after the sixth century BC, based on when this, originally Assyrian, word was thought to have been introduced into western Arabia (Winnett 1937: 51; Winnett & Reed 1970: 115–116; but see Graf 1990: 140; and most recently Rohmer, forthcoming). Another source for the dating of the inscriptions has been the so-called *Hierodulenlisten* from Maᶜīn, which list the marriages between Minaean men and foreign women, among them a 'free woman from Liḥyān' and women from Dadan (the woman from Liḥyān occurs in Maᶜīn 93 side B line 46, and the women from Dadan occur in Maᶜīn 93 West side lines 31; 36; South side lines 9/10; 16; 42/43; North side line 8; Maᶜīn 94 line 4; Maᶜīn 95 line 16; Maᶜīn 98 line 5/6), but the dating of this text is uncertain (for discussions see Bron 1998:102–103; and more recently Rohmer & Charloux 2015: 302). As pointed out by the reviewer, it is worth mentioning that after Gaza, the women from Dadan are the most numerous in the list, but there is only one from Liḥyān. Based on the style of statues found at Dadan and the name *Tlmy* of one or more of the kings of Liḥyān, Tarn (1929) argued for a strong Ptolemaic influence at the oasis during the third and second centuries BC, but this has since been shown to be unlikely (for a discussion of the evidence see Rohmer, forthcoming). Based on archaeological evidence from the sites of ancient Dadan and Ḥegrā (Madāʾin Ṣāliḥ), Rohmer and Charloux argue convincingly that the Lihyanite kingdom flourished between the sixth and fourth centuries BC (2015: 309) and entered a phase of decline in the third century BC (2015: 313). This would supposedly push back the period of the kings who identify themselves as *mlk ddn* 'king of Dadan' even further than that.

[2] See for example Winnett 1939 for a general discussion of the chronology of the Minaean kingdom. In that article Winnett argued that the Minaeans eventually took over political control of Dadan, but in a later work he showed that Minaean-Dadanite relations were probably friendly (Winnett & Reed 1970: 117–118). See Robin & de Maigret 2009 for a discussion of early archaeological evidence of the Minaean kingdom.

is JSLih 049, in which a priest of Wd, one of the main deities of the Minaeans, dedicates a boy to Ḏġbt, the local deity of Dadan.[3] The inscription is carved in relief in the Dadanitic script and language and uses Dadanitic dedicatory formulae.

1. JSLih 049[4]

ᶜbdwd//ʾfkl/w//d/w bn-h//s¹lm/w z//dwd/hw//dqw/h-ġ// lm/s¹lm/h-//[m]ṯlt/l-//ḏġbt// f-rḍy-h//m----
ᶜbdwd priest of Wd and his two sons S¹lm and Zdwd offered the boy S¹lm as a {substitute} to Ḏġbt so may he favour them....

An inscription discovered more recently and published by Abū ʾl-Ḥasan (2005), uses Dadanitic formulae and the Dadanitic language[5] but is expressed in the Minaic script. The inscription is deeply incised on the prepared face of a stone. It is interesting that even though the author of the text apparently chose to carve it in Minaic letters, he clearly had knowledge of the Dadanitic language and formulae, unless the person who composed the text and the one who carved it were not one and the same. This would still suggest, however, that the mason was not simply copying the letter shapes he saw on the exemplar he was given.

2. AHUD 1 (Fig. 1)

----t/ḥrym/bn/ḥyw/ḏ ᶜ//mrtᶜ/ḥggt/ḏġbt/f rḍ-h//m/ wʾḫrt-hm/w s¹ᶜd-hm/s¹nt//ṯlṯn/b-rʾy/ᶜtdn/lḏn/bn//hnʾs¹/ mlk/lḥyn/f ᶜrr ḏ//ġbt/ᶜrr/h-s¹fr/ḏt
----t Ḥrym son of Ḥyw of the lineage of ᶜmrtᶜ[6] performed the pilgrimage to Ḏġbt so favour them and their offspring and aid them year thirty during the *rʾy* of ᶜtdn, Lḏn son of Hnʾs¹ king of Liḥyān and may Ḏġbt dishonour the one who dishonours this inscription[7]

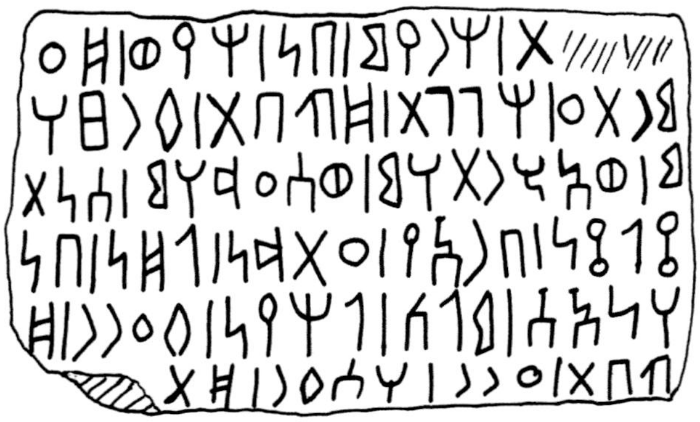

Figure 1. *AHUD 1. Abū ʾl-Ḥasan's tracing. (2005: 31, fig. 1). From OCIANA.*

Figure 2. *JSLih 220. Jaussen and Savignac's hand copy (1909–1922, ii: pl. CXXXIII). From OCIANA.*

Other evidence for at least some measure of familiarity with both scripts appears in several graffiti that were carved using a mixture of Dadanitic and Minaic letter shapes. In JSLih 220, for example, the author used a typical Minaic *z* and ʾ, but a Dadanitic *h*.

3. JSLih 220 (Fig. 2)

zydʾlhn

Finally, there is a Minaic legal inscription which, even though it is heavily damaged, clearly lays out the status of the children of a Minaean woman and a Dadanite man, thus suggesting close personal relationships between the Minaeans and the Dadanites.

[3] For a brief discussion of the meaning of *[m]ṯlt* 'substitute' in relation to the possible practice of dedicating the first born to *ḏġbt*, see the commentary in the record of JSLih 049 in OCIANA (accessed 4 March 2018).

[4] The editorial apparatus is as follows: [ ] indicates a restored letter; { } indicates a damaged letter; ---- indicates a part of the inscription that is broken off or too heavily damaged to suggest a reading; / indicates a word divider; // indicates a line break.

[5] The only difference from other Dadanitic texts is the feminine demonstrative *ḏt* referring to the noun *h-s¹fr*, which is otherwise masculine in the Dadanitic inscriptions (Abū ʾl-Ḥasan 2005: 32). This may have been a slip by the author of the text due to interference from the Minaic equivalent *ṣḥft* 'document' which is feminine and occurs regularly in Minaic inscriptions.

[6] Note that *ᶜmrtᶜ* is a lineage group which is well attested at Dadan both in the Minaic inscriptions (e.g. JSMin 69, 86, 94, etc.) and the Dadanitic (e.g. JSLih 245; U 072, and for more examples see the commentary in the OCIANA record for JSLih 245, accessed 4 March 2018). The use of this family name therefore further supports the idea that the inscription was commissioned or made by a person with a Minaean and Dadanite background.

[7] Even though both forms of *ᶜrr* look the same, the first should be interpreted as a perfective with an optative meaning 'may he dishonour', while the second represents an active participle 'the one who dishonours'.

4. M 360

[... ...]w{ġ}nhn{ʾ}[... ...] mᶜnm w-bhn[... ...]//[... ...]s^1 ddny{m}{ʾ}[..]{b}n b{ʾ}[.] ḏ-{ʾẖ}rh [... ...] //[... ...]{m} ᶜnyt k-ddny w-k-ḏ ʾẖrh [... ...] //[... ... m]{ᶜ}nm w-bhn-s^1m {w}-bhnt-s^1m w[... ...] //[... ... s^1]ᶜrb kl wld tld mᶜnyt k-kl ḏ- {ʾẖrhʾ}[... ...] //[... ...]

[... ...] *nhn(ʾ)* [... ...] Maᶜīn and the sons [... ...] // [... ...] a {Dadanite man} [... ...] of the {descent} [... ...] // [... ...] a {Minaean woman} to a Dadanite man and for those of descent [... ...] // [... ...] {Maᶜīn} and their sons and their daughters [... ...] //[... ...] offer all the children that a Minaean woman will have for all that {descent} [... ...] //[... ...][8]

These inscriptions testify to the close relations between the Dadanite and Minaean communities at the oasis, and particularly to Minaean participation in Dadanite cultural practices. While the graffiti with mixed Dadanitic/Minaic letter shapes show that people were exposed to both scripts, their mixing could be due to imperfect learning of either script independently, or playful use of the variation rather than the purposeful creation of a mixed register (so far only attested in graffiti), as it seems to be unpredictable which glyphs are exchanged.[9]

Contact between scribal schools?

Despite the apparent close contact between the Minaeans and the Dadanites and their epigraphic habits, their scribal schools seem to have had little impact on each other. In her 2014 paper Irene Rossi noted that the language and orthography of the Marginal Minaic texts, found beyond the Minaean homeland, barely diverge from those of Central Minaic (Rossi 2014: 114). Most of the differences that do occur are in the formulae that are used in the inscriptions (2014: 114).[10] Rossi sees this as a testament to a strongly maintained Minaean identity in the communities established abroad and the important role of the central scribal schools in the maintenance of this identity (2014: 119).

Dadanitic contains several features that set it apart from other ANA varieties: it is the only ANA script used to carve monumental inscriptions in relief; and formal Dadanitic inscriptions are the only ANA variety in which word dividers are used consistently (Macdonald 2008: 186). Dadanitic is also the only ANA script that regularly uses *matres lectionis* (2008: 105). While Dadanitic orthography is unique among ANA writing practices in its consistent use of these features they are common in Ancient South Arabian (ASA) inscriptions (Macdonald 2015: 15; Robin 2015: 99). Since there are other ANA varieties that make use of word dividers — they are also found in Taymanitic and Dumatic (Macdonald 2008: 186) — it seems unlikely that Dadanitic borrowed this practice from Minaic. It is difficult to say, however, exactly how the use of word dividers spread throughout the Arabian Peninsula and what role the Minaean presence at Dadan may have had in promoting their more consistent use in the Dadanitic inscriptions. The use of *matres lectionis* in Dadanitic on the other hand, must have developed independently. While Minaic and Dadanitic both represent final /-ū/ and /-ī/ with *-w* and *-y*[11] respectively, Dadanitic clearly uses *-h* to represent final /-ā/ (Drewes 1985: 167–68; followed by Farès-Drappeau 2005: 62–63), which sets its system apart from Minaic (Stein 2011: 1049).[12] Moreover, while Minaic clearly represents word-internal diphthongs, Dadanitic does not.[13]

---

[8] The transliteration and translation follow DASI (accessed 29 September 2017). The translation of lines 3–5 is based on Grimme's interpretation (1932: 236–237), except for the translation of *ḏ- ʾẖrh*, which he translated as 'what follows'.

[9] Only thirteen of the twenty-eight glyphs in the Dadanitic script are clearly distinguishable from their equivalents in the Minaic script (*ʾ ṯ g ḥ ẖ ḏ z ṣ ḍ ṭ ẓ f h*). In addition, /s^1/ and /s^3/ had merged in Dadanitic whereas they were distinct in Minaic and so had separate glyphs.

[10] While there seems to be an overlap in genres of inscriptions (legal, religious, and construction texts), at present a direct link between Dadanitic and Minaic formulae is difficult to demonstrate.

[11] There is some variation in the spelling of word internal triphthongs in III-y verbs. Both *rḍyt* (AH 288) and *rḍt* (JSLih 036) 'may she favour [someone]' and *rḍy-h* (e.g. AH 213) and *rḍ-h* (e.g. U 038) 'may he favour him' are attested. This suggests that at some point during the history of the Dadanitic corpus the triphthongs collapsed. The fact that no variation is attested in the spelling of word-final triphthongs, suggests that at the time when the triphthongs collapsed word-final *-y* came to be used as a *mater lectionis* for [-ē] as Drewes suggested (1985: 170). Since this development took place during the time span in which the Dadanitic inscriptions were produced, it is unclear in which cases *-y* was intended to represent a final diphthong or triphthong, and in which a final long vowel.

[12] Minaic has what is called the 'parasitic *h*'. This can be found infixed in some plural forms *bhn* 'sons (of…)'; *ʾnṯhtn* 'the women' (Stein 2011: 1049). It has been suggested that its possible occurrence in feminine external plurals might point to a vocalization /ā/ word internally (Stein 2011: 1049; referencing Frantsouzoff 2003: 42); it has also been suggested it might represent final short /-a/, based on its occurrence in the construct state (Stein 2011: 1051–1052), e.g. *b-byth ᶜṯtr ḏ-Qbḍ* 'at the temple of ᶜAṯtar of Qbḍ' (M 302). While its exact vocalization is still unclear, it was not used consistently to represent final /-ā/ as in Dadanitic.

[13] Cf. for example Dadanitic *bt* 'temple' (e.g. JSLih 077; AH 197) and *ym* 'day' (Al-Saᶜīd 1420/1999: 3–14, no. 1) to Minaic *byt* (M 338; M 356) and *ywm* (M 316; M 366). Based on the currently available evidence it is impossible to tell whether this difference is purely orthographic, or whether it reflects a difference in pronunciation. There are some personal names in which the diphthong may be represented (e.g. *rᶜnʾws*^{1} [JaL 156l]; *yṯbqws*^{1} [Al-Saᶜīd 1419/1999: 28–30, no. 5]; *zydẖrg* [JaL

This shows that both Dadanitic and Minaic had strongly established scribal practices that, despite their being in contact, seem to have had little influence on each other. Generally, language, script, and formulae were strongly connected within Dadanitic on the one hand and Minaic on the other, and only occasionally do there seem to have been crossovers, as we have seen in AHUD 1 and in the mixing of Dadanitic and Minaic letter forms in some of the graffiti. Two Minaic inscriptions, however, might shed more light on the existence of bilingualism at the oasis. If the interpretation proposed below is correct, JSMin 145 and JSMin 166 would be the first linguistically mixed Minaic/Dadanitic texts using the Minaic script and orthography, to be recognized.

Commentary on the texts

Both inscriptions were discovered by Jaussen and Savignac. They note that the inscriptions are irregularly but deeply carved into the rock (1909–1922, ii: 339–340; 347). Unfortunately, only their copies of the inscriptions are available (1909–1922, ii: pls CXXV and CXXVII respectively).

5. JSMin 145

nḥs^{1}ṭb dṯʾ ʾgr wd//{ʾ}ṣnʿ s^{1}tṭr ʿl mtbr//ʾwdq k-ḥmyn brn
Nḥs^{1}ṭb [of the lineage of] Dṯʾ servant of Wd, the artisan, has traced on the quarry a dedication for *ḥmyn brn*

6. JSMin 166

nḥs^{1}ṭb//ḏ dṯʾ//ṣnʿ wd //s^{1}tṭr ʿl mtbr//ʾwdq
Nḥs^{1}ṭb, he of the lineage of Dṯʾ, the artisan of Wd, has traced on the quarry a dedication

Since JSMin 166 is a briefer version of JSMin 145, the commentary will focus on JSMin 145, referring to the other inscription when needed.

Line 1: the personal name *nḥs^{1}ṭb* is most commonly found in Nabataean inscriptions (Negev 1991: 43; cf. Macdonald 1999: 280). It is also attested once in Dadanitic (JSLih 230) and once in the Safaitic corpus available on OCIANA (MEG 5). Including JSMin 145 and JSMin 166 it occurs six times in Marginal Minaic.

ʾgr can be more closely associated with the South Arabian realm. It never occurs in Dadanitic as a noun and only once as a personal name (Graf Abū al-Ḍibāʿ 1). In Minaic it occurs with the meaning 'servant, employee'. See for example:

7. Shaqab 1/6–8

{w}-//fqḍ kl mʿn ḥr w-[ʾ]//[g]r w-ġbr[14]
And they were those appointed [for the tributes?] of all Maʿīn, free men and employees and farmers[15]

8. M 401/3

kl mʿnm ḥrm w-ʾgrm w-ms^{2}km
...all Maʿīn, free men, servants, salaried employee[s] and the assembly of the officials (?)[16]

It is not surprising that the author of JSMin 145 used a form more common in Minaic than in Dadanitic to indicate his relationship with the Minaean deity Wd, and it firmly places this phrase in the Minaean cultural and linguistic realm.

Line 2: the reading of the *alif* at the beginning of line 2 in JSMin 145 is considered uncertain, even though it is clearly visible on Jaussen and Savignac's hand copy (1909–1922, ii: pl. CXXV). In the commentary on the DASI website[17] it is noted that, based on comparison with JSMin 166, the *alif* in line 2 was not considered part of the inscription. This is partly due to the fact that the *alif* was carved slightly above the line, but also because it poses a problem for the linguistic interpretation of the inscription if the language is considered to be Minaic. A plural form would not make sense here, and other functions for a prefixed *alif* are not available in Minaic. In JSMin 166 *ṣnʿ* occurs in construct with the name of the deity Wd while it occurs independently in JSMin 145, therefore we cannot conclude a priori that the *alif* in JSMin 145 does not belong to the inscription.

Instead I would propose to interpret *ʾṣnʿ* as a Dadanitic form and read the ʾ- as a definite article. Although this is not the most common form of the definite article in

161b]). In the case of personal names, it is difficult to be certain of the exact vocalization of the form. Moreover, since the linguistic situation in the oasis was not homogeneous (see Kootstra 2018: 210–214 for a discussion of the linguistic diversity at Dadan), it is not certain that these spellings and a possible retention of the diphthong would have been representative of the pronunciation of the majority of the inhabitants of the oasis. I would like to thank Jérôme Norris for asking me about 'marginal' spellings of diphthongs in Dadanitic.

[14] Note that the ʾ and *g* of *ʾgr* have been restored and the stone has broken off where the letters would have been. It has probably been restored based on the phrase in M 401, as there are no clear parallels in other ASA languages.

[15] Translation following CSAI (accessed 29 September 2017).

[16] Translation following CSAI (accessed 29 September 2017); *ʾgr* also occurs twice in Qatabanic as 'dignitary' of a deity (MuB 36 and TC 1046).

[17] Accessed 29 September 2017.

Dadanitic, it occurs in several inscriptions as can be seen in the following examples.[18] If this interpretation is correct, this may tell us something about the spoken register of Dadanitic. Since the author of this inscription was clearly not strictly following any set formula, it is likely that he was basing himself more closely on spoken language than the highly formulaic dedicatory inscriptions. This may lend further support to the idea that there was a more archaic written register present in the Dadanitic inscriptions (using the more common *h(n)-* definite article) and a spoken register of which we sometimes see traces in the inscriptions (such as the ʾ-definite article).[19] For example:

9. JSLih 276 (part)

f-ʿrr/ḏġbt/ʿrr/ʾ-sfr/ḏh
So may Ḏġbt dishonour whoever dishonours this inscription

10. AH 119/3–4

ʾẓlt ʾ-ẓll ḏh
she performed this *ẓll* ceremony

11. AH 074/2–3

ʿm/bnt/bs^2 *ʾẓlt ʾ-ẓll*
ʿm daughter of Bs^2 performed the *ẓll* ceremony

This solves the apparently awkward syntax in JSMin 145 in which the author seemed to be identifying himself with an indefinite noun. Further support for a Dadanitic origin of the noun *ṣnʿ* can be found in the fact that while it is one of the more commonly mentioned occupations in the Dadanitic corpus,[20] it does not seem to occur as such in the ASA inscriptions.[21] Instead, the root is found with different meanings, for example 'to fortify, to reinforce' (CIAS 39.11; Gr 1; Gr 219; Ir 32) or 'to save' (Ir 13) in Sabaic; *ʾṣnʿ* is attested once in Central Minaic with the meaning 'firmest' (as-Sawdāʾ 27) and once as a noun in Hadramitic *h-ṣnʿ* 'the help' (KR 6);[22] Beeston et al. mention *ʾṣnʿ* as a plural noun meaning 'fortification' (1982: 143).

The t-stem of the root *s*^{1}*ṭr* in JSMin 145 is rarely found in either corpus. There is one attestation in a broken context in Dadanitic:

12. AH 207

---- *s*^{1}*tṭr/b-mṣd* ----
---- he wrote at the sanctuary ----[23]

The verbs in JSMin 145 and JSMin 166 are the only two occurrences of *s*^{1}*tṭr* in Minaic, and there is one in Hadramitic (Qāniʾ 4). The root is, however, quite widely attested in Minaic, while it only occurs once in Dadanitic as a G-stem verb (JaL 061 f). In Minaic it mostly occurs as a noun *s*^{1}*ṭr* 'inscription' (e.g. al-Jawf 04.37; Gr 326; M 43). It therefore seems clear that the verb was not part of the common formulae of either corpus but could have come from either language.

The preposition *ʿl* 'on, upon' is separated from *mtbr* by a word divider in JSMin 166, but not in JSMin 145. It is clearly the same phrase, however. Jamme compares *mtbr* to Classical Arabic *mutabbar* 'broken up' from the D-stem *tabbara* 'to break, break into pieces', and interprets it as 'quarry' (Jamme 1974: 104) following the translation proposed by Jaussen and Savignac (1909–1922, ii: 339–340). In relation to this, Jaussen and Savignac mention that some metal was found close to where the two inscriptions were discovered, which suggested to them that in ancient times this location may have been used as a quarry (1909–1922, ii: 340). The root *tbr* does not seem to occur elsewhere in Dadanitic or in ASA.[24]

[18] The most common form of the definite article in Dadanitic is a prefixed *h-* with the unassimilated form *hn-* before laryngeals (Farès-Drappeau 2005: 65), but Dadanitic also contains examples of a ʾ- and an unassimilated *ʾl-* definite article (for more on the variation of the definite article in ANA, see Al-Jallad, forthcoming).

[19] For a more elaborate discussion on variation and possible different registers in the Dadanitic inscriptions see Kootstra 2018: 215.

[20] It occurs eleven times, e.g. AH 213; JSLih 074; al-Ḫuraybah 12.

[21] After a search for the root in DASI (accessed 29 September 2017).

[22] All attestations and translation are based on DASI (accessed 29 September 2017).

[23] For the translation of *mṣd* as 'sanctuary', see Lundberg 2015: 136. Note that this text (AH 204) is damaged and fragmentary. Abū ʾl-Ḥasan 2005: 36–37 translates *h-mṣd* as 'the high red mountain', which he interprets as a reference to the red stone of Jabal Umm Daraj where almost all the inscriptions mentioning *mṣd* are found, except for JSLih 085 which was found at Al-Khuraybah. Note that JSLih 085 was found at the entry to 'the ancient sanctuary' (provenance notes in the OCIANA record, accessed 7 March 2018). Abū ʾl-Ḥasan's identification of *h-mṣd* with the location of Jabal Umm Daraj is probably correct, based on the distribution of the texts containing this word. Based on the etymology of the word (discussed in Lundberg 2015: 136) and its occurrence in relation to the sanctuary in Al-Khuraybah a translation as 'sanctuary' is more appropriate in JSLih 085, with the important note that in most cases the sanctuary at Jabal Umm Daraj seems to have been meant.

[24] This is based on the lack of occurrences in DASI, OCIANA, and the online Sabaic dictionary (http://sabaweb.uni-jena.de/SabaWeb, accessed 29 September 2017). Note that Aramaic *tbr* 'to break' (CAL, accessed 29 September 2017) comes from the root *√ṯbr (cf. Sab *ṯbr* 'to destroy, to damage, to crush' [Beeston et al. 1982: 149] and Classical Arabic *ṯabara-hu* 'he destroyed him' [Lane, 330c]). It is unclear why

Line 3: *ʾwdq* is translated by Jaussen and Savignac as a broken plural meaning 'the cuttings' (1909–1922, ii: 339–340) and in this they were followed by Jamme (1974: 103–104) who, however, interprets it as a reference to the inscription itself. Jamme notes that it is syntactically awkward that there is no definite article on this noun (1974: 104). He suggests that the possibility of omitting the definite article is due to 'Lihyanite' (i.e. Dadanitic) influence. He gives the example *b-ḥqwy/kfr* 'on two sides of [the] tomb' (JSLih 075 and JSlih 077) to illustrate the fact that if the object referred to was sufficiently clearly defined from context, the definite article could be omitted in Dadanitic. As an additional example he mentions *ʾṣfḥt* 'rock faces' in JSLih 065 (= JaL 133). He dismisses the possibility that we might be looking at a ʾ- definite article. According to him, this inscription cannot be compared to JSLih 066 *ʾḫḏ h-ṣfḥt ḏt* 'he took this rock face', since the demonstrative pronoun is lacking in JSLih 065 (Jamme 1974: 101).

The occurrence of the phrase *b-ḥqwy/kfr* could suggest that *kfr* was so well defined to the author of the inscriptions in this particular genitive construction, that it functioned as a proper name. The noun *mṣd* 'sanctuary' (see note 23 for a discussion of the term) is the only other form that can be used in a similar way, omitting the definite article.[25] This suggests that these words were so closely connected to the place they indicated that they had become (almost) equivalent to toponyms. Based on the two occurrences of the phrase *b-ḥqwy kfr*, it is difficult to be sure that such a specific meaning existed. But regardless of whether or not both forms can be considered proper names, this phenomenon is so restricted in its use in Dadanitic that it seems unlikely that it influenced Minaic.

Once again, I would propose instead to interpret this unique form in Minaic as a nominal form derived from a fairly common Dadanitic dedicatory verb *ʾdq* (√wdq) 'to offer'. This root occurs in several different forms in Dadanitic. It is attested both as a C-stem verb *ʾdq* *ʾawdaq(a) and *hdq* *hawdaq(a) and as a CD-stem verb *hwdq* *hawaddaq(a).[26] The representation of the diphthong in this inscription is probably due to the use of the Minaic script. Unlike Dadanitic, Minaic *does* represent word internal diphthongs.[27] Orthographic rules are dictated by the script used and not by the language.[28] The fact that the *w* is represented in the Minaic script here therefore suggests that it was intended to represent a form /ʾawdaq(a)/, indicating that the diphthong was pronounced in the Dadanitic form.[29] If the interpretation of *ʾwdq* as a causative verb 'to dedicate' is correct, this inscription can be related to more common formulae in the oasis used in dedicatory texts.

13. JSLih 061/3–4

ʾdq/l-l//h/{h}-ṣlmn
He dedicated to Lh {the} two statues

14. JSLih 063/2

ʾdq/{l}-ḏġ{b}t/hn-ʾṣl[m]
He dedicated {to} {Ḏġbt} the {statues}

15. Private collection 2/3–5

ʾdq/h-m//gmrt/l-//ḏġbt
He dedicated the incense burner to Ḏġbt

While it is unusual to find the object of a dedication in an indefinite form, it is syntactically possible. Interpreting it as an indefinite form, however, would be an awkward reading if *ʾwdq* referred back to the inscription itself as Jamme suggested (1974: 103–104).

The preposition *k-* 'for' is typically Minaic (Arbach 1993: 40; Stein 2011: 1062) and does not occur in Dadanitic.

Ḥmyn is a common name in Safaitic (147 attestations in the OCIANA database);[30] it is attested once in Dadanitic (U 109), and occurs seven times in Minaic and once in Sabaic (Haram 18).[31] The name *brn* is less well attested but occurs five times in Safaitic (e.g. KRS 2451, 1784), once in Dadanitic (JSLih 105), and once in Hismaic (KJB 11).[32] It is also attested in Qatabanic (Ja 361), Sabaic

the etymological /ṯ/ would be represented with a *t* in this word in either Minaic or Dadanitic, which both preserved their interdentals, but there are a few examples of etymological interdentals being represented as stops in Dadanitic (Kootstra 2018).

[25] Both *b-h-mṣd* (e.g. AH 208, 217, 221) and *b-mṣd* (AH 202, 207) 'at the sanctuary' occur.

[26] Dadanitic clearly did not represent word internal diphthongs (see n. 13). Thus, the *w* in *hwdq* most likely represents something else. CD-stems can also be found in Ge'ez (A_2 stem) (Weninger 2011: 1131); Akkadian (Soden 1952: §95); and possibly Modern South Arabian (Dufour 2017: §4).

[27] For some examples see n. 13.

[28] Cf. for example, the Safaitic script which did not represent diphthongs, but from Greek/Safaitic bilinguals, we know that they were most likely pronounced. In an inscription from Jordan a man called Taym wrote his name in Greek as Θαιμος while he represented his name in Safaitic as *tm* (Al-Jallad & Al-Manaser 2016: 56).

[29] Note that the fact that word-internal diphthongs are not represented in the Dadanitic orthography does not necessarily mean that they were not pronounced.

[30] Accessed 29 September 2017.

[31] DASI accessed 29 September 2017.

[32] OCIANA accessed 29 September 2017.

(Robin-Kāniṭ 3), and Hadramitic (RES 2693), but does not seem to have been very common.[33] Based on these occurrences, however, it seems to be the case that *ḥmyn brn* was a person and not the epithet of a deity.

Discussion

If the interpretation proposed above is correct, JSMin 145 and JSMin 166 are two linguistically mixed inscriptions, probably written by someone of Minaean descent, based on his identification as a servant of the Minaean deity Wd, the use of Minaic as the main language of the inscription, and the use of the Minaic script. The words he chose to substitute with Dadanitic words or phrases suggest that he was borrowing specific cultural terms from Dadanitic. One might even suggest that he was code-switching, since he used the Dadanitic noun together with the Dadanitic definite article (Myers-Scotton 1997). The fact that the author chose to use a Dadanitic term for an occupation that is regularly attested in the Dadanitic inscriptions may suggest that he was part of the Dadanitic workforce and this was simply how his job was referred to in day to day interactions. Clearly, this can be no more than speculation and it must be noted that none of the artisans who give their name in the Dadanitic inscriptions bears the name *nḥs¹ṭb*. It should also be noted that the other possible Dadanitic term in the text, *ʾwdq* 'he dedicated', is closely tied to Dadanitic cultural practices and may therefore also be considered a cultural loan.

Conclusions

The new interpretation of JSMin 145 and JSMin 166 points to the bilingualism of the Minaean author of the inscriptions. This is of course to be expected in a situation such as the one at Dadan, where a trading colony was established in a foreign oasis, but this is the first clear example of it in the epigraphic record. Since the author's Dadanitic insertions are probably based on the spoken language, as he is clearly diverging from written formulae, his usage of the ʾ-definite article may tell us something about the spoken register at the oasis. We only have this one example, however, and it is therefore unclear whether this would have been the common spoken register for all the Dadanitic-speaking inhabitants of the oasis. Finally, the use of the Minaic script and orthographic conventions may reveal something about the phonology of Dadanitic. The fact that the author wrote the *w* in the form *ʾwdq*, representing the word-internal diphthong, seems to suggest that the underlying Dadanitic form preserved the diphthong in this position, which was not orthographically represented in the Dadanitic script.

[33] DASI accessed 29 September 2017.

Acknowledgements

I would like to thank Benjamin Suchard, Jérôme Norris, and Marijn van Putten for their comments on the first draft of the paper. I would also like to thank Ahmad Al-Jallad for our helpful discussions about inscriptions and writing traditions. Finally, I would like to thank Michael Macdonald and the anonymous reviewer for their comments and corrections. All errors are of course my own.

Sigla

AH	Dadanitic inscriptions in Abu ʾl-Ḥasan 1997.
AHUD	Minaic inscription published in Abū ʾl-Ḥasan 2005.
CAL	Comprehensive Aramaic Lexicon, http://cal.huc.edu/
CIAS	Ancient South Arabian inscriptions published in Beeston, Pirenne & Robin 1977–1986.
CSAI	Corpus of South Arabian Inscriptions, part of DASI.
DASI	Digital Archive for the Study of pre-Islamic Arabian Inscriptions http://dasi.humnet.unipi.it/
Gr	Ancient South Arabian inscriptions published in Grjaznevič 1978.
Graf Abū al-Ḍibāʿ	Dadanitic inscriptions published in Graf 1983.
Haram	Ancient South Arabian inscriptions published in Robin 1992.
al-Ḫuraybah	Dadanitic inscriptions published in Al-Theeb 2013.
Ir	Ancient South Arabian inscriptions published in Al-Iryānī 1990.
Ja	Ancient South Arabian inscriptions published in Jamme 1963.
JaL	Dadanitic inscriptions published in Jamme 1974.
al-Jawf	Ancient South Arabian inscriptions published in Arbach & Schiettecatte 2006.

JSLih	Dadanitic inscriptions in Jaussen & Savignac 1909–1922.
JSMin	Minaic inscriptions in Jaussen & Savignac 1909–1922.
KJB	Hismaic inscriptions published in King 1990.
KR	Ancient South Arabian inscriptions published in Avanzini 2008.
KRS	Safaitic inscriptions recorded by G.M.H. King in 1990 on the Basalt Desert Rescue Survey and published in OCIANA.
Lane	Lane 1863–1893.
M	Minaic inscriptions in Garbini & Capuzzi 1974 and available in DASI.
Maʿīn	Minaic inscriptions in Bron 1998.
MEG	Safaitic inscriptions published in Macdonald 1991.
MuB	Qatabanic inscriptions published in Avanzini et al. 1994.
OCIANA	Online Corpus of the Inscriptions of Ancient North Arabia http://krcfm.orient.ox.ac.uk/fmi/webd#ociana
Private collection	Dadanitic inscriptions from a private collection published in OCIANA.
Qāniʾ	Ancient South Arabian inscriptions from ancient Qāniʾ published in Ryckmans G. 1939.
RES	*Répertoire d'épigraphie sémitique*. (8 volumes). Paris: Imprimerie nationale, 1900–1968.
Robin-Kāniṭ	Ancient South Arabian inscriptions from the ancient site of Kāniṭ in Robin 1982.
as-Sawdāʾ	Ancient South Arabian inscriptions published in Avanzini 1995.
Shaqab	Ancient South Arabian inscriptions from Shaqab al-Manaṣṣah available in DASI.
TC	Ancient South Arabian inscriptions from the Timnaʿ cemetery in Cleveland 1965.
U	Dadanitic inscriptions from al-Udhayb in Sima 1999.

References

Abū ʾl-Ḥasan Ḥ.A.D. 1997. *Qirʾah li-kitābāt liḥyāniyyah min Jabal ʿIkma bi-minṭaqat al-ʿUlā*. Riyād: maktabat al-malik Fahd al-waṭaniyyah.

Abū ʾl-Ḥasan Ḥ.A.D. 2005. Dirāsah taḥlīliyyah li-naqsh maʿīnī jadīd min al-ʿUlā. *Adumatu* 12: 29–38.

Arbach M. 1993. Le Maḏābien: Lexique, onomastique et grammaire d'une langue de l'Arabie méridionale préislamique. PhD thesis, Université de Provence, Aix-en-Provence. [Unpublished].

Arbach M. 2003. La situation politique du Jawf au Ier millénaire avant J.-C. *Arabian Humanities* 11: 1–8.

Arbach M. & Schiettecatte J. 2006. *Catalogue des pièces archéologiques et épigraphiques du Jawf au musée national de Ṣanʿâʾ / Ṣanʿâʾ National Museum*. Ṣanʿāʾ: Centre français d'archéologie et de sciences sociales de Ṣanʿâʾ.

Avanzini A. 1995. *As-Sawdāʾ*. (Inventaire des inscriptions sudarabiques, 4). Paris: De Boccard/Rome: Herder.

Avanzini A. 2008. Notes for a history of Sumhuram and a new inscription of Yashhurʾil. Pages 609–641 in A. Avanzini (ed.), *A port in Arabia between Rome and the Indian Ocean (3rd c. BC–5th c. AD). Khor Rori Report 2*. (Arabia Antica, 5). Rome: 'L'Erma' di Bretschneider.

Avanzini A., Bāfaqīḥ M., Bāṭāyiʿ A. & Robin C.J. 1994. Materiali per il Corpus Qatabanico. *Raydān* 6: 17–36.

Beeston A.F.L. 1979. Some observations on Greek and Latin data relating to South Arabia. *Bulletin of the School of Oriental and African Studies* 42: 7–12.

Beeston A.F.L., Pirenne J. & Robin C.J. 1977–1986. *Corpus des inscriptions et antiquités sud-arabes*. (2 volumes in 4 parts). Louvain: Peeters.

Beeston A.F.L., Al-Ghul M.A., Müller W.W. & Ryckmans J. 1982. *Sabaic Dictionary (English-French-Arabic)*. Louvain-la-Neuve: Peeters.

Bron F. 1998. *Maʿīn*. (Inventaire des inscriptions sudarabiques, 3). Paris: De Boccard/Rome: Herder.

Cleveland R. 1965. *An Ancient South Arabian necropolis. Objects from the second campaign (1951) in Timnaʿ cemetery*. (Publications of the American Foundation for the Study of Man, 4). Baltimore, MD: Johns Hopkins Press.

Drewes A.J. 1985. The phonemes of Lihyanite. Pages 165–173 in C. Robin (ed.), *Mélanges linguistiques offerts à Maxime Rodinson par ses élèves, ses collègues et ses amis*. (Comptes rendus du Groupe Linguistique d'études chamito-sémitiques, Supplément 12). Paris: Geuthner.

Dufour J. 2017. How can MSA tell us something about the Semitic verb? Paper presented at the 45th North Atlantic Conference on Afroasiatic Linguistics, Leiden University. Available at www.academia.edu/33457152/How_can_Modern_South_Arabian_tell_us_something_about_the_Semitic_verb

Farès-Drappeau S. 2005. *Dédan et Liḥyān: Histoire des Arabes aux confins des pouvoirs perse et hellénistique (IVe–IIe s. avant l'ère chrétienne)*. (Travaux de la Maison de l'Orient et de la Méditerranée, 42). Lyon: Maison de l'Orient et de la Méditerranée.

Frantsouzoff S. 2003. En marge des inscriptions de Raybūn. Remarques sur la grammaire, le lexique et le formulaire de la langue ḥaḍramoutique épigraphique. *Arabia* 1: 39–58.

Garbini G. & Capuzzi A. 1974. *Iscrizioni Minee* (Pubblicazioni del Seminario di Semitica, Ricerche, 10; Iscrizioni sudarabiche, 1). Naples: Istituto Orientale di Napoli.

Graf D.F. 1983. Dedanite and Minaean (South Arabian) inscriptions from the Ḥisma. *Annual of the Department of Antiquities of Jordan* 27: 555–569.

Graf D.F. 1990. Arabia during Achaemenid times. Pages 131–148 in H. Sancisi-Weerdenburg & A. Kuhrt (eds), *Achaemenid History IV: Centre and periphery. Proceedings of the Groningen 1986 Achaemenid history workshop.* Leiden: Nederlands Instituut voor het Nabije Oosten.

Grimme H. 1932. Die Bedeutung des Eigennamens *ʾʾs²r* in Glaser 1155 und 1083 sowie weiteres zu Gl. 1155. *Wiener Zeitschrift für die Kunde des Morgenlandes* 39: 227–245.

Grjaznevič P.A. 1978. *Materiali ekspedicii P.A. Grjazneviča 1966–1967 Gg. Južnaja Aravija*. (Pamjiatniki Drevney Istorii i Kultury, 1). Moscow: Glavnaja redakzija vostočnoj literatury.

Al-Iryānī M. 1990. *Fī taʾrīkh al-Yaman. Nuqūš musnadiya wa-taʿliqāt*. Ṣanaʿāʾ: Markaz al-dirāsāt wa-ʾl-buḥūth al-yamanī.

Al-Jallad A. (forthcoming). What is Ancient North Arabian? In D. Brinstiehl & N. Pat-El (eds), *Re-engaging comparative Semitic and Arabic studies*. Wiesbaden: Harrassowitz.

Al-Jallad A. & Al-Manaser A. 2016. New epigraphica from Jordan II: Three Safaitic-Greek partial bilingual inscriptions. *Arabian Epigraphic Notes* 2: 55–66.

Jamme A. 1963. *The al-ʿUqlah Texts*. (Documentation sud-arabe, 3). Washington: Catholic University of America Press.

Jamme A. 1974. *Miscellanées d'ancient* [sic] *Arabe*. vii. Washington, DC. [Privately produced].

Jaussen A. & Savignac M.R. 1909–1922. *Mission archéologique en Arabie*. (5 volumes). Paris: Leroux/Geuthner.

King G.M.H. 1990. Early North Arabian Thamudic E. A preliminary description based on a new corpus of inscriptions from the Ḥismā desert of southern Jordan and published material. PhD thesis, School of Oriental and African Studies, University of London. [Unpublished].

Kootstra F. 2018. *Ẓ* and *ṭ* in the Dadanitic inscriptions. Pages 202–217 in L. Nehmé & A. Al-Jallad (eds), *To the Madbar and back again: Studies in the languages, archaeology, and cultures of Arabia dedicated to Michael C.A. Macdonald.* (Studies in Semitic Languages and Linguistics, 92). Leiden: Brill.

Lane E.W. 1863–1893. *An Arabic-English Lexicon, derived from the best and most copious Eastern sources*. London: Williams & Norgate.

Lundberg J. 2015. Prepositional phrases in the Dadanitic inscriptions. *Arabian Epigraphic Notes* 1: 123–138.

Macdonald M.C.A. 1991. Epigraphic gleanings from the archive of the Palestine Exploration Fund. *Palestine Exploration Quarterly* 123: 109–116.

Macdonald M.C.A. 1999. Personal names in the Nabataean realm. A review article. *Journal of Semitic Studies* 44: 251–289.

Macdonald M.C.A. 2008. Ancient North Arabian. Pages 197–224 in R.D. Woodard (ed.), *The ancient languages of Syria-Palestine and Arabia*. Cambridge: Cambridge University Press.

Macdonald M.C.A. 2015. Arabs and empires before the 6th century. With contributions by A. Corcella, T. Daryaee, G. Fisher, M. Gibbs, A. Lewin, D. Violante, & C. Whately. Pages 11–89 in G. Fisher (ed.), *Arabs and Empires before Islam*. Oxford: Oxford University Press.

Myers-Scotton C. 1997. *Duelling languages: Grammatical structure in code switching*. Oxford: Clarendon.

Negev A. 1991. *Personal names in the Nabatean realm*. (Qedem, 32). Jerusalem: Institute of Archaeology, Hebrew University of Jerusalem.

Robin C.J. 1982. *Les hautes-terres du nord-Yémen avant l'Islam*. (2 volumes). (Uitgaven van het Nederlands Historisch-Archaeologisch Instituut te Istanbul, 50). Istanbul: Nederlands Historisch-Archaeologisch Instituut te Istanbul.

Robin C.J. 1992. *Inabbaʾ, Haram, al-Kāfir, Kamna et al-Ḥarāshif.* (Inventaire des inscriptions sudarabiques, 1). Paris: De Boccard/Rome: Herder.

Robin C.J. 1998. La fin du royaume de Maʿīn. In R. Gyselen & F. Aubaile-Sallenave (eds), Parfums d'orient. *Res Orientales* 11: 177–188.

Robin C.J. 2015. Before Ḥimyar: Epigraphic evidence for the kingdoms of South Arabia. Pages 90–126 in G. Fisher (ed.), *Arabs and empires before Islam*. Oxford: Oxford University Press.

Robin C.J. & de Maigret A. 2009. Le royaume sudarabique de Maʿīn: Nouvelles données grâce aux fouilles italiennes de Baraqīsh (l'antique Yathil). *Comptes Rendus de l'Académie des Inscriptions et Belles-Lettres*: 57–96.

Rohmer J. (forthcoming). Foreign powers and local kingdoms in northwest Arabia: New insights into the political history of Dadan, Ḥegrā and Taymāʾ in the later 1st millennium BC. In M. Luciani (ed.), *The archaeology of the Arabian Peninsula 2: Connecting the evidence. Proceedings of the International Workshop Held in Vienna on April 25*. (Oriental and European Archaeology). Vienna: Austrian Academy of Sciences Press.

Rohmer J. & Charloux G. 2015. From Liḥyān to the Nabataeans: Dating the end of the Iron Age in North-West Arabia. *Proceedings of the Seminar for Arabian Studies* 45: 297–320.

Rossi I. 2014. The Minaeans beyond Maʿīn. Pages 111–124 in O. Elmaz & J.C.E. Watson (eds), *Languages of southern Arabia.* (Supplement to volume 44 of the Proceedings of the Seminar for Arabian Studies). Oxford: Archaeopress.

Ryckmans G. 1939. Inscriptions sud-arabes. Sixième série. *Le Muséon* 52: 297–319.

Al-Said S.F. 1419/1999. Dirāsah taḥlīliyyah li-nuqūsh liḥyāniyyah jadīdah [I]. *Majallat jāmiʿat al-malik Saʿūd* 11/*al-ādāb* 2: 1–38.

Al-Said S.F. 1420/1999. Nuqūš liḥyāniyyah ghayr manshūrah min al-matḥaf al-waṭanī al-Riyāḍ, al-mamlakah al-ʿarabiyyah al-saʿūdiyyah. *Nashrah baḥthiyyah* 14/1: 3–14.

Sima A. 1999. *Die lihyanischen Inschriften von al-ʿUḏayb (Saudi Arabien)*. (Epigraphische Forschungen auf der Arabischen Halbinsel, 1). Rahden/Westfalen: Leidorf.

Soden W. von 1952. *Grundriss der akkadischen Grammatik*. (Analecta Orientalia, 33). Rome: Pontificium Institutum Biblicum.

Stein P. 2011. Ancient South Arabian. Pages 1042–1073 in Weninger et al. 2011.

Tarn W.W. 1929. Ptolemy II and Arabia. *Journal of Egyptian Archaeology* 15: 9–25.

Al-Theeb [Al-Dhiyīb] S.A. 2013. *Al-Khuraybah (Dadan) ʿāṣimat mamlakatay Dadān wa-Liḥyān. Al-taqrīr al-ʿUlā li-l-mawsim al-ṯhāmin 2011m.* (Silsilat al-dirāsāt al-athariyyah al-maydāniyyah, 1). Riyāḍ: Iṣdārāt al-jamīʿah al-suʿūdiyyah l-l-dirāsāt al-athariyyah.

Weninger S. 2011. Old Ethiopic. Pages 1124–1142 in Weninger et al. 2011.

Weninger S., Khan G., Streck M.P. & Watson J.C.E. (eds). 2011. *The Semitic languages. An international handbook.* (Handbücher zur Sprach- und Kommunikationswissenschaft, 36). Berlin/Boston: De Gruyter Mouton.

Winnett F.V. 1937. *A study of the Lihyanite and Thamudic inscriptions*. (University of Toronto Studies — Oriental Series, 3). Toronto: University of Toronto Press.

Winnett F.V. 1939. The place of the Minaeans in the history of pre-Islamic Arabia. *Bulletin of the American Schools of Oriental Research* 73: 3–9.

Winnett F.V. & Reed W.L. 1970. *Ancient records from North Arabia*. (Near and Middle East Series, 6). Toronto: University of Toronto Press.

Author's address

Fokelien Kootstra, Leiden University, Leiden Institute for Area Studies, Room no. 0.11, Matthias de Vrieshof 4, 2311 BZ Leiden, Netherlands.
e-mail f.kootstra@hum.leidenuniv.nl

M.C.A. Macdonald (ed.), *Languages, scripts and their uses in ancient North Arabia.* (Supplement to volume 48 of the Proceedings of the Seminar for Arabian Studies). Oxford: Archaeopress, 2018: 31–38

'Literacy in literate societies': the scribe in Nabataean and other Aramaic contexts

John F. Healey

Summary
This paper reviews the key role of scribes reflected in surviving documents in late Aramaic, including Nabataean. The approach is to examine the explicit and implicit role of scribes in the drawing up of Nabataean legal documents such as those found in the Babatha archive and lying in the background of the Ḥegrā tomb inscriptions, which appear to be summaries of archived documents. This material has a clear affinity with earlier Aramaic scribal tradition and with the Jewish Aramaic Babatha documents, as well as with some slight evidence from Palmyra and more substantial evidence in early Syriac. All of these data can be exploited to build a fuller picture of the scribal culture of the region in the Graeco-Roman period. The discussion is framed by the ambiguities in the use of the terms 'literacy in oral societies' and 'literacy in literate societies'. In the latter, scribes might have been among the relatively few literates, but they fulfilled a specific role in what were really *literate* societies. The terms used for 'scribe' are also examined.

Keywords: scribes, law, Aramaic, Nabataean, Syriac, literacy

The discussion of literacy in the ancient world in general, and in the ancient Near East and Arabia in particular, cannot be usefully conducted on the basis of a binary choice or zero-sum game in which we conclude that a certain percentage of people within a society were or were not literate. The issue of 'literacy in an oral environment' was magisterially surveyed in a well-known paper by Michael Macdonald (2005; see also Macdonald 2017, a detailed review of Wise 2015). My concern here is the role of specialist scribes in what I would call 'literate societies' in the areas of northern Arabia and Syria where Aramaic was commonly used. Apart from general works on literacy and Macdonald 2005, a number of studies have been devoted to the subject in the context of the Greco-Roman world and Palestine (Harris 1989; Bowman 1991; Millard 2000; Hezser 2001; Wise 2015), although most interest in the subject has focused on the editors and transmitters of literary texts (e.g. Oppenheim 1964: 228–287; Toorn 2007).

It is possible to try to arrive at estimates of the percentages of literates in particular ancient societies (for the pitfalls see Macdonald 2017), but I see two faults in the logic of this way of thinking: firstly, the use of percentages implies an analogy with modern measures of literacy in which the question asked is 'How many ordinary citizens, excluding very small children, are functionally literate in the sense of being able to read comfortably and write effectively, even if slowly?' In this simplified version of the modern question, no distinction is made between men and women or farm labourers and lawyers. But one presumes that even in a country which has in absolute terms low levels of literacy, 100% of the lawyers will be literate, although one should note the case of Petaus cited by Macdonald (2005: 53), a village 'scribe' who had difficulty signing his name. Thus, even in the modern context any 'percentage' hides a more complex reality (unless literacy is virtually at the 100% level throughout the population).

In relation to ancient societies, there are other factors to be taken into account in trying to quantify literacy. The society may exclude females from all education related to writing: if so, the society has no *intention* of enabling them to read and write. Thus, it might achieve 100% literacy for men and have only a low level for women. In such a case, it is not meaningful to say that the society has achieved 50% literacy.

Until relatively recently in western Europe, it was not thought necessary for working-class people to read and write. The Protestant Reformation is often credited with the widening of access to these skills, since even working-class salvation depended on reading the Bible, (see in this context the discussion of Sweden and Scotland in Macdonald's paper [2005: 54–56]). Perhaps it is less obvious that upper-class aristocrats in earlier times did not really need to read and write either: they did not do their own reading (before Gutenberg) and any significant writing would be put into the hands of specialists trained in the art of writing.

Secondly, in citing modern-style percentages, we are also in danger of ignoring the central role played by such specialists, the scribes. If you had access to good scribes, you did not need to learn to read and write (but no doubt it might save a lot of time and mistakes if you did).

Writing was regarded as a specific skill and its origin was mythologized in the sense that it was said to have been invented or taught to mankind by the gods, like other magic arts: in Mesopotamia by the goddess Nisaba or the god Nabû, in Egypt by Thoth, later interpreted as identical with Hermes. Literacy was not regarded as a skill to which all should aspire, however, and it was not uniquely valued in society. In fact, there is a view that literacy in cuneiform was quite widespread in some periods in ancient Mesopotamia, although perhaps restricted largely to state officials in the Neo-Assyrian period (Veldhuis 2011: 73; Charpin 2010: 53–65). Tiglath-Pileser III, however, would not have been bothered in the least to be told, say, that only 5% of his people could read and write and that all of those were men — 5% might have been more than enough.[1] The point in the present context is that, even if literacy was not totally restricted to them, scribes had a specific function in societies like this, just as soldiers or weavers did, and there was no need for everyone to be a scribe or a soldier or a weaver.

Veldhuis's discussion distinguishes functional, technical, and scholarly literacy (Veldhuis 2011): we should note for present purposes that the term 'scribe' in the ancient context covers at least two different phenomena, that of the literary scribe and that of the legal or administrative scribe. The literary scribe was often, it seems, the editor or even in some sense the author of the work he wrote down. A good example of this is Ilimilku, the Ugaritic scribe who wrote down or even perhaps composed the main mythological and legendary texts (Wyatt 1998: 145–146 on KTU 1.6 vi 54–58, and also pp. 114, 241, and 278). This kind of scribe has a higher level of learning and the title 'scribe' becomes an honorific, applied, for example, to 'Ezra the scribe' in the Old Testament (e.g. Ezra 7: 11; Neh. 8: 4), 'Enoch the scribe' elsewhere in the Jewish tradition (see below) and perhaps also in evidence at Ḥatra in the period we are concerned with (as we will also see below).

The other kind of scribe is much more prosaic: he was a legal practitioner occupying a non-prestige role in society as the one to turn to locally if you needed some writing done, especially writing connected with a contract. He was expert, not in composing mythological texts or even writing them elegantly, but in the prosaic drawing up of legal documents. He had been trained in this specific skill, even if it is not always clear to us how such training was organized. The evidence of training is implicit, consisting above all in the broad formal uniformity of legal texts over a long period of time and a wide area (see Démare-Lafont & Lemaire 2010 for a series of discussions of the formulaic legal language).

Thus, I would argue that measuring literacy for ancient societies using percentages of literacy in the modern sense is fundamentally misguided. Such measures would tell us little about the society in question even if they could be discovered. To discover the role of literacy in society we need to look at the role of scribes as well as the absolute numbers of literates. In fact, it is almost impossible to estimate percentages of the latter, but it is feasible to discuss the former on the basis of surviving documents. And a society can be literate without having many literates, since literacy can have a major, dominating role in a society in which literates are few (see Macdonald 2005: 45). Macdonald, for example, states firmly and, I believe, correctly, that Nabataea was a literate society (2005: 94), although this does not mean that illiterates were only a small minority (see also Macdonald 2017: 841–842).

The case of the Nabataeans can be studied on the basis of surviving Nabataean material and by making some comparisons with neighbouring contemporaries who, like the Nabataeans, shared in the Aramaic tradition of scribal literacy.

This Aramaic scribal tradition goes back to the beginning of the first millennium BC (see the surveys of Aramaic and the Aramaeans by Gzella 2015 and those edited by Niehr 2014). It is virtually commensurate with the history of Aramaic, which is known in written evidence from about 900 BC. From this early period, there is no evidence at all of widespread literacy although scribal practice reflected in the work of stone carvers is already clearly established. The first extensive text, the ninth-century BC Tell Fekheriye inscription, is a bilingual monumental inscription in Aramaic and Assyrian (Abou-Assaf, Bordreuil & Millard 1982). Although it is a monumental official inscription, its form and existence clearly imply an already established scribal milieu: the text uses formulaic language paralleled elsewhere; it is bilingual, with the Aramaic evidently derived at least in part from the Assyrian; and it is carved in a confident style reflective of a well-established scribal tradition.

[1] Arguably, the developmental and economic advantages of widespread literacy were underappreciated, just as the future significance of the computer was underappreciated in 1975 when I first saw one.

As we move on in time through the later Assyrian and Neo-Babylonian periods to the Achaemenid, we are presented with extensive administrative use of writing in Aramaic, for example in the fifth-century BC texts of the Jewish community in Elephantine and in other Aramaic texts from Egypt, and as far away as fourth-century BC Bactria (Porten et al. 1996: 74–267; Naveh & Shaked 2012). The texts from Egypt are written on papyrus, the use of which already implies the ephemeral character of writing for everyday purposes (as opposed to stone-carved display inscriptions). At the same time, however, the many formal letters to governors and petitions which survive in this archive also have a formulaic character and were carefully composed and written, either by specialist scribes or by particularly skilled members of the Jewish community.

A little later, in the fourth century BC, we have the Wadi Daliyeh legal papyri (Gropp in Gropp et al. 2001: 1–116). These are mostly slave sales and follow similar formularies, but they do not explicitly mention the names of scribes, possibly because the documents had official status through having been executed before local officials.

Turning now to the period of the surviving Nabataean texts, there are large numbers in the general category 'Nabataean', from both before and after the end of the Nabataean kingdom in AD 106, and there are a large number of graffiti, especially from the Sinai peninsula, which are of uncertain date. These graffiti were discussed by Macdonald in the context of the playful use of writing, since most of them seem to have been scribbled 'idly' on suitable rocks close to where travellers or herdsmen passed or, more probably, camped (Macdonald 2005: 94).

Many of the more substantial Nabataean texts which have survived are legal in character. In passing, we may note that this is true of the tomb inscriptions from Ḥegrā/Madā'in Ṣāliḥ (Healey 1993a; 1993b; Nehmé 2015, i: 100–104), although these are not legal texts in the full sense but, rather, summaries of legal documents. They use legal language, but they are not witnessed and do not have the same status as the original papyrus documents on which they are based and to which there is an allusion in one inscription mentioning a copy of the full document being preserved in archives (Healey 1993a: no. 36/9). Although these tomb texts are not themselves legal documents, it is likely that the summarizing of the originals was carried out by a scribe, who used his skill to extract the key points from the original.

The other main source here is the Babatha archive found in a cave on the western side of the Dead Sea and published in 2002 (Yadin et al. 2002: 169–276). This Nabataean Babatha material is from an archive containing other documents which are also scribal and legal in character. These other legal documents, carried around by the unfortunate Babatha, are in Jewish Aramaic and Greek and share broadly the same scribal culture as that of the Nabataean texts and other Greek texts of the same Dead Sea region.

These texts contain a number of details relevant to the issue of literacy. For example, there is reference to substitute signatories being used for principals in legal documents who, as the texts say, 'do not know how to write'. This applied to Babatha herself, as we know from *P.Yadin* 15/35. What is especially important to note here is that the inability to write did not prevent someone like Babatha from engaging in complex legal arrangements, owning property, and conducting disputes in a Roman court. The use of literate substitutes who could at least sign for them was normal in Roman-period documents from Egypt. Harris (1989: 142) quotes a figure of 1500 references to such illiteracy in the Greek papyri from Egypt (Greenfield 1993; Czajkowski 2017: 63–66).

There is an illuminating discussion of the finer shades of illiteracy in K. Czajkowski's recently published book (2017: 62–65), in particular in relation to examples of the writing of one's own legal documents, as evidenced from the Babatha archive and elsewhere. Notably Babatha's husband, Judah son of Elᶜazar, appears to have written the marriage contract himself (*P.Yadin* 10/20). And some people may have been able to read but not write (2017: 64). These facts should caution us against any overly simple view of literacy in particular societies, as does the discussion of Veldhuis of functional, technical, and scholarly literacy in the Mesopotamian context (2011).

Note also that, despite the fact that in some cases in Aramaic and Greek documents from the Near East (e.g. also in early Syriac documents) the illiterates were women, women could own and transfer property quite independently in Nabataea. Often they could not write and maybe did not want to learn to write (if my view of literacy is correct). You did not have to be literate in order to participate fully in a literate society, since you had scribes to do the writing for you. Legally, the ability to speak was essential, but the ability to write was not. Property contracts were essentially oral transactions.

Words for 'scribe'

Two words for 'scribe' are used in Nabataean texts. We have a small group of inscriptions in which the term *ktb*ᵓ, probably to be vocalized as *kātᵉbā*, the emphatic state *pe*ʿ*al* participle of KTB, may be used for 'scribe'. Some of the inscriptions in question are among the Nabataean graffiti in Sinai. Most of these are hard to date, but most probably post-date the end of the Nabataean kingdom in AD 106, so that they do not give us incontrovertible evidence for the earlier period.

The two fairly clear examples from Sinai are *CIS* ii 825, *ʾltqbw br qymw ktbʾ*, and 2667 (reread in Negev 1977: 223, pl. 32 A, no. 7), *ʿbydw ktbʾ*. The latter example is especially suggestive that the title *ktbʾ* refers to a specific profession (rather than more informally 'the writer, the one who wrote'), since the same inscription also mentions other professions: an *ʾpklʾ/apkallā*-priest and a *mbqrʾ/mebaqqerā*.[2] This inscription is from the Jebel Moneijah complex — apparently the site of a Nabataean temple — discussed by Avraham Negev (1977). The inscriptions from this site often mention professions related to the local cult: *ʾpklʾ/apkallā, 'apkallā*-priest' (seven times), *khnʾ/kāhenā*, 'priest' (once), and *mbqrʾ/ mebaqqerā*, 'examiner of sacrificial victims' (?) (four times). As previously indicated, dating is difficult, but one of the inscriptions in the group (*CIS* ii 2666 = Negev 1977: 222–223, pl. 31 E, no. 6) is dated to the year 113, probably in the era of the Roman Province of Arabia, thus indicating AD 219.

There are also two inscriptions, one from Petra and the other from Ḥegrā, which could refer to the scribal profession, although it seems unlikely. The first is *CIS* ii 416 (re-edited in Nehmé 2012: MP 138), *šlm qrʾʾ wktbʾ*. Here we might translate 'Peace to the reader and the scribe', but a simpler translation would be 'Peace to the one who reads and the one who wrote'. It is interesting to find here reference to the reader *and* the writer and there is an implication of a casual reader and therefore some level of literacy in the passing population. The same formula, I understand, also appears in early Arabic inscriptions. Similarly, the second inscription at Madā'in Ṣāliḥ/Ḥegrā, JS I 190, has *šlm ktbʾ dy ktb wʾlw*, 'Peace to the scribe who wrote [this], Wāʾilu'. But here the context of clear reference to the inscription itself carved on the rock by Wāʾilu makes it again improbable that a professional scribe is involved. Rather he is just the casual 'writer' of a graffito.[3]

The second small, but more secure group of references to scribes in Nabataean appears in a very different kind of context, that of legal texts. Here the word which is used is *sprʾ* — probably to be vocalized as *sāperā* — not *ktbʾ*. This too, like *kāṭebā*, is a nominalized emphatic state *pe*ʿ*al* participle form, but it always means 'scribe' and does not correspond to a normal productive verbal root in Aramaic. This noun's origin is not altogether clear. Koehler and Baumgartner (1994–2000: 1939–1940) assumed it was borrowed from Akkadian *šāpiru*, the title of an official (CAD Š/1: 453–458), but Sokoloff (2009: 99) has with good reason argued the reverse, in other words, that Akkadian *sepīru*, 'a scribe who writes in alphabetic script', was borrowed from Aramaic (see CAD S: 225-226). In any case it became the normal word for 'scribe' in Aramaic, occurring well over 100 times, for example, in the Aramaic from Elephantine and in many later Aramaic dialects (see Hoftijzer & Jongeling 1995: 798–799). In Nabataean, *sprʾ/ sāperā* occurs a handful of times in the Nabataean legal papyri of the Babatha archive, always in a formal context connected with the drawing up of a legal text.

Thus in *P.Yadin* 1/59, 66, *ḥwrw br ʿwtw sprʾ*, 'Ḥuwaru son of ʿAwtu, the scribe', which appears at the end of the signatures of the witnesses, and *P.Yadin* 2/49 and *P.Yadin* 3/55, *ʿzwr br ʿwtw sprʾ* , 'ʿAzūr son of ʿAwtu, the scribe', also at the end of the list of signatories on the verso of the document. The name of the scribe ʿAzūr son of ʿAwtu is also restored in *P.Yadin* 4/26 (see also Czajkowski 2017: 73).

It is important to note here that the Nabataean papyri involve legal formularies and practices which are entirely consonant with other Aramaic legal texts of the same period and earlier. They are part of a common legal tradition going back, as was shown long ago in relation to the papyri from Elephantine, to models in Neo-Assyrian and Neo-Babylonian law. The *sāperā* had a central role in this tradition of law and frequently signs off the legal document with his name and title after the names of the legal witnesses.

This kind of legal scribe — indeed some term like the English word 'notary' might best convey his role, since he is not a mere writer and not a composer of literary works, but a skilled drafter of watertight legal contracts — was essential to the working of complex agricultural societies in which land ownership and its transfer were centrally important. Even if many men and some women were able to write their own signature, they were not literate in the modern sense and therefore depended on trained scribes for legal documents, as indeed we still do today.[4]

[2] This word is also found in *CIS* ii 2661/4, where *mbqrʾ* can be read with confidence in the light of Negev 1977: nos. 2, 8, and 9. Note that as well as *mebaqqerā* the form *ʾal-mubaqqirū* is found (*CIS* ii 2723, although the reading is uncertain); see also Teixidor 1979: 357–358.

[3] Cantineau (1930–1932, ii: 108) takes *ktbʾ* as a participle in JS I 142 (although adding a question mark), but a personal name *tymlktbʾ* is more likely.

[4] Our modern-day concern with literacy has nothing to do with avoiding

These pieces of Nabataean evidence for scribes are meagre but fortunately, as with many aspects of Nabataean society, we can use other sources to fill in some of the gaps left by the sporadic character of our extant information.

Thus, we have Jewish documents, also from the Judaean Desert materials, in which the scribe plays a role, although the naming of the scribe is not a common feature. Scribes are, however, mentioned in legal contexts in several texts. Thus, *ʾlʿzr br mtth sprh* in a well-known deed of sale from AD 134 (according to Milik 1957: 264–268[5]) and ... *br yhwsp sprʾ* in a marriage contract (Benoit, Milik & de Vaux 1961: no. 21/22). We may note also *ktb spryʾ* in a third text (Cotton & Yardeni 1997: no. 50/18), although the meaning is obscure. *Yhwdh br ʾlʿzr hs(w)pr* (with the Hebrew definite article) appears in an ossuary inscription, naming the deceased and his professional status (*CIIP* § 244). The Aramaic of the Dead Sea Scrolls provides us with other material, including repeated references to 'Enoch the distinguished scribe' (*ḥnwk spr pršʾ*) (Milik 1976: 315 in 4QEnGiants[a] ar frag. 8/4, and 305 in 4QEnGiants[b] ar 21–22 [frag. 2/14]). In this last case we are clearly dealing with the use of the word 'scribe' to mean 'learned man'.

Since the term *sprʾ* is very much a Mesopotamian term, whether of Akkadian or Aramaic origin, it is not surprising that it also appears in other Aramaic evidence from further north, specifically in early Syriac (so-called Old Syriac) legal texts and in Hatran inscriptions. As far as the early Syriac legal parchments are concerned, from the AD 240s the term is used in exactly the same way as in Nabataean as the descriptor of the legal notary who drew up the contract (Drijvers & Healey 1999: 231–248):

> P1/29–30: *mrqws ʾwrlys blšw br mqymw sprʾ ktbt šṭrʾ hnʾ*, 'Marcus Aurelius Bēlšu, son of Muqīmu, the scribe, I wrote this document'
> P2/29–30: *ʾnʾ br bsʾ sprʾ br brbʿšmyn ktbt šṭrʾ hnʾ*. 'I, Bar Bassa, the scribe, son of Barbaʿšamīn, wrote this document'
> P3/26–27: *mrqws ʾwrlys gdʾ sprʾ br gdʾ ktbt šṭrʾ hnʾ*, 'Marcus Aurelius Gadda, the scribe, son of Gadda, I wrote this document'

From Ḥatra we have no legal documents for direct comparison, but the title 'scribe' appears surprisingly often in inscriptions on stone. In some cases, the reference may be to a high official rather than a mere writer of documents (Beyer 1998: 181):

> Ḥatra 215/1: *dkyr ʾšṭṭ sprʾ*, 'Remembered be Aštaṭ the scribe'
> Ḥatra 221/2: *dkyr gdyhb rbytʾ wʾšṭṭ sprʾ*, 'Remembered be Gadyahb the major-domo and Aštaṭ the scribe'
> Ḥatra 289a/3: *dkyr zbdy sprʾ*, 'Remembered be Zabday the scribe'
> Ḥatra 408/9 (= Healey 2009: no. 66/9): *dkyr ʿqʾ sprʾ*, 'Remembered be ʿAqā the scribe'

There are cases where a higher official, a 'learned' scribe, is implied:

> Ḥatra 35/3 (= Healey 2009: no. 75/3): *nšrʿqb sprʾ dbrmryn*, 'Nišrʿaqab, the scribe of [the god] Barmārēn' is clearly an official of a temple,

and

> Ḥatra 389/1-2: *dkyr ddʾ lṭb wlšnpyr qdm nbw sprʾ* (readings uncertain), 'Remembered be Dadā for good and for wellbeing before [the god] Nabû the scribe' where it is the god who is called 'scribe', the patron of the scribal art.

Neither in early Syriac nor in Hatran does *kātᵉbā/ktbʾ* appear as the word for 'scribe', although it may form part of a Hatran personal name (Beyer 1998: 178) and the *verb* KTB is used in the Syriac legal texts for the action of the scribe (P1/30; P2/30; P3/27). In later Syriac (i.e. Classical, Christian Syriac) *sāfᵉrā* or *sōfᵉrō* is retained for 'legal scribe, notary, learned man', while *kāṯōvā* or *kōṯōvō* is much rarer (Sokoloff 2009: 1035, 661).

An argument could be made that the term *sāpᵉrā* is closely linked with the Mesopotamian legal tradition, which was adopted by the Aramaic-speaking peoples of the Near East from the Assyrian period onwards. This tradition was highly formulaic and the standard term for a scribe was *sāpᵉrā*. We would probably be right to assume that the *sāpᵉrā* came into Nabataean tradition ultimately from this Aramaic and Mesopotamian legal tradition. The term *kātᵉbā*, by contrast, is used more loosely and it is not used for 'scribe' in the legal texts. It appears only in post-Nabataean (i.e. post-AD 106) contexts and its use is often ambiguous: even the best cases of its use as a professional title are weak, as we have seen.

I hesitate to venture into questions of Arabic, but I note that Arabic *sāfir*, which belongs to the same Semitic root as Aramaic SPR, only rarely has meanings connected with the

the use of solicitors: we learn to read and write with other purposes in mind.

[5] Note, however, that Cotton and Yardeni (1997: no. 8a) read *mmrh* for *sprh*.

scribal art (although it is, of course, used in relation to the role of the *safīr*, 'mediator' or 'ambassador'), and in both Classical Arabic (Lane 1863–1893: 1371c) and in Safaitic there are derivatives related to writing (al-Jallad 2015: 340). I was led by my colleague Rex Smith to Lane's entry on *sāfir* (1863–1893: 1371c), which notes the meaning 'writer, scribe', and cites the form *sāfirā*, connecting it with what it calls 'the Nabathaean language' (giving reference, of course, to standard lexicographical sources). This obviously cannot refer directly to the classical Nabataeans, who were long dead, but to the Aramaic of the indigenous population of Mesopotamia. Thus, it implies that it is a borrowing from some form of Aramaic and the continued survival of the older technical meaning of the word in Classical Arabic. There, however, *kātib* is the word normally used for 'scribe, notary, writer, etc.'. It is possible that this difference of usage reflects a difference between areas of Mesopotamian and Arabian influence.

Much of the above has concentrated on explicit evidence of Nabataean scribes and scribes in other late-Aramaic-using contexts (Syriac, Hatran, etc.). But there is also indirect, implicit, evidence, which suggests that the scribal profession was well organized and must have involved systematic training. Several circumstantial details point to this:

1. The existence of legal archives (referred to in inscriptions from Ḥegrā, Palmyra [PAT 2759, 2760] and Edessa [P1/18-20 and *P.Euphr*. 7/33]) implies a central registry for property transactions. These must have been administered. Indeed, in the Syriac documents there is a reference to the 'inspector' of documents connected to the archive, the *mbḥrʾ/m*^{e}*baḥ(ḥ)*^{e}*rā* (P1/26).
2. Within the Nabataean tradition there is a high degree of legal uniformity, which makes it hard to avoid the conclusion that scribes were trained within a well-defined tradition. It is true that for Nabataean we only have the Babatha archive, but the legal language of the Ḥegrā tomb inscriptions points in the same direction. In terms of legal formulae and practice, the Nabataean legal texts are conservative. They represent the legal tradition already evidenced by Achaemenid Aramaic texts from Elephantine. It must have been handed down through some process of training.
   On a wider canvas, we may note that this 'professional' repertoire of legal formularies and practices was shared with other forms of contemporary Aramaic. The Babatha Aramaic documents are drawn up in a style which would be immediately intelligible in Judaea or Palmyra or Edessa, despite the fact that the Nabataean legal texts were drawn up locally in the backwater of Maoza near Zoar at the southern end of the Dead Sea, not in Petra. A good illustration of the fact that an international set of norms for legal texts was being followed is the feature that the surviving contracts are double documents, following the age-old tradition of such scribal practice found all over the Aramaic-speaking world. This kind of practice could only have reached Zoar by way of scribal training within a long tradition.
3. The *form* of Aramaic in use in Nabataea was conservative and not much different from Achaemenid Aramaic. The standard hypothesis is that the Nabataeans wrote their documents and inscriptions in a rather fossilized form of Aramaic, in line with the fact that most of them did not speak Aramaic, but some form of Arabic. Thus, the formal Nabataean language of the legal documents was a learned language or dialect, not one acquired by the scribe at his mother's knee.

The conclusion seems inevitable that there was a system of scribal training. Of course, we do not know how such scribal training worked. At one extreme, there might have been centralized schools at places like Petra and Ḥegrā, associated perhaps with the archives. At the other, it is possible that local scribes passed on their craft from generation to generation locally, although one might then expect much greater variety to develop and innovations to creep in. Either way, scribes were the key to Nabataean society's literate character.

Sigla

CAD	*Chicago Assyrian Dictionary,* see Gelb I.J. et al. 1956–2010.
CIIP	*Corpus Inscriptionum Iudaeae et Palaestinae*, see below under Cotton et al. 2010–
CIS ii	Nabataean inscriptions in *Corpus Inscriptionum Semiticarum. Pars II. Inscriptiones Aramaicas continens*. Paris: Imprimerie nationale, 1889–1954.
Ḥatra	Hatran inscriptions in Beyer 1998.
JS	Nabataean inscriptions in Jaussen & Savignac 1909–1914.
KTU	Ugaritic texts in Dietrich, Loretz & Sanmartín 2013.

MP	(Milik Pétra) Nabataean inscriptions in Nehmé 2012.
P	Syriac documents on parchment in Drijvers & Healey 1999.
PAT	Palmyrene inscriptions in Hillers & Cussini 1996.
P.Euphr.	Greek and Syriac papyri in Feissel, Gascou & Teixidor 1997.
P.Yadin	Nabataean papyri in Yadin et al. 2002.

References

Abou-Assaf A., Bordreuil P. & Millard A.R. 1982. *La statue de Tell Fekherye et son inscription bilingue assyro-araméenne*. (Études assyriologiques). Paris: Éditions Recherche sur les civilisations.

Benoit P., Milik J.T. & de Vaux R. 1961. *Les grottes de Murabba ᶜât*. (Discoveries in the Judaean Desert, 2). Oxford: Clarendon Press.

Beyer K. 1998. *Die aramäischen Inschriften aus Assur, Hatra und dem übrigen Ostmesopotamien*. Göttingen: Vandenhoeck & Ruprecht.

Bowman A.K. 1991. Literacy in the Roman Empire: Mass and mode. Pages 119–131 in J.H. Humphrey (ed.), *Literacy in the Roman world.* (Journal of Roman Archaeology Supplement, 3). Ann Arbor, MI: Journal of Roman Archaeology.

Cantineau J. 1930–1932. *Le Nabatéen.* (2 volumes). Paris: Leroux.

Charpin D. 2010. *Reading and writing in Babylon*. Cambridge, MA/London: Harvard University Press.

Cotton H.M. & Yardeni A. 1997. *Aramaic, Hebrew and Greek documentary texts from Naḥal Ḥever and other sites*. (Discoveries in the Judaean Desert, 27). Oxford: Clarendon Press.

Cotton H.M. et al. 2010–. *Corpus Inscriptionum Iudaeae et Palaestinae*. Berlin: De Gruyter.

Czajkowski K. 2017. *Localized law: The Babatha and Salome Komaise archives*. (Oxford Studies in Roman Society and Law). Oxford: Oxford University Press.

Démare-Lafont S. & Lemaire A. (eds). 2010. *Trois millénaires de formulaires juridiques*. (École Pratique des Hautes Études, Sciences historiques et philologiques II; Hautes études orientales Moyen et Proche Orient, 4/48). Geneva: Droz.

Dietrich M., Loretz O. & Sanmartín J. 2013. *Die keilalphabetische Texte aus Ugarit, Ras Ibn Hani und anderen Orte.* (Dritte erweiterte Auflage). (Alter Orient und Altes Testament, 360/1). Münster: Ugarit-Verlag.

Drijvers H.J.W. & Healey J.F. 1999. *The Old Syriac inscriptions of Edessa and Osrhoene*. (Handbuch der Orientalistik, 1. Der Nahe und Mittlere Osten, 42). Leiden: Brill.

Feissel D., Gascou J. & Teixidor J. 1997. Documents d'archives romains inédits du Moyen Euphrate (IIᵉ s. après J.-C.). II. Les actes de vente-achat (*P.Euphr*. 6 à 10). *Journal des Savants*: 3–57.

Gelb I.J., Jacobsen T., Landsberger B, & Oppenheimer A.L. 1956–2010. Assyrian dictionary of the Oriental Institute of the University of Chicago. Chicago, IL: Oriental Institute of the University of Chicago.

Greenfield J.C. 1993. 'Because he/she did not know letters': Remarks on a first millennium C.E. legal expression. *Journal of the Ancient Near Eastern Society of Columbia University* 22: 39–44.

Gropp D.M., Bernstein M., Vanderkam J.C. & Brady M. 2001. *Wadi Daliyeh II: The Samaria Papyri from Wadi Daliyeh and Qumran Cave 4. XXVIII: miscellanea, part 2*. (Discoveries in the Judaean Desert, 28). Oxford: Clarendon Press.

Gzella H. 2015. *A cultural history of Aramaic from the beginnings to the advent of Islam*. (Handbuch der Orientalistik, 1. Der Nahe und Mittlere Osten, 111). Leiden/Boston, MA: Brill.

Harris W.V. 1989. *Ancient literacy*. Cambridge, MA/ London: Harvard University Press.

Healey J.F. 1993a. *The Nabataean tomb inscriptions of Madaʾin Salih*. (Journal of Semitic Studies Supplements, 1). Oxford: Oxford University Press.

Healey J.F. 1993b. Sources for the study of Nabataean law. *New Arabian Studies* 1: 203–214.

Healey J.F. 2009. *Aramaic inscriptions and documents of the Roman period*. (Textbook of Syrian Semitic Inscriptions, 4). Oxford: Oxford University Press.

Hezser C. 2001. *Jewish literacy in Roman Palestine*. (Texts and Studies in Ancient Judaism, 81). Tübingen: Mohr Siebeck.

Hillers D.R. & Cussini E. 1996. *Palmyrene Aramaic texts*. (Publications of The Comprehensive Aramaic Lexicon Project). Baltimore, MD: Johns Hopkins University Press.

Hoftijzer J. & Jongeling K. 1995. *Dictionary of the North-West Semitic inscriptions*. (Handbuch der Orientalistik, 1. Der Nahe und Mittlere Osten, 21.1–2). Leiden/New York: Brill.

al-Jallad A. 2015. *An outline of the grammar of the Safaitic inscriptions*. (Studies in Semitic

Languages and Linguistics, 80). Leiden/Boston, MA: Brill.

Jaussen A. & Savignac M.R. 1909–1914. *Mission archéologique en Arabie I–II*. Paris: Leroux/Geuthner.

Koehler L. & Baumgartner W. 1994–2000. *The Hebrew and Aramaic lexicon of the Old Testament.* (5 volumes). Leiden/New York: Brill.

Lane E.W. 1863–1893. *An Arabic-English lexicon, derived from the best and most copious Eastern sources*. London: Williams & Norgate.

Macdonald M.C.A. 2005. Literacy in an oral environment. Pages 49–118 in P. Bienkowski, C. Mee & E. Slater (eds), *Writing and Ancient Near Eastern society: Papers in honour of Alan R. Millard.* (Library of Hebrew Bible/Old Testament Studies, 426). New York/London: T. & T. Clark. [Reprinted with addenda and corrigenda as article I in M.C.A. Macdonald, *Literacy and identity in pre-Islamic Arabia*. (Variorum Collected Studies 906). Farnham: Ashgate, 2009.]

Macdonald M.C.A. 2017. Review of Wise 2015. *Journal of Roman Archaeology* 30: 836–846.

Milik J.T. 1957. Deux documents inédits du Désert de Juda. *Biblica* 38: 245–268.

Milik J.T. (ed. with the collaboration of M. Black) 1976. *The Books of Enoch: Aramaic fragments of Qumrân Cave 4*. Oxford: Clarendon Press.

Millard A.R. 2000. *Reading and writing in the time of Jesus*. (The Biblical Seminar, 69). Sheffield: Sheffield Academic Press.

Naveh J. & Shaked S. 2012. *Aramaic documents from ancient Bactria (fourth century BCE)*. London: The Khalili Family Trust.

Negev A. 1977. A Nabatean sanctuary at Jebel Moneijah, southern Sinai. *Israel Exploration Journal* 27: 219–231.

Nehmé L. (with the collaboration of J.T. Milik & R. Saupin) 2012. *Pétra: atlas archéologique et épigraphique. 1. De Bāb as-Sīq au Wādī al-Farasah.* Paris: Académie des Inscriptions et Belles-Lettres.

Nehmé L. 2015. *Les tombeaux nabatéens de Hégra.* (2 vols). Paris: Académie des Inscriptions et Belles-Lettres.

Niehr H. (ed.). 2014. *The Aramaeans of Ancient Syria.* (Handbuch der Orientalistik, 1. Der Nahe und Mittlere Osten, 106). Leiden/Boston, MA: Brill.

Oppenheim A.L. 1964. *Ancient Mesopotamia: Portrait of a dead civilization*. Chicago/London: Chicago University Press.

Porten B., Farber J.J., Martin C.J. & Vittmann G. 1996. *The Elephantine papyri in English: Three millennia of cross-cultural continuity and change*. (Documenta et Monumenta Orientis Antiqui, 22). Leiden/New York: Brill.

Sokoloff M. 2009. *A Syriac lexicon: A translation from the Latin, correction, expansion, and update of C. Brockelmann's* Lexicon Syriacum. Winona Lake, IN/Piscataway, NJ: Eisenbrauns/Gorgias Press.

Teixidor J. 1979. Bulletin d'épigraphie sémitique 1978–1979. *Syria* 56: 353–405.

Toorn K. van der. 2007. *Scribal culture and the making of the Hebrew Bible*. Cambridge, MA/London: Harvard University Press.

Veldhuis N. 2011. Levels of literacy. Pages 68–89 in K. Radner & E. Robson (eds), *The Oxford handbook of cuneiform culture*. Oxford: Oxford University Press.

Wise M.O. 2015. *Language and literacy in Roman Judaea. A study of the Bar Kokhba documents*. (The Anchor Yale Bible Reference Library). New Haven, CT: Yale University Press.

Wyatt N. 1998. *Religious texts from Ugarit: The words of Ilimilku and his colleagues*. Sheffield: Sheffield Academic Press.

Yadin Y., Greenfield J.C., Yardeni A. & Levine B.A. 2002. *The documents from the Bar Kokhba period in the Cave of Letters. Hebrew, Aramaic and Nabatean-Aramaic papyri*. (Judean Desert Studies). Jerusalem: Israel Exploration Society/Hebrew University/Shrine of the Book.

Author's address
John F. Healey, Middle Eastern Studies, University of Manchester, Oxford Road, Manchester M13 9PL, UK
e-mail john.healey@manchester.ac.uk

M.C.A. Macdonald (ed.), *Languages, scripts and their uses in ancient North Arabia.* (Supplement to volume 48 of the Proceedings of the Seminar for Arabian Studies). Oxford: Archaeopress, 2018: 39–49

The role of Aramaic on the Arabian Peninsula in the second half of the first millennium BC

PETER STEIN

Summary

Epigraphic records from ancient Arabia comprise not only inscriptions in the local languages and scripts of the region, but also texts in Aramaic. Only recently, places such as Taymāʾ in the north and Mleiha (Mulayḥah) in the east of the Peninsula have been shown to be remarkable examples of places where the Aramaic language and script were used during the Achaemenid and Seleucid periods. The evidence from these sites raises several questions, which will be addressed in this paper: when did writing in Aramaic begin in these places, and why there specifically? How much mutual influence can be seen between Aramaic and the local languages and scripts in each of those regions? What is the relationship between the foreign and local languages in terms of their use for administrative, social, and religious purposes?

Keywords: Aramaic, Taymāʾ, Mleiha, Hasaitic, Taymanitic

Speak, I pray thee, to thy servants in Aramaic; for we understand it. And talk not with us in the local language in the ears of the people that are on the wall.

2 Kings 18: 26[1]

This famous scene from the siege of Jerusalem by Sennacherib's troops in the year 701 BC, as recorded in the Hebrew Bible, illustrates well the situation we are confronted with on the Arabian Peninsula some centuries later. There is a local population (here the Judaeans of the southern part of Ancient Palestine) speaking their own language, and a foreign force of an entirely different language tradition (the Assyrians), communicating with each other by means of an intermediary language (Aramaic) which is not the mother tongue of either party. This intermediary language is apparently understood by the Assyrian official (the *rabshākēh* who is addressing those on the city walls) as well as by the Judaean representatives, among whom are explicitly mentioned the 'major-domo' of the royal palace (*ʾᵃšer ʿal habbayit*), a scribe (*sōper*), and a secretary (*mazkīr*, lit. 'the man who remembers, records', 2 Kings 18: 18). It is particularly the mention of the latter two which is remarkable in our context. Why were these two sent to negotiate with the Assyrian envoy?[2] It must surely have been because they could speak the language used in international communication. By contrast, ordinary people — officers as well as soldiers — who were following the scene from the city walls, were said to be able to communicate only in their mother tongue. This was the situation in Palestine around 700 BC. Let us now turn to the Arabian Peninsula, where documentation of Aramaic only starts later, apparently in the course of the sixth to fourth centuries BC. The earliest evidence which can be dated with certainty originates in the oasis of Taymāʾ.

Taymāʾ

The famous Taymāʾ stele, discovered by Charles Huber and Julius Euting in 1880 and subsequently brought to the Musée du Louvre (Teima 1[3] = *CIS* ii 113 = KAI 228), is a document in fine Aramaic language and script (Fig. 1). From a palaeographical point of view, it appears to be one of the earliest instances of the Aramaic script in the

[1] Adapted from the King James Version of the Bible. The Hebrew original contains the word 'Judaean' (*yəhūdīt*) instead of 'local language', which I have changed here to make the sense more general.

[2] It is perhaps not only their belonging to 'the ruling elite' which explains these men's understanding of Aramaic (thus e.g. Gallagher 1999: 50–51), but their particular profession as scribes. It is not even necessarily true that the Judaean major-domo named Eliakim was himself fluent in Aramaic. Since the text states that the three men together addressed the request to the *rabshākēh*, it is quite possible that Eliakim could only talk to the Assyrians with the help of his two colleagues interpreting.

[3] Note the numbering of Imperial Aramaic inscriptions from Taymāʾ follows that in Schwiderski 2004: 410–413.

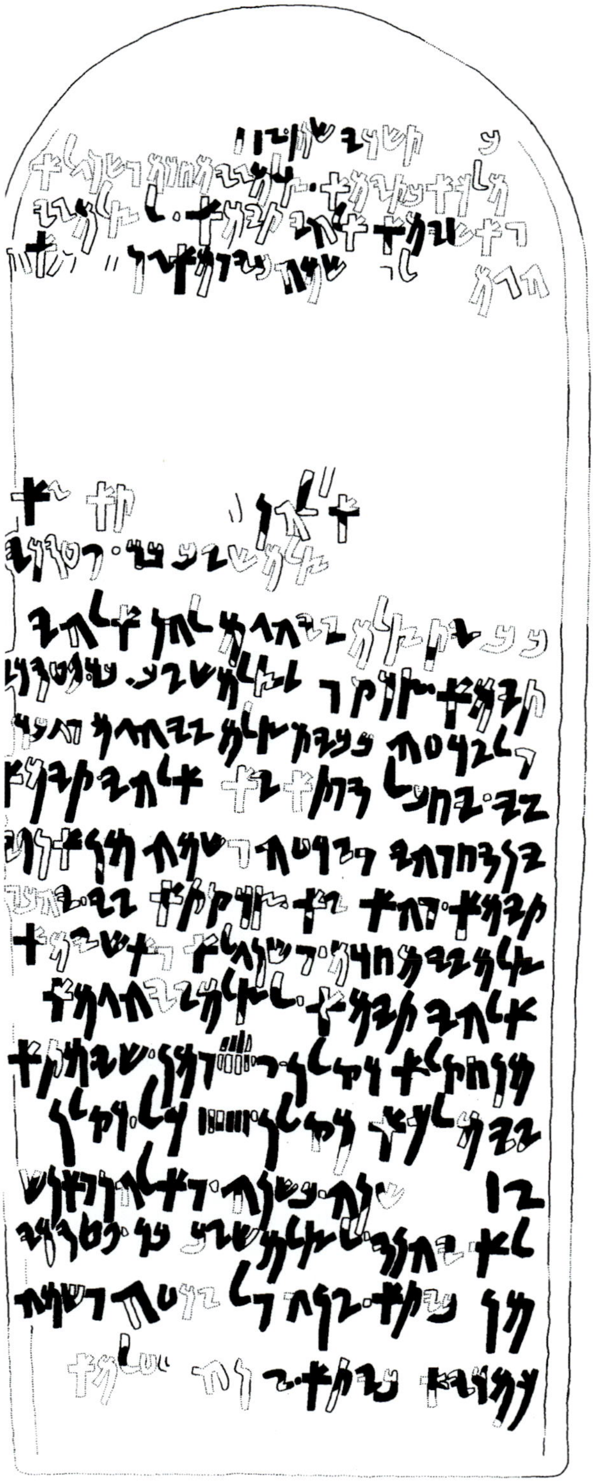

Figure 1. *Teima 1 = CIS II 113 = KAI 228: a legal inscription from Taymāʾ (facsimile P. Stein).*

Figure 2. *TA 2382: a fragmentary votive (?) inscription from Taymāʾ (photograph Deutsches Archäologisches Institut, Orient-Abteilung, J. Kramer).*

region. Historically, it can be dated to the Achaemenid period, probably to the beginning of the fifth century BC,[4] hence more or less contemporary with the rich documentary evidence in Imperial Aramaic from Egypt, which mainly dates from the fifth century BC. Apart from the Louvre stele, some ninety-five inscriptions and fragments which can be said to have been carved in the so-called Imperial or Official Aramaic script have so far

[4] The dating formula in line 1 of the inscription refers to year 22 (or somewhat later) of an Achaemenid king (Stein 2014: 225–226, and here the quotation below, with n. 15). This king has previously been identified as Artaxerxes II (405–359 BC), which would give a date for the carving of the stele in the early fourth century BC (Stein 2014: 225–226, with n. 29), but the discovery in 2015 by the Saudi-British-German project Epigraphy and Landscape in the Hinterland of Taymāʾ of an Imperial Aramaic graffito at al-Muqayil, about 40 km south-east of Taymāʾ, requires us to revise this picture. The fine script of this graffito by an official of the Babylonian king Nabonidus closely resembles that of the stele Teima 1, which means that the time span between the two inscriptions cannot have been very large (Stein, forthcoming, a, with fig. 1 there). The text, which has been given the siglum ELHT.37.IA.1, is to be published in Macdonald, forthcoming, a.

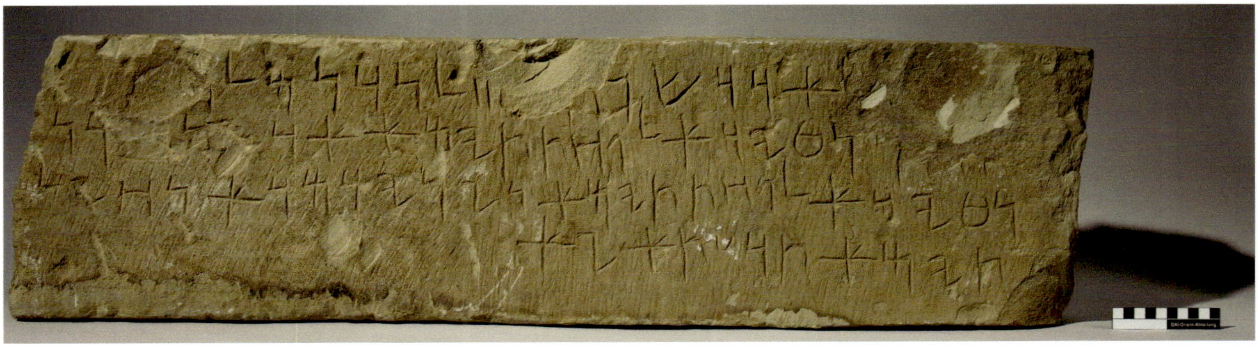

FIGURE 3. *TA 964: a building inscription from Taymāʾ (photograph Deutsches Archäologisches Institut, Orient-Abteilung, J. Kramer).*

been unearthed in Taymāʾ, the majority during the Saudi-German excavations between 2004 and 2015.[5] Although most of these consist of short inscriptions on gravestones or indeterminate fragments, there are a number of elaborate texts such as votive inscriptions (about twenty-five items),[6] a few building inscriptions, and — if one agrees with the interpretation — one record of a legal deed, the transfer of agricultural property to the family of a priest (Teima 1; see Stein 2014). All these inscriptions, including the numerous tombstones, belong to a formal register of script[7] intended for display in the public sphere (Figs 2 & 3). The same can be said for the cuneiform inscriptions from Taymāʾ stemming from the ten years' residence in the oasis of the Babylonian king Nabonidus (556–539 BC).[8] While some Aramaic inscriptions appear to have been written already under Nabonidus' rule,[9] Aramaic must eventually have superseded Akkadian as the written language in Taymāʾ sometime after that. It is quite possible that this change took place in the course of the replacement of Babylonian supremacy by the Persians in the late sixth century BC.[10]

What of the language of the local people of Taymāʾ at that time? Indeed, some of the proper names, particularly in the more prestigious texts such as building or votive inscriptions, are of foreign origin. We find Babylonian (Nabûnādinaḫi in TA 2675 and perhaps, if not Aramaic, Ṣalm(u)šēzib in Teima 1), Egyptian (Petosiris in Teima 1),[11] and Aramaic names (Ṣalmyahab in TA 8827+8828 and elsewhere, and Naṭīrʾel in TA 964), which testify that the foreign ruling power had not only established its own administration but also installed (at least parts of) the required personnel. Names of local origin, which can clearly be attributed to an 'Arabian' pattern, do also occur, most often in the less monumental inscriptions such as tombstones (e.g. ʿAzīzū in TA 8947 and Taym son of Zayd in Teima 23).

That the indigenous population of Taymāʾ spoke a local language of its own is obvious from the numerous graffiti in a particular dialect and script, which is commonly called 'Taymanitic'.[12] The traditional linguistic affiliation of this

[5] For a preliminary report on these excavations, see Eichmann, Schaudig & Hausleiter 2006. The inscriptions from these campaigns, with the siglum 'TA', are published in Stein, forthcoming, a (31 items); and Macdonald, forthcoming, b (17). In addition, there are another thirty-one inscriptions in Imperial Aramaic in the Taymāʾ Museum (Macdonald & al-Najem, forthcoming). For the older publications, see the list in Schwiderski 2004: 410–413, to which the late, but definitely not 'Nabataean', votive inscription in Beyer & Livingstone 1987: 290–292 should be added, as well as those in al-Theeb 1993 and 2007.

[6] See the list in Stein, forthcoming, a: table 2.2. The vagueness in the numbers of texts is due to the fact that some of the fragmentary texts cannot be attributed with certainty to one genre or the other.

[7] A helpful characterization of the different uses of script for public and private purposes in both formal and informal registers, respectively, has recently been given by Macdonald (2015: esp. 28–30).

[8] On the cuneiform evidence of Nabonidus' residence in Taymāʾ, see H. Schaudig in Eichmann, Schaudig & Hausleiter 2006: 169–174; Schaudig 2011; Hausleiter & Schaudig 2016; and Schaudig, forthcoming.

[9] Namely the Aramaic graffito by a Babylonian official (see n. 4) and perhaps also the Babylonizing votive inscription TA 2675 (Stein, forthcoming, a). It is certainly not impossible that, besides Akkadian, Aramaic had already been in use as a written language for administrative purposes in the chancellery of the Babylonian court at Taymāʾ (Gzella 2015: 194) although so far, we have no direct evidence for that.

[10] That the Achaemenids did indeed supersede the Babylonians as the political power in Taymāʾ is strongly suggested by the completely Achaemenid formula in the inscription of the Louvre stele Teima 1 (see below, with n. 14). There is no reason to identify the date in this inscription with a Liḥyanite king, as recently argued by Rohmer, forthcoming. Nevertheless, the Achaemenid occupation may have been a rather short interlude of perhaps hardly more than half a century, since the local dynasty of Liḥyān could already have taken over power in Taymāʾ by the first half of the fifth century BC; see Stein, forthcoming, a.

[11] For the relationships between Taymāʾ and Egypt see Sperveslage & Eichmann 2012; Sperveslage 2016.

[12] The most comprehensive and up-to-date study of these inscriptions and the language behind them is Kootstra 2016.

dialect to the Ancient North Arabian language group has recently been questioned by F. Kootstra (2016: 104–107) in favour of a closer relationship with the North-west Semitic languages, which include Aramaic, of course. On the other hand, the particular (North Arabian) script speaks for a completely separate tradition in writing that local language. Written documentation of this language, however, is limited to what we may call at best 'commemorative' graffiti — short notices recording the presence of the author on the occasion of a certain event such as participation in a war, and sometimes involving short religious statements. As far as we can see, there is almost no overlap with the genres of the inscriptions in Aramaic and Akkadian: while documents of public relevance such as building activities, votive acts in the temple, and so on are exclusively expressed in the foreign written language, spontaneous expressions of personal character like graffiti are basically executed in the local language and script.[13] It remains an open question whether the administrative correspondence, which must have existed in the city at least from the time of Nabonidus' residence onwards, was written in the foreign 'public' language as well. Common sense would suggest that this was in fact the case, although no evidence for that has so far been unearthed.

That this administrative language had a really strong impact in the oasis is supported by its continued use, undiminished even under changing political conditions. It should be remembered that so far, the oldest datable Aramaic document from the oasis, the large stele Teima 1, was in all probability erected under the rule of an Achaemenid king. The introductory dating formula, although severely damaged, clearly resembles other royal inscriptions from the Achaemenid empire:[14]

> ⌜*b-*⌝[xx *l-tšr*]*y* *š*⌜*n*⌝*t* *22*[xxxxxxxx] | [*m*]*l*[*kʾ b-tym*]*ʾ*
> On [(day) ... of (the month) Tišr]ī of year 22(?) [of Darius/Artaxerxes (?), the k]i[ng, in Taym]āʾ (Teima 1/1–2, cf. Fig. 1)

As we have seen, the most probable date for this inscription is the early fifth century BC. In several other inscriptions from Taymāʾ which, from a palaeographical point of view, are definitely later than this stele, we find introductory dating formulae which follow a different, local era based on the regnal years of the kings of Liḥyān:

> *b-10 l-šbṭ dy | šnt 20 tlmy | mlk lḥyn*
> On (day) 10 of (the month) Šəbāṭ of year 20 of Tulmay, king of Liḥyān (TA 2382/1–3, see Fig. 2)[15]

> [*b-... šn*]*t 3 mšʿwdw mlk lḥyn*
> [On (day) ... of yea]r 3 of Masʿūdū, king of Liḥyān (TM.TAr.004/1)[16]

Interestingly enough, the political centre of that kingdom, the oasis of Dadan located only 140 km from Taymāʾ, has not revealed any noteworthy written evidence in Aramaic.[17] In contrast to Taymāʾ, inscriptions for public purposes — as well as private graffiti — are written there in the

[13] See also Gzella 2015: 194–195. In fact there is only one short Taymanitic inscription which might document the erection of a standing stone (and thus be similar to a dedicatory inscription such as TA 2675; (see also the much more extensive Teima 20): *[...]{k}frl b zbd | {n}ṣb yd-h [h-]'lht* '[...]KFRL son of Zabīd set up (with) his own hand a standing stone [representing the] goddess' (TM.T. 020/1–2, interpretation adapted after the OCIANA database http://krc.orient.ox.ac.uk/ociana/corpus/pages/OCIANA_0040444.html, accessed 26 July 2017). Compared with the almost 500 inscriptions in Taymanitic script known so far (according to OCIANA), this single instance is certainly a marginal exception. The authors of the OCIANA entry point out that the stone block on which this particular inscription was incised is a reused pillar once crowned by a capital, which was found, however, only in a secondary context. By contrast, graffiti in the Aramaic language and script are rather scarce in the region; see Teima 11, 13, 15, 17–19 and the three additions by Sima (1999), most of them originating not from Taymāʾ proper but from the environs as far as Dadan (al-ʿUlā). See also below, with n. 20, for JSNab 334, 335, and 337.

[14] See the parallels referred to by Stein (2014: 225–226). Previous discussions even focused on a possibly earlier date (Nabonidus) based on archaeological and iconographical arguments (see the references in Stein 2014: 222 with n. 13). An identification of the ruler in this text with a Lihyanite king, based on the dating formulae in the newly found inscriptions from Taymāʾ as quoted in what follows above (see most recently Rohmer, forthcoming), ignores the different construction of the dating formulae in both contexts. While the apposition to the king's name in Teima 1/2 can hardly be restored otherwise than to the emphatic *mlkʾ* 'the king' followed by the particular location in which the inscription was set up (as clearly paralleled in a number of other Achaemenid royal inscriptions), in those dated to the regnal years of Lihyanite kings, the royal title is always rendered in the construct state (*mlk lḥyn*) without a respective location ('in Taymāʾ'). The apparent similarity between both formulae is thus restricted to the numerical data, which are not at all distinctive.

[15] Two other inscriptions from the same find spot have a similar formula, differing only in the particular year (TA 4916 and TA 4915, dated to year 30 and 40 respectively of the same king). This might refer to a certain ritual regularly carried out in the temple every ten years (Stein, forthcoming, a: chapter 1.1). Other Aramaic inscriptions from Taymāʾ are dated according to other Lihyanite kings such as Lawḏān (TA 964) and two different kings named Šahrū (in TA 8827+8828 and TA 17431, respectively; for the latter, see below, with note 36).

[16] The inscription, a three-line dedication to the god Ṣalm, was an accidental find during building work in the town of Taymāʾ and is housed in the Taymāʾ Archaeological Museum (registration no. 488); it will be published as TM.TAr.004 in Macdonald & al-Najem, forthcoming.

[17] For the few Aramaic graffiti from the environs of Dadan, see the references given in n. 13. The fact that Aramaic does not seem to have spread much beyond Taymāʾ could be taken as an indication that the political influence of the Persian Empire did not stretch beyond that oasis. The comparatively rich amount of epigraphic documentation from Taymāʾ may even suggest that the oasis, the furthest outpost in the south-western corner of Persian influence in Arabia, was an administrative centre for the entire region (see Knauf 1990: 206–207).

local language and script called Dadanitic. This idiom, like Taymanitic traditionally affiliated to the Ancient North Arabian group, is documented in many hundreds of inscriptions from Dadan and its surroundings.[18] Irrespective of their political hegemony over Taymāʾ, which lasted probably from the mid-fifth to the second century BC,[19] the Lihyanite kings did not use their mother tongue in the neighbouring oasis, but continued to make use of the writing system that had been established there generations earlier. Moreover, the kings of Liḥyān even adapted this language and script for their private practice, as can be seen in some graffiti from al-Khabū al-Gharbī and al-Khabū al-Sharqī, some 10 km south-west of Taymāʾ:

mšʿwdw mlk lḥyn | *ktb dnh*
Masʿūdū, king of Liḥyān, wrote this (JSNab 334/1–2)[20]

That the king who left his mark here is identical with that in the votive inscription TM.TAr.004 (cf. above) is fairly probable.[21] It is interesting to note that the Lihyanite king makes use of the foreign Aramaic script not only in a prestigious public context in the city but also in private graffiti (which are otherwise executed in the local language, Taymanitic) — probably even written in his own hand. While the local language and script (Dadanitic) were employed for all kinds of writing in the political centre of the Lihyanite kingdom at Dadan, Aramaic must already have gained such a high prestige in Taymāʾ by that time, that neither the local idiom (Taymanitic) nor the written language of the actual political power (Dadanitic) had a chance to supersede the foreign language there.[22]

Moreover, the adoption of foreign customs by the Lihyanite kings is not restricted to the Aramaic script and some formulaic expressions, but also affects the administrative system as a whole, as can be deduced from the following inscription:

1. [*b*-xxx] ⌜*l*-⌝*ʾdr* *š*⌜*nt*⌝[xx]*1*?+*2* *lwdn* *ml*⌜*k*⌝
2. [*l*]⌜*ḥ*?*yn*⌝ *nṭyrʾl* *pḥt* *tymʾ* *ʾ*⌜*d*?*y*?*n*?⌝[x?ʾ?]⌜*k*⌝*n*
3. *nṭyrʾl* *pḥt* *tymʾ* *w-zkyr* *mrʾ* *w-ḥ*⌜*y*⌝*l*
4. *tymʾ* *trʿtʾ* *zʾ*

1. [On day ...] of (the month) ʾĀdār of the year [...] of Lawḍān, the king of
2. [Li]ḥyān. Naṭīrʾel, the governor of Taymāʾ. At that time
3. Naṭīrʾel, the governor of Taymāʾ — be remembered the lord and the garrison
4. of Taymāʾ! — [has er]ected this gate (TA 964, see Fig. 3)[23]

The author, clearly the leading official of the city under the Lihyanite king, designates himself not with a genuine local term for 'chief', but rather with the common Aramaic word *pḥt* = *pēḥā* 'governor, satrap'. This functionary title, probably introduced by the Persian administration,[24] was maintained under the rule of the subsequent political power. Once the administrative structures had been taken over, the language of the chancellery continued to be the *lingua franca*, Aramaic.

[18] To date, the OCIANA database (http://krc.orient.ox.ac.uk/ociana/index.php/database) contains almost 2000 entries under the label 'Dadanitic' (accessed 27 July 2017).

[19] Cf. the arguments given in Stein, forthcoming, a: chapter 1.2. That the Achaemenids must have abandoned the region in the course of the fourth century BC at the latest is supported by the fact that the former Persian possessions in North Arabia no longer played any role in the time of Alexander the Great (Jacobs 1994: 167–168).

[20] Cf. also JSNab 335 and 337 (Jaussen & Savignac 1914: 220–222). Although they placed them in the Nabataean corpus, Jaussen and Savignac recognized that they are not in the Nabataean script but in a particular (late) ductus of Imperial Aramaic (Jaussen & Savignac 1914: 221; Starcky 1966: cols 906–907; and most recently Rohmer & Charloux 2015: 301, with references). There is no reason to denote this Lihyanite king as a 'Schattenkönig' of the Nabataeans, as referred to by Hackl, Jenni and Schneider who date the inscription 'am wahrscheinlichsten' to the second quarter of the first century BC (2003: 308 with n. 946).

[21] The same can be said for Šahrū, king of Liḥyān, who is likewise known by a rock graffito in the environs of Taymāʾ (published in al-Theeb 2014: 34–35) and by a monumental inscription in the oasis proper (TA 17431, see nn. 15 and 36). Although the ductus of the inscriptions, depending on the different genre and support, is slightly different, the basic palaeographical features do not speak against a close chronological relationship of both texts, the script of which can be attributed to Macdonald's 'Taymāʾ Aramaic' (Macdonald, forthcoming, c). Reservations on the royal character of the two rulers Masʿūdū and Šahrū, as expressed by Rohmer and Charloux (2015: 301–302: 'self-proclaimed kings with doubtful ties to the historical core of the Lihyanite kingdom'), are out of place; these kings were clearly well established as rulers, like their forerunners, at least in and around the oasis of Taymāʾ. Whether they had a fixed residence, be it in Dadan, Taymāʾ, or elsewhere, or were itinerant between the oases within their realm (Rohmer, forthcoming) remains a different question.

[22] Robin (2010: 125) concludes that Aramaic must have served as the spoken language ('langue parlée') of parts of the population (particularly the elites) in Taymāʾ as well as among the Nabataeans.

[23] TA 964, published in Stein, forthcoming, a.

[24] This widely accepted view was questioned by Graf (1990: 140), recently followed by Rohmer and Charloux (2015: 299) and Rohmer, forthcoming. They argue that the title *pḥh/pḥt* had already been in use in the Neo-Babylonian period. The argument put forward in favour of this is the occurrence of the word *pḥh*, commonly interpreted as this particular functionary title, in the Aramaic letter KAI 266/9 from Egypt (about 600 BC). The context there, however, is damaged and the term occurs without a following attribute so that the actual jurisdiction of the 'governor' remains unclear.

Figure 4. *Mleiha 10: a bilingual tomb inscription (Aramaic-Hasaitic) from Mleiha (from Overlaet, Macdonald & Stein 2016: 131; photograph B. Overlaet).*

Mleiha

Let us now turn to the other side of the Arabian Peninsula, the Arabian Gulf coast. Although the evidence for the Aramaic script is relatively poor in this region,[25] there is at least one place which can be compared with Taymāʾ — not so much by the number of extant inscriptions but by the distribution of text genres — namely Mleiha (Mulayḥah) in the United Arab Emirates. This site, apparently resettled during the third century BC after a gap in occupation, and finally abandoned in the third century AD,[26] is located some 50 km inland from the eastern coast of the Arabian Gulf. The situation here is markedly different from that at Taymāʾ inasmuch as at Mleiha we find two written languages which were used equally for public inscriptions: Aramaic and Hasaitic. The two languages typically occur side by side in bilingual tomb inscriptions (see, for example, Fig. 4) not only in Mleiha but also on the Saudi-Arabian Gulf coast (al-Ḥasā), the core region of the Hasaitic inscriptions.[27]

Apart from tombstones, other public inscriptions are written in Aramaic as well as Hasaitic (although separately and not as bilinguals on the same support). These are votive inscriptions, dedicated to the main local deity Lāt (spelled hal-Lāt and han-ʾIlāt, respectively) and always punched onto small plaques of metal such as bronze or an even more precious material. Two dedications on bronze tablets (one only fragmentary) are in Aramaic (Mleiha 8 and 9, see Fig. 5) and one, on a silver plaque, is in Hasaitic, but not in the well-known monumental ductus of the South Arabian script but in the minuscule or *zabūr*, the script that was used in Ancient Yemen for everyday

[25] The evidence of inscribed material in Aramaic from the Gulf region is summarized by Healey and Bin Seray (1999–2000) as amounting to twenty-two or twenty-three items (excluding coinage). To this corpus must be added the recently discovered Hasaitic-Aramaic bilingual tomb inscription from Mleiha (Mleiha 10; see Overlaet, Macdonald & Stein 2016).

[26] On the archaeological evidence and chronological development of the site see the relevant chapters in Mouton 2010 and Mouton & Schiettecatte 2014.

[27] Among the Aramaic inscriptions from the Gulf collected by Healey and Bin Seray (1999–2000; see n. 25 above), four or five are bilingual with Hasaitic. In Mleiha itself, five tomb inscriptions have been discovered so far, two or three of them bilingual (Mleiha 10 and two unpublished), the rest only in Hasaitic (Mleiha 2 and one unpublished). For an up-to-date collection of the published inscriptions from the site, see Stein, forthcoming, b.

Figure 5. *Mleiha 8: a votive inscription on a bronze tablet from Mleiha (Sharjah Archaeological Museum, Inv. SM 3001; photograph P. Stein).*

correspondence on wooden sticks (Mleiha 11; see Stein 2017). The formula of the Hasaitic dedication is clearly based on a South Arabian model, as the characteristic verbal form *hqn(y)t* 'she dedicated' (literally 'she gave into possession') shows. This parallel fits with a number of indicators suggesting a direct borrowing of this script from South Arabia. Since people from the Gulf commissioned large dedicatory inscriptions in their own (Hasaitic) language in the centres of South Arabia such as Mārib and the Wādī al-Jawf around 300 BC,[28] they must have been established there for a certain time, probably engaging in commercial activities. This being said, we may assume that they consequently adopted the mode of documenting their business in written form from their South Arabian partners. Of course, they could have used Aramaic for that purpose as well, since they were also familiar with it in their home region in the Gulf, but they probably never attempted to do so. Since the South Arabian writing culture had already been firmly established in Yemen for centuries, it was certainly not suitable for foreign merchants like those from East Arabia to communicate with their South Arabian partners in another, completely foreign, language and script. It is therefore no wonder that not a single trace of Aramaic has been discovered in South Arabia in the entire first millennium BC.[29]

But what of the status of Aramaic in the Gulf region? The bilingual tomb inscriptions and particularly the votive inscriptions on the bronze plaques from Mleiha prove that Aramaic — along with Hasaitic — had been established there as a written language for public purposes. While the general layout of the bronze plaque as well as some characteristic formulaic traits are clearly based on South Arabian patterns (as is their Hasaitic counterpart on the silver plaque Mleiha 11),[30] the Aramaic language must have found its way to the Gulf from elsewhere. Since some of the inscriptions left by East Arabian traders in Mārib and other places in Yemen were dated by the regnal years of king Seleucos I (305–281 BC), a Seleucid supremacy over the home region of their authors can be assumed, and this could have been the reason that Aramaic advanced in that region. Indeed, Aramaic could already have been introduced into the region by the Achaemenids, as is suggested by a single Aramaic inscription from Bahrain from probably the fifth–fourth century BC (Gzella 2008: 123–124). Once established, some chancelleries here and there producing Aramaic texts could have continued working under the political successors of the Persian Empire, even though the impact of this might have been rather weak, as the political influence of the Seleucids in the southern Gulf was certainly not very strong (Robin

[28] These are votive inscriptions on stone blocks, some of them dated to the first years of the Seleucid era (see below). While the language of these texts is clearly akin to that of the Hasaitic inscriptions from the Gulf, their script is definitely South Arabian, not 'Hasaitic', which means that the authors commissioned a local mason (as one might expect). For the evidence, see Stein 2017: 117; forthcoming, b and the references there.

[29] Aramaic would penetrate South Arabia only in the course of increasing Jewish influence in the fourth century AD. But even then, its influence remained restricted to some monotheistic vocabulary and formulaic quotations in Aramaic (or Hebrew) texts within inscriptions, which were otherwise clearly Sabaic.

[30] The lexical and formulaic borrowings from South Arabia in Mleiha 8 are discussed in Stein 2018: 48–58.

2016: 240–241). Moreover, the South Arabian writing culture would have been much more influential in the trading offices, as we have seen, since the merchants from East Arabia who engaged in international trade had clearly established close and long-term relationships, including local representations, with that region. Using Aramaic was thus not so much a matter of daily business (as it might have been in Taymāʾ), since the daily written language was the local Hasaitic (in the foreign South Arabian script).[31] Rather, Aramaic was used much more as a language and script of prestige, restricted to really prominent inscriptions for public display. This was the conclusion drawn by Michael Macdonald with respect to the Aramaic language of the legends on the Abiʾel coins from the central Gulf area and the Oman peninsula. He emphasizes the enormous status of Aramaic, which was 'the venerable language of imperial government and diplomacy in this region', concluding that 'regardless of whether or not Aramaic was in general use in the area Abiel ruled, it was the natural language and script to choose for coin legends in that region in the Seleucid and Parthian periods' (Macdonald 2010: 408).

Conclusion

The situation of Aramaic in the two corners of the Arabian Peninsula — Taymāʾ in the north-west and Mleiha in the east — is thus quite similar on the one hand, but markedly different on the other. In both cases, the foreign idiom must have been introduced as a written language by a supra-regional power — probably the Persians (Achaemenids), perhaps also the Babylonians under Nabonidus (in Taymāʾ). The basic requirement for the long-term survival of this foreign language — more than 300 years at least in Taymāʾ — was an established administrative system, a chancellery which regularly had to record documents of economic and social life (of which no single piece has so far been discovered in the entire region) and ensure a minimum of public expression in the form of (more or less) monumental inscriptions.

On the other hand, we have a second language in both places — apparently the idiom spoken by the local people (Taymanitic and Hasaitic, respectively). While this idiom in Taymāʾ was not officially written but restricted to informal, private graffiti and some grave stelae, it was used as a regular written language for public purposes — alongside Aramaic — in Mleiha.[32] In Taymāʾ, Aramaic thus appears to have been the only language suitable for business and administrative purposes, and needed to be properly maintained. The observation that some authors of official inscriptions from Taymāʾ still under the rule of the kings of Liḥyān bear Aramaic names suggests that the former bonds with the international Aramaic network continued to exist even after the political conditions had completely changed.

In contrast to this, Aramaic was apparently less firmly anchored in the Gulf region, since there was another written language competing with it. The great advantage of this second language was probably that it was not foreign but was the spoken idiom with which the population was basically familiar. The number of extant inscriptions suggests that the local language was also more important for written communication, leaving only a secondary role for Aramaic.[33] Why, then, was Aramaic not totally abandoned after Hasaitic had been implemented as a written language? Certainly because of its prestige, its importance as *the* internationally understood idiom, a veritable *lingua franca*. Using this prestigious language besides the common local idiom would have given the displayed documents a considerably higher significance.[34]

Finally, another important aspect of Aramaic in Arabia should be mentioned, which is perhaps an outcome of the curious role which this language played on the Peninsula. In Taymāʾ as well as apparently in the eastern Gulf, we have evidence of continuity in writing Aramaic beyond the early Hellenistic period, thus bridging the gap of written evidence in the third to second century BC ('the two dark

[31] Moreover, the numerous North and South Arabian influences in the Aramaic inscriptions suggest that Aramaic was not deeply anchored in daily writing in the region. Apart from the Arabian onomastics, some lexical, morphological, and syntactic features of apparently Arabian origin can be detected in the Aramaic texts from Mleiha (particularly Mleiha 8 and 9; see the evidence and explanation in Stein 2018). It is not entirely clear, however, whether all these peculiarities are characteristics of the local (Hasaitic) language or part of the (stereotypical) formulae which have been borrowed from South Arabia.

[32] Curiously enough, the characteristic genre for writing the local idiom in Taymāʾ, the personal graffito, has not yet been documented in Mleiha and the Gulf region at all. Short notes, such as possession marks on vessels and so on, however, were written in the Hasaitic monumental script as well as in Aramaic (the few examples of the latter are still unpublished).

[33] This situation may well be compared with that of late eighth-century Jerusalem referred to at the beginning of this paper, as there was in fact a written language, besides Aramaic, in the country: the contemporary form of Hebrew, which is documented not so much by public inscriptions (as in the Gulf) but rather by numerous private texts in ink (mainly on ostraca) such as letters, accounts, and other documents of daily life.

[34] The employment of a local written language such as Ḥasaitic and a foreign administrative language (here, Aramaic) side by side even in public registers such as votive inscriptions mirrors the situation in Greco-Roman Syria, where the Aramaic vernacular was used as a language of prestige and cultural identity beside the foreign Greek, for instance in memorial inscriptions (Gzella 2015: 215–216).

centuries') that exists for Aramaic documentation in the rest of the world (Gzella 2015: 214 and 220). It is also the case in Taymāʾ[35] where quite a number of inscriptions, most of them from recent excavations, exhibit a ductus of script that clearly tends towards Nabataean, although the inscriptions proper are still composed in the tradition of Imperial Aramaic.[36] As clearly Nabataean inscriptions are also well attested in Taymāʾ, apparently continuing to be in use far into the Roman period,[37] we have reason to assume an unbroken tradition of writing in the oasis from the Imperial to the Middle Aramaic period. Could Taymāʾ thus have even been a catalyst for the development of Nabataean writing? The fact that the language of the Nabataean inscriptions is considered more 'conservative', that is, more closely related to Imperial Aramaic than the other contemporary variants of so-called 'Middle Aramaic',[38] could easily be explained by assuming a continuity in a traditional chancellery language eventually to be traced back to the Babylonian/Persian administration in the sixth–fifth century BC. The oasis of Taymāʾ is certainly a good candidate for localizing a continued transmission of Aramaic as a written language far beyond the administrative structures of the Persian Empire and its successors. Indeed, traces of local writing traditions of the third to first centuries BC can also be found elsewhere in the realm of Nabataean occupation, such as Elusa (Negev) and the Ḥawrān (Macdonald 2003: 44–46). The extraordinarily dense documentation from Taymāʾ, however, suggests this site had a key position in the development of Aramaic at the end of the first millennium BC.

[35] The evidence in Mleiha is less conclusive due to the small number of texts. Moreover, the bilingual tomb inscription, Mleiha 10, is probably from the late third century BC according to the dating formula in the text (Overlaet, Macdonald & Stein 2016: 138–139). Although the two bronze inscriptions (Mleiha 8 and 9) lack a particular dating formula, they must belong to the same period from a palaeographical point of view (Stein 2018). Since the occupation of the site flourished up to the third century AD (see above, with n. 26), further discoveries of Aramaic inscriptions may be expected in future.

[36] See Macdonald, forthcoming, b. The most striking example is certainly TA 17431, a four-line votive or building inscription commissioned under the rule of a certain 'Šahrū, king of Liḥyān'. The particular dating formula in line 1 of the text follows the same pattern as those of the earlier inscriptions set up under Lihyanite rule in Taymāʾ as referred to above. There is no indication that the political situation in the oasis had already changed towards Nabataean supremacy, although the letter forms of this and other inscriptions from Taymāʾ clearly anticipate what is later called the 'Nabataean' script (see above, with n. 20, on JSNab 334).

[37] An illustrative example of the use of Nabataean as a written language in the Roman period is given by the tomb inscription of a Jewish 'chief of' Taymāʾ (*rʾš tymy*) dating from the year 203 AD, published by al-Najem and Macdonald (2009).

[38] Cf. Gzella (2011), who prefers the label 'Late Imperial Aramaic' for that group.

Acknowledgements

I would like to express my gratitude to the participants of the 2017 Seminar for Arabian Studies for fruitful discussions and helpful advice, in particular Michael Macdonald, Sulaiman al-Theeb, Jérôme Rohmer, and Arnulf Hausleiter. Above all I am most grateful to Michael Macdonald for a critical review of this paper, which helped to clarify my argumentation in many ways.

Sigla

CIS ii: *Corpus inscriptionum semiticarum. Pars secunda: Inscriptiones aramaicas continens. Tomus 1*. Paris: Imprimerie nationale, 1889–1954.

JSNab: Nabataean inscriptions published in Jaussen & Savignac 1914.

KAI: Inscriptions in Donner & Röllig 1962–1964.

Mleiha: Inscriptions from Mleiha as numbered in Stein, forthcoming, b.

TA: Inscriptions discovered during the Saudi-German excavations at Taymāʾ 2004–2015 and published in Stein, forthcoming, a and Macdonald, forthcoming, d.

TM: Inscriptions in the Taymāʾ Museum to be published in Macdonald & al-Najem, forthcoming.

Teima: Imperial Aramaic inscriptions from Taymāʾ as numbered in Schwiderski 2004: 410–413.

References

Beyer K. & Livingstone A. 1987. Die neuesten aramäischen Inschriften aus Taima. *Zeitschrift der Deutschen Morgenländischen Gesellschaft* 137: 285–296.

Donner H. & Röllig W. 1962–1964. *Kanaanäische und aramäische Inschriften. Mit einem Beitrag von O. Rössler.* (3 volumes). Wiesbaden: Harrassowitz.

Eichmann R., Schaudig H. & Hausleiter A. 2006. Archaeology and epigraphy at Taymāʾ (Saudi Arabia). *Arabian Archaeology and Epigraphy* 17: 163–176.

Gallagher W.R. 1999. *Sennacherib's campaign to Judah. New studies*. (Studies in the History and Culture of the Ancient Near East, 18). Leiden/Boston: Brill.

Graf D.F. 1990. Arabia during Achaemenid times. Pages 131–148 in H. Sancisi-Weerdenburg & A. Kuhrt (eds), *Achaemenid History IV: Centre and periphery.*

Proceedings of the Groningen 1986 Achaemenid History Workshop. Leiden: Nederlands Instituut voor het Nabije Oosten.

Gzella H. 2008. Aramaic in the Parthian period: The Arsacid inscriptions. Pages 107–130 in H. Gzella & M.L. Folmer (eds), *Aramaic in its historical and linguistic setting.* (Veröffentlichungen der Orientalischen Kommission der Akademie der Wissenschaften und der Literatur Mainz, 50). Wiesbaden: Harrassowitz.

Gzella H. 2011. Late Imperial Aramaic. Pages 598–609 in S. Weninger, G. Khan, M.P. Streck & J.C.E. Watson (eds), *The Semitic languages. An international handbook*. (Handbücher zur Sprach- und Kommunikationswissenschaft, 36). Berlin/Boston: De Gruyter Mouton.

Gzella H. 2015. *A cultural history of Aramaic. From the beginnings to the advent of Islam.* (Handbuch der Orientalistik, 1/111). Leiden/Boston: Brill.

Hackl U., Jenni H. & Schneider Ch. 2003. *Quellen zur Geschichte der Nabatäer. Textsammlung mit Übersetzung und Kommentar*. (Novum Testamentum et Orbis Antiquus, 51). Freiburg: Universitätsverlag/Göttingen: Vandenhoeck & Ruprecht.

Hausleiter A. & Schaudig H. 2016. Rock relief and cuneiform inscription of king Nabonidus at al-Ḥāʾiṭ (Province of Ḥāʾil, Saudi Arabia), ancient Padakku. *Zeitschrift für Orient-Archäologie* 9: 224–240.

Healey J.F. & Bin Seray H. 1999–2000. Aramaic in the Gulf: Towards a corpus. *Aram* 11–12: 1–14.

Jacobs B. 1994. *Die Satrapienverwaltung im Perserreich zur Zeit Darius' III*. (Beihefte zum Tübinger Atlas des Vorderen Orients, B.87). Wiesbaden: Steiner.

Jaussen A. & Savignac M.R. 1914. *Mission archéologique en Arabie. ii. El-ᶜEla, d'Hégra à Teima, Harra de Tebouk*. (Publications de la Société des Fouilles Archéologiques). Paris: Geuthner.

Knauf E.A. 1990. The Persian administration in Arabia. *Transeuphratène* 2: 201–217.

Kootstra F. 2016. The language of the Taymanitic inscriptions & its classification. *Arabian Epigraphic Notes* 2: 67–140. Available at https://openaccess.leidenuniv.nl/handle/1887/42063

Macdonald M.C.A. 2003. Languages, scripts, and the uses of writing among the Nabataeans. Pages 36–56, 264–266 (endnotes), 274–282 (references) in G. Markoe (ed.), *Petra rediscovered: Lost city of the Nabataeans*. New York: Abrams.

Macdonald M.C.A. 2010. The 'Abiel' coins of eastern Arabia: A study of the Aramaic legends. Pages 403–547 in M. Huth & P.G. van Alfen (eds), *Coinage of the Caravan Kingdoms. Studies in Ancient Arabian monetization.* (Numismatic Studies, 25). New York: The American Numismatic Society.

Macdonald M.C.A. 2015. On the uses of writing in ancient Arabia and the role of palaeography in studying them. *Arabian Epigraphic Notes* 1: 1–50. Available at https://openaccess.leidenuniv.nl/handle/1887/37060

Macdonald M.C.A. (forthcoming, a). Report on the first and second seasons, 2013 and 2015, of the Epigraphy and Landscape in the Hinterland of Taymāʾ project. *Atlal*.

Macdonald M.C.A. (forthcoming, b). The Imperial Aramaic inscriptions found in the 2010–2015 seasons. Section 3 in M.C.A. Macdonald, forthcoming, d.

Macdonald M.C.A. (forthcoming, c). The Taymāʾ Aramaic inscriptions. Section 5 in M.C.A. Macdonald, forthcoming, d.

Macdonald M.C.A. (forthcoming, d). *Catalogue of the inscriptions discovered in the Saudi-German excavations at Taymāʾ, 2004–2015*. With contributions by A. Hausleiter, F. Imbert, H. Schaudig, P. Stein & F. Tourtet. In *Taymāʾ II*. Oxford: Archaeopress.

Macdonald M.C.A. & al-Najem M. (forthcoming). *Catalogue of the inscriptions in the Taymāʾ Museum*. With contributions by F. Imbert & P. Stein. In *Taymāʾ III*. Oxford: Archaeopress.

Mouton M. 2010. Mleiha et le peuplement de la péninsule d'Oman à la période pré-Islamique récente. Pages 181–211 in A. Avanzini (ed.), *Eastern Arabia in the first millennium BC.* (Arabia Antica, 6). Rome: 'L'Erma' di Bretschneider.

Mouton M. & Schiettecatte J. 2014. *In the desert margins. The settlement process in ancient South and East Arabia.* (Arabia Antica, 9). Rome: 'L'Erma' di Bretschneider.

al-Najem M. & Macdonald M.C.A. 2009. A new Nabataean inscription from Taymāʾ. *Arabian Archaeology and Epigraphy* 20: 208–217.

Overlaet B., Macdonald M.C.A. & Stein P. 2016. An Aramaic-Hasaitic bilingual inscription from a monumental tomb at Mleiha, Sharjah, UAE. *Arabian Archaeology and Epigraphy* 27: 127–142.

Robin C.J. 2010. Langues et écritures. Pages 119–131 in A.I. Al-Ghabban, B. André-Salvini, F. Demange, C. Juvin & M. Cotty (eds), *Routes d'Arabie. Archéologie et histoire du royaume d'Arabie saoudite*. Paris: Somogy.

Robin C.J. 2016. Gerrha d'Arabie, cité séleucide. Pages 223–250 in F. Duyrat, F. Briquel-Chatonnet, J.-M. Dentzer & O. Picard (eds), *Henri Seyrig (1895–1973)*. Actes du colloque Henri Seyrig (1895–1973) tenu les 10 et 11 octobre 2013 à la Bibliothèque nationale de France et à l'Académie des inscriptions et belles-lettres, Paris (Syria Supplément, 3). Beirut: Presses de l'Institut français du Proche-Orient.

Rohmer J. (forthcoming). Foreign powers and local kingdoms in northwest Arabia: new insights into the political history of Dadan, Ḥegrā and Taymāʾ in the later 1st millennium BC. In M. Luciani (ed.), *The Archaeology of the Arabian Peninsula 2: Connecting the evidence. Proceedings of the international workshop held in Vienna on April 25, 2016*. (OREA Series). Vienna: Austrian Academy of Sciences Press.

Rohmer J. & Charloux G. 2015. From Liḥyān to the Nabataeans: Dating the end of the Iron Age in north-west Arabia. *Proceedings of the Seminar for Arabian Studies* 45: 297–320.

Schaudig H. 2011. Cuneiform texts from Taymāʾ. Pages 113–115 in R. Eichmann, A. Hausleiter, M.H. al-Najem & S.F. al-Said, Taymāʾ — Autumn 2005 and 2006 (Spring and Autumn). 3rd Report on the Joint Saudi Arabian-German Archaeological Project. *Atlal* 21: 64–118, pls 4.1–4.23.

Schaudig H. (forthcoming). Cuneiform texts from Taymāʾ: Seasons 2004–2015. Section 1 in M.C.A. Macdonald, forthcoming, d.

Schwiderski D. 2004. *Die alt- und reichsaramäischen Inschriften.* Band 2: *Texte und Bibliographie*. (Fontes et Subsidia ad Bibliam pertinentes, 2). Berlin/New York: De Gruyter.

Sima A. 1999. Aramaica aus Dedan und Taymāʾ. *Arabian Archaeology and Epigraphy* 10: 54–57.

Sperveslage G. 2016. Intercultural contacts between Egypt and the Arabian Peninsula at the turn of the 2nd to the 1st millennium BCE. Pages 303–330 in J.C. Moreno García (ed.), *Dynamics of production in the Ancient Near East 1300–500 BC*. Oxford/Philadelphia: Oxbow Books.

Sperveslage G. & Eichmann R. 2012. Egyptian cultural impact on north-west Arabia in the second and first millennia BC. *Proceedings of the Seminar for Arabian Studies* 42: 371–384.

Starcky J. 1966. Pétra et la Nabatène. Cols. 886–1018 in H. Cazelles & A. Feuillet (eds), *Supplément au Dictionnaire de la Bible*. vii. Paris: Letouzey & Ané.

Stein P. 2014. Ein aramäischer Kudurru aus Taymāʾ? Pages 219–245 in M. Krebernik & H. Neumann (eds), *Babylonien und seine Nachbarn in neu- und spätbabylonischer Zeit. Wissenschaftliches Kolloquium aus Anlass des 75. Geburtstags von Joachim Oelsner. Jena, 2. und 3. März 2007*. (Alter Orient und Altes Testament, 369). Münster: Ugarit.

Stein P. 2017. South Arabian *zabūr* script in the Gulf: Some recent discoveries from Mleiha (Sharjah, UAE). *Arabian Archaeology and Epigraphy* 28: 110–123.

Stein P. 2018. Die aramäischen Bronzeinschriften aus Mleiha (Sharjah, VAE). *Zeitschrift der Deutschen Morgenländischen Gesellschaft* 168: 41–66.

Stein P. (forthcoming, a). Die reichsaramäischen Inschriften der Kampagnen 2005–2009 aus Taymāʾ. Section 2 in M.C.A. Macdonald, forthcoming, d.

Stein P. (forthcoming, b). Languages and scripts in the Arabian Gulf in the Hellenistic period: The epigraphic evidence from Mleiha (Sharjah, U.A.E.). In G. Hatke & R. Ruzicka (eds), *Ancient South Arabia: Kingdoms, tribes, and traders. Proceedings of an international conference at the Austrian Academy of Sciences, Vienna, 31 August–2 September 2016*. Vienna: Austrian Academy of Sciences.

Al-Theeb (= Al-Dhiyīb) S.A. 1993. *Aramaic and Nabataean inscriptions from north-west Saudi-Arabia*. Riyadh: King Fahd National Library.

Al-Theeb (= Al-Dhiyīb) S.A. 2007. *Nuqūš Taymāʾ al-ʾārāmiyyah*. Al-Riyāḍ: Maktabat al-malik Fahd al-waṭaniyyah.

Al-Theeb (= Al-Dhiyīb) S.A. 2014. *Nuqūš mawqiʿ Sarmadāʾ muḥāfaẓat Taymāʾ*. Al-Riyāḍ: Jāmiʿat al-malik Saʿūd.

Author's address

Peter Stein, Friedrich-Schiller-Universität Jena, Theologische Fakultät, Fürstengraben 6, D 07743 Jena, Germany
Universität Erfurt, Katholisch-Theologische Fakultät, Domstraße 10, D 99089 Erfurt, Germany
e-mail Peter.Stein@uni-jena.de

The use of languages and scripts among nomads

M.C.A. Macdonald (ed.), *Languages, scripts and their uses in ancient North Arabia.* (Supplement to volume 48 of the Proceedings of the Seminar for Arabian Studies). Oxford: Archaeopress, 2018: 53–69

New research on the 'Thamudic' graffiti from the region of Ḥimā (Najrān, Saudi Arabia)

ALESSIA PRIOLETTA

with a note by Christian J. Robin

Summary
The region of Ḥimā includes a wide area located in the desert about 100 km north-east of Najrān. In antiquity, this was on the route leading from South Arabia to the north of the Arabian Peninsula and thus has an exceptional archaeological ensemble of graffiti, rock drawings, and funerary structures. Since 2007 the Saudi-French mission to Najrān has been conducting explorations and epigraphic surveys in Ḥimā and has already exhaustively recorded the area of ᶜAn Jamal, ᶜAn Halkān, and Jabal as-Sammā. In 2016 C.J. Robin achieved the complete decipherment of the graffiti in the 'Southern Thamudic' script and sketched their basic linguistic features. Through a preliminary study of the material recorded by the Saudi-French mission, this paper provides a new, general overview of the graphic and linguistic features of these texts. The new data, combined with what was previously known (script, palaeographic varieties, chronology, formulae, and language) are presented and examined and compared with Ancient South Arabian and with the scripts and languages from northern Arabia.

Keywords: Ancient South Arabian, Ancient North Arabian, Thamudic, graffiti, Najrān region

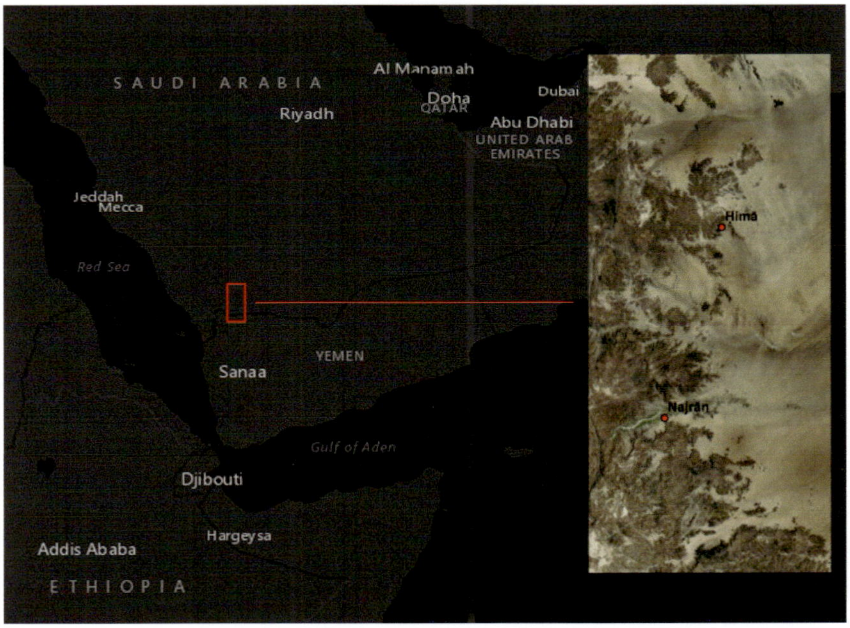

FIGURE 1. *A map of the Ḥimā area, north-north-east of Najrān.*

Introduction

This paper provides a general overview of the graphic and linguistic features of graffiti from the region of Ḥimā (Fig. 1). These are in a script which used to be called 'Southern Thamudic',[1] but which has now been sufficiently studied to be identified as a distinct Ancient North Arabian

[1] 'Thamudic' is not in fact a script but a conventional label for all the Ancient North Arabian scripts that await a more precise classification (Macdonald & King 2000; Macdonald 2000: 43–44).

Les alphabets sabéen et ḥimaʾite

	transcription latine	sabéen	T1	T2	T3	ḥimāʾite T4 T5	T6	T7	T8	T9
1.	ʾ									
2.	ʿ									
3.	b									
4.	d									
5.	ḏ									
6.	ḍ									
7.	f									
8.	g									
9.	ġ									
10.	h									
11.	ḫ									
12.	ḥ									
13.	k									
14.	l									
15.	m									
16.	n									
17.	q									
18.	r									
19.	s¹									
20.	s²									
[21.	s³	]								
22.	ṣ									
23.	t									
24.	ṯ									
25.	ṭ									
26.	w									
27.	y									
28.	z									
[29.	ẓ	]								

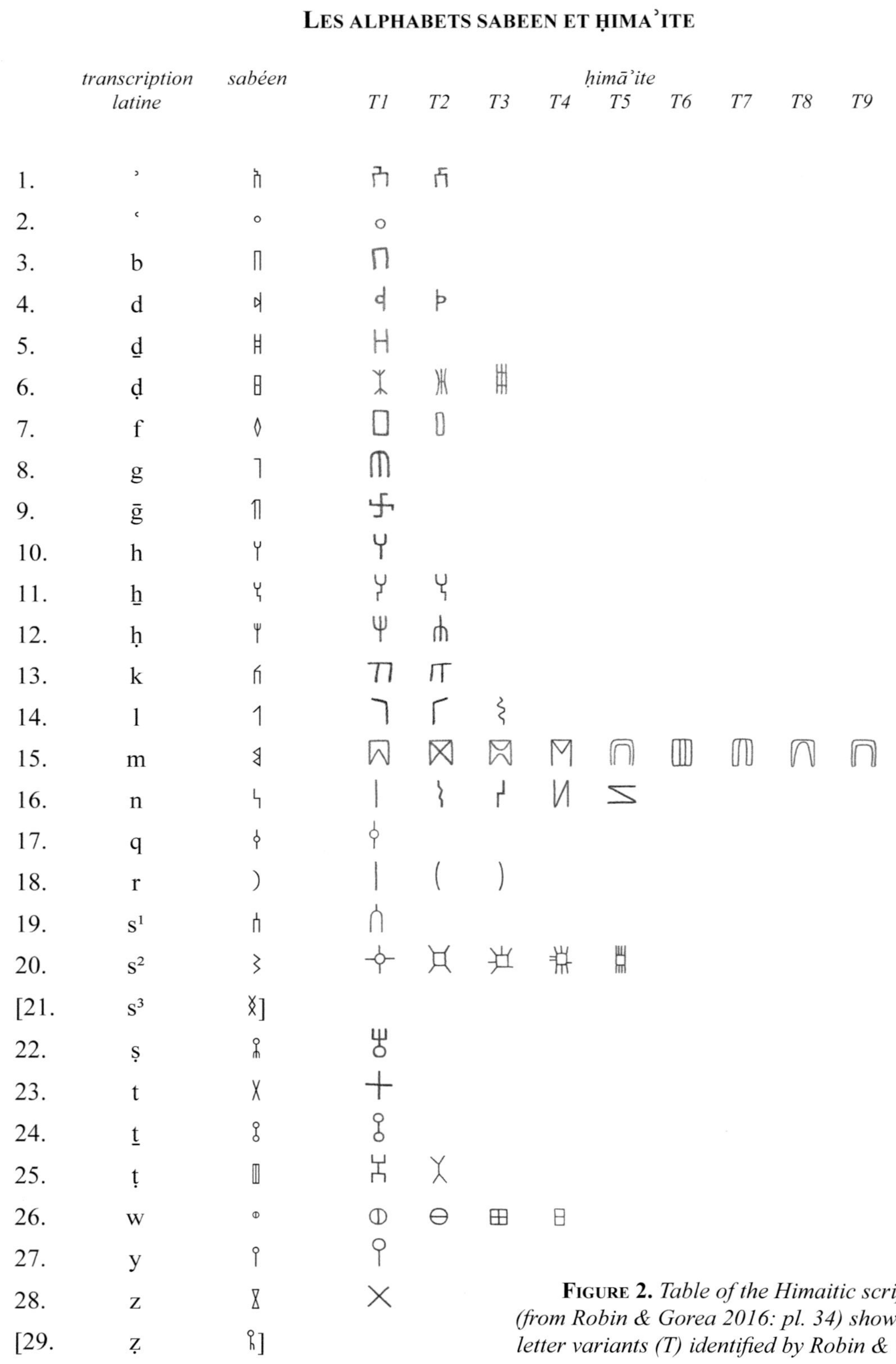

Figure 2. *Table of the Himaitic script (from Robin & Gorea 2016: pl. 34) showing the letter variants (T) identified by Robin & Gorea.*

(ANA) script type which has been labelled 'Himaitic'. The Saudi-French archaeological and epigraphic mission has worked in the province of Najrān since 2007, and from 2011 has concentrated its research exclusively on the area of Ḥimā, located about 100 km north-north-east of Najrān.[2] This area had already been identified and investigated by Harry St.J.B. Philby in 1936 (Philby 1952; van den Branden 1956), the Philby-Ryckmans-Lippens expedition (PRL) in 1951–1952 (Lippens 1956; Ryckmans J 1956, Ryckmans G 1957; Grohmann 1962),[3] the Saudi Department of Antiquities and Museums from the 1970s (Kabāwī et al. 1999), and a Japanese team in the early 2000s (Kawatoko, Tokunaga & Iizuka 2005).[4]

As a preliminary remark, it should be emphasized that this paper discusses the author's ongoing research and therefore many of the statements in it may be susceptible to modifications in the future, as fieldwork continues and the texts already recorded are more thoroughly scrutinized.[5]

Script

The non-Ancient South Arabian (ASA) script used in the Ḥimā area has traditionally been called 'Southern Thamudic' (Ryckmans J 1956: 5–17). Since its decipherment by Christian Robin (Robin & Gorea 2016), however, it can now be removed from the 'Thamudic' pending file and Robin has suggested the name 'ḥimāʾite' (Robin, Al-Ghabbān & Al-Saʿīd 2014: 1062), in English 'Himaitic'.[6] The alphabet is made up of twenty-seven glyphs (Fig. 2). So far, none has been identified for the letters s^3 and *ẓ*.[7] In completing his decipherment of the alphabet, Robin corrected the interpretation of some signs that had been provided by the epigraphists of the Japanese mission (*l*, *ṣ*, *ṭ*, *g*, s^2, *r*, and *n*), identified the letter *ḍ*, and confirmed the value of the 'swastika' as a *ġ* (Robin & Gorea 2016: 310–375).[8]

The description of the *ductus* and of the individual glyphs has already been provided in Robin's exhaustive study; I will therefore not go into detail here and will simply limit myself to some additional remarks. The direction of writing is predominantly right to left, and only very rarely does one encounter texts written downwards (Fig. 3) or from left to right. All the glyphs have a vertical stance, with the exception of the *m* which is oriented horizontally as in most examples of Thamudic B, C, and D. No word dividers are used to separate the words. The letters are mostly formed by single continuous strokes, but in some cases by two parallel strokes or by a series of dots.[9] The most common carving techniques are incising or pecking the sandstone with a hard, sharp stone (on this subject, see Arbach et al. 2015: 26–27).

Two main graphic variants can be distinguished: a formal and an informal. In the formal, the characters are usually large and have angular and regular forms, and there are some examples where the letters are particularly carefully shaped and often highly decorated.[10] The informal[11] are normally small and often more difficult to read. Some letter-forms are the same in both variants,

[2] A detailed report on the major results of the 2007–2011 seasons was published in Arbach et al. 2015: 11.

[3] For the rock drawings, see Anati 1968a; 1968b; 1972; 1974.

[4] The largest collection was made by the PRL expedition that copied (and occasionally photographed) nearly 8000 inscriptions. The plates illustrating these texts were prepared by J. Ryckmans but were never published. Only a few of them appear in Robin, Al-Ghabban & Al-Saʿīd (2014), and in Robin et al. (in preparation). These copies, made in difficult conditions but generally of good quality, formed the initial documentary database. To this documentation were added the 300 texts published by the Japanese mission (Kawatoko, Tokunaga & Iizuka 2005), and a handful of graffiti that have appeared in various publications, notably in the Saudi journal *Aṭlāl* (Kabawi et al. 1999) and two volumes published by A. Jamme (1965; 1966). For its part, the Saudi-French mission has studied about 10,000 texts, nearly half of which were already known from these previous publications.

[5] Christian Robin, however, has both undertaken extensive work on the historical-cultural content of the corpus of inscriptions and graffiti found at Ḥimā (Robin, Al-Ghabban & Al-Saʿīd 2014), and has achieved the full decipherment of the alphabet of the Himaitic graffiti and has made a preliminary sketch of the linguistic evidence they provide (Robin & Gorea 2016: 310–375). A lengthy introduction to the corpus of graffiti located in the area of ʿĀn Jamal will appear in Robin et al. (in preparation).

[6] During a meeting in Riyadh organized in May 2015 by the Saudi Commission for Tourism and Cultural Heritage (SCTH) in order to launch the ambitious project *TADWIN*, the more neutral, 'pending' label 'Thamudic F' was preferred by the participants.

[7] Only a few examples of these two letters have been found even in the ASA graffiti from this area.

[8] The identification of the swastika with the letter *ġ* had been suggested by Jacques Ryckmans (1956: 10; 1960: 202) and retained in van den Branden's publication (1956). The reading of the *g* and *ṭ* is now confirmed by the discovery of an extremely interesting abecedary from Qaryat al-Fāw, which is carved in ASA characters except for these two glyphs that are in the Himaitic script (Al-Saʿīd, in preparation).

[9] A nice example of the dotted stroke is reproduced in Robin & Gorea 2016: pl. 2.

[10] This style is defined as 'ostentatoire' in Robin & Gorea 2016: 331 where good examples are shown on plates 13 and 27.

[11] Robin and Gorea (2016: 331) call this 'cursive' and explain in footnote 83: 'Nous donnons à cursif son sens habituel, celui d'écriture qui "court", c'est-à-dire tracée rapidement, et non celui d'écriture dans laquelle les lettres sont attachées. L'écriture "cursive" est celle du quotidien, par opposition à l'écriture "ostentatoire" qui est celle des grandes occasions'.

Figure 3. *Two graffiti carved vertically downwards to the right of a human figure and reading:* l-grmt *and* ymt *(©MAFSN).*

while other shapes can be modified: generally in the informal variant, angular letters (such as the ᵓ, *b*, s^1, and *ṭ*) become rounded; the appendixes of ᵓ and *ḫ* become wavy lines; the *f*, usually a rectangle, takes the shape of a bow; the vertical line of the *r* becomes curved; the *z*, basically a St Andrew's cross, becomes wavy lines (Fig. 4).

The letters that exhibit the most numerous variations are the *m*, followed by the s^2, the *n*, the *w*, and the *ḍ*.[12] It seems that, with the stylistic modifications described above, all these variants are used interchangeably in both the formal and informal scripts. Texts in a mixture of Himaitic and ASA letter forms are also not rare. Usually, these exhibit the ASA forms of ᵓ, *ḏ*, and *m*. No evident motivation for such a choice is apparent, except that it is this limited range of characters and that it appears mostly in the formal script.[13] In the absence of any certain chronological span, it is impossible to attempt any palaeographic approach and establish whether at least some of these variants represent ideal forms of different graphic phases. Even when two variants of the same letter are found in one text — which

[12] So far, thirteen variants of the *m* have been encountered, eight of the s^2, six of the *n*, four of the *w*, and three of the *ḍ*. Further variants of these glyphs have been found since the publication of the alphabetic chart in Robin & Gorea 2016: pl. 34, reproduced as Figure 2 here.

[13] See Robin & Gorea 2016: pl. 1. In the graffito reading *mrᵓlᶜzy*, the ᵓ has its form in the ASA script.

Figure 4. *A group of graffiti in the informal style (© MAFSN).*

Figure 5. *A graffito carved above a camel and reading from right to left:* ms^{1}k wqr-h 'Ms^{1}k *carved it'; the* r *has reversed ends (©MAFSN).*

often happens, especially for the *m* — it cannot be assumed that one is a transitional form of the other.[14] Furthermore, at the current stage of our research, we are not yet able to infer whether these variants are associated with different families, an approach that is proving to be particularly fruitful in the case of Safaitic inscriptions.[15] On the other hand, unlike the Safaitic corpus, the relatively restricted area of the Ḥimā region and the mingled distribution of such variants over the different zones would tend to exclude the hypothesis of geographical variation as a reason for the different styles.[16]

Chronology

The chronological frame of the Himaitic graffiti is very vague and this topic will not therefore be addressed at length here. Robin has already explored some useful approaches, at least for establishing a relative chronology, such as the study of superimpositions and of the link between text and drawing.[17] Even if palaeography were to be excluded as a dating tool,[18] some clues are available when a Himaitic letter takes obvious inspiration from a corresponding ASA character. Two examples have been found, in which the ASA letter is particularly diagnostic and can therefore provide a *terminus post quem* for the carving of the Himaitic graffito. One text has an *r* with reversed ends, which is not attested in the ASA script before the fourth century AD (Fig. 5). The second example is even more interesting: the author who carved the Himaitic graffito drew inspiration from a text in the late ASA script carved on the same rock. He then not only produced a graffito in a mixed ASA and Himaitic script, but also took over the shape of the ASA letter *b* — a

[14] See Macdonald, this volume, for a discussion of a similar situation in the Dadanitic inscriptions.

[15] This was something explored by Chiara della Puppa in her paper at the Special Session and which she will discuss in more detail in her doctoral thesis.

[16] This cannot definitely be proved to be true, however, until the systematic survey of the Ḥimā complex is completed and the data are fully digitized in a database allowing text/corpus analyses.

[17] See, in particular, the chapter 'La datation des gravures' in the introduction to the ᶜĀn Jamal volume (Robin et al., in preparation), where Robin distinguishes between direct and indirect dating methods. In the latter category the criteria useful for a relative classification of the engravings are: 'surimposition des gravures', 'patine des panneaux', 'mouvements de la roche', 'évitement'; those useful for the absolute classification are: 'diffusion de l'écriture', 'paléographie', 'mention explicite d'une date', 'passage à l'islam', 'introduction, domestication, disparition d'espèces'.

[18] This issue has been readdressed lately in Macdonald 2015: 17–27.

shape that appears approximately in the third century AD — and used it to represent the Himaitic *m*.[19]

Geographical extent and origin of the script

In his decipherment, Robin points out that the Himaitic alphabet shares numerous 'isoglosses', on the one hand with ASA, and on the other with Thamudic D (Robin & Gorea 2016: 323–324). He therefore assumes that it could have developed either from the ASA script used by the settled populations of southern Arabia including Najrān and Qaryat al-Faw, or from Thamudic D, which was employed by some nomads of the Arabian Desert. In either case, the shared letters are seen as borrowed as a result of the contact of the local population with foreign people crossing Ḥimā for commercial reasons.

Some further comments can be made on this point. Firstly, many of the glyphs that the Himaitic script shares with the ASA script in fact either belong to the common repertoire of the South Semitic script family or are shared with the other ANA scripts, especially Thamudic B. Secondly, two of the five glyphs that have no parallels in ASA are graphic isoglosses with Thamudic D (*ġ* and *s²*). Finally, three of the letters distinguishing the Himaitic script from Thamudic D (*f*, *ẖ*, and *z*) are also found in Taymanitic and in Dispersed Oasis North Arabian (see Macdonald 2000: 29, 33–36), and could constitute the original forms of the South Semitic script as well.[20]

Moreover, preliminary studies conducted on the graffiti from Maʾsal and other sites of Najd south-west of Riyadh inventoried by the Saudi-French mission in 2015 and 2016, have revealed a script similar or possibly identical to that of Ḥimā.[21] Only the direction of the writing — mostly vertical — is different and is for the most part similar to the sub-varieties of Thamudic C from northern Najd.[22] Incidentally, this latter point makes clear that the horizontal ductus of Himaitic is most probably secondary and influenced by the ASA script.[23] All these elements taken together seem to substantiate the idea that Himaitic belongs to the North Arabian writing tradition, of which it constitutes an independent branch.[24] If one adds that a similar script was also used in at least two sites of the ʿAsīr province, namely Wādī Tathlīth and Jabjab,[25] this not only extends the geographical range of this variety, but also adds more weight to the hypothesis that the origin of this branch is to be placed somewhere in central Arabia.[26]

Grammatical notes

This section lists the linguistic data that has so far been drawn from the graffiti from Ḥimā, some of which has already been noted by previous scholars. Only the most indisputable data are considered here, either because they occur regularly or for grammatical reasons, but further information is expected to appear in future, since there are a number of longer sequences which do not seem to be simply lists of names. It should be remembered that many of these data have been found in onomastics and therefore cannot be taken as a secure source for a grammatical sketch, as they might not necessarily reflect the language spoken by the people who carved the graffiti.

Little can be said on orthography, except that the reflexes of diphthongs in word-internal position were not marked in the script. This phenomenon — which may suggest a collapse of internal diphthongs in pronunciation or be simply a writing practice — is attested in the onomasticon and is especially evident in theophoric

[19] See Robin & Gorea 2016: pl. 31. Even if the letter shapes are abstract enough to have been produced independently, the borrowing from ASA into Himaitic is likely, not only in view of the ASA text carved next to the Himaitic one, but also because this particular shape of the ASA *b* makes it very similar to the Himaitic *m*.

[20] Ahmad Al-Jallad has reminded the author that in a recently published Thamudic B abecedary discovered in Jordan, the letter *ẖ* has a particular shape, which seems to be 'a compromise between the South Arabian [?] and the X-shaped glyph common in many ANA scripts, including Thamudic B'. In the same work, he and his co-author wonder whether 'The present shape could reflect an archaic form, ancestral to the X-shaped *ẖ* of other ANA scripts' (Al-Jallad & Al-Manaser 2015: 7).

[21] This alphabet has the compact ʾ, the *ġ* in the shape of a swastika, the crossed *m*, the *s²* as a sunburst, and the *ṯ* as a vertical line with a circle on each end. Besides the script there are similar formulae, such as (PN) *wdd* PN. These graffiti were presented by the author during the 20th Rencontres Sabéennes held in Perugia in June 2016.

[22] Examples of Thamudic C are in Al-Theeb 1421a/2000 (e.g. no. 105, fig. p. 191), 1421b/2000 (e.g. no. 68, fig. 204), and 1422/2002 (e.g. no. 62, fig. 194). Macdonald and King identified two different scripts in this category, C^1 and C^2 (2000: 138). Recently, Al-Jallad has attempted a further refinement of the first variant (Al-Jallad, in preparation).

[23] Theoretically, local people who wrote in Himaitic could have encountered the ASA inscriptions left by South Arabian travellers at Ḥimā as early as the eighth to seventh century BC.

[24] The existence of a family of ANA scripts, and therefore of a proto-script ancestor of all its varieties, was questioned by Al-Jallad at the Special Session.

[25] For the former corpus, see Al-Qaḥṭānī 2007; photographic samples of graffiti from Jabjab were kindly provided to the author by Florent Egal; see also Robin & Gorea 2016: pls 28–30.

[26] Robin has already remarked that, 'il est manifeste qu'une certaine proximité culturelle existait entre les gens de Himà et les populations des steppes et des déserts plus au nord' and 'elle se traduit notamment dans l'écriture' (Robin & Gorea 2016: 325).

names (*zdmnt* vs. *zydlt*, *tmlt* vs. *tymlt*, *ṯbn* vs. *ṯwbn*, etc.) (Robin & Gorea 2016: 328).

The only sure example of the omission of prosthetic vowels in the script is provided by the verbal form *tqr* (compared to Arabic *ittaqara*). The rare occurrences of the noun *bn* 'son'[27] and some other examples found in personal names (*Mrʾlqs¹*, compared to Arabic *Imruʾ al-Qays*) are less certain, as they could be parallel to forms found in Arabic (*bin and *marʾ) and would not necessarily reflect the structure of Classical Arabic.[28]

As far as phonology is concerned, it has already been mentioned that the Himaitic alphabet seems to lack independent glyphs for the reflexes of the Proto-Semitic affricate /s³/ and of the emphatic interdental /ẓ/.[29] This is not surprising when one considers that both these phonemes are, so far, missing in Thamudic B, C, and D, and that there is no /ẓ/ in Taymanitic (Macdonald 2008: 191). On the other hand, unlike Thamudic C and D, the presence of the letters *ḏ* and *z* in personal names and especially the rare use of the determinative pronoun *ḏ* prove that Himaitic retained the voiced interdental.[30]

Sporadic fluctuations in the spelling of the letter *ġ* have also been noticed in personal names (Robin & Gorea 2016: 328–329): some examples point to the replacement of *ġ* with *g* (*gzlt* instead of *ġzlt*, both names occurring), others show the opposite phenomenon (*ġḏmt* instead of *gḏmt*, both attested). We also find *mġwyt* compared to the ASA *mʿwyt*.[31] At present, however, the frequency of such alternations cannot be assessed and therefore their phonological implications are still uncertain.

There is only a limited amount of evidence on nominal morphology and it is important to note that in some ways it conflicts with that inferred from the onomasticon. As we have not yet compiled the inventory of all the personal names attested in the graffiti, no detailed outline of the onomasticon from Ḥimā can be defined on statistical grounds. Nevertheless, besides the theophoric names already mentioned, the vast majority are one-word names or names consisting of prepositional phrases[32] and a preliminary inquiry using the OCIANA database[33] showed that a large number of them are indeed common in the ANA corpora while they are often missing in ASA.[34]

Like the ASA names, however, the personal names found at Ḥimā may bear the *-m* or the *-n* endings. On this point Robin observes that, while the use of the former is not regular — as the same name can often appear with or without mimation (*whbm* vs. *whb*, *ʿdym* vs. *ʿdy*) — the names with *-n* seem to be more numerous (*ġmrn*, compared to Arabic *al-ghamr*). He then postulates that, as in ASA, these endings marked the indefinite and definite states of the noun, although he argues that the definite article in the local language was probably a variety of the prefixed forms *hal- or *al-, of which a few occurrences are also known from personal names (Robin & Gorea 2016: 327–328).[35]

While this assumption must necessarily wait to be confirmed by new, non-onomastic data, the discovery of a graffito depicting a lion and accompanied by a text mentioning its author, the verb 'to carve' (*yqr*), and the substantive 'lion' (*lbʾ*) as the direct object, suggests a different scenario. The unmarked noun *lbʾ* could be indefinite, but the presence of the drawing makes it more likely that the noun here is definite (Fig. 6). Since most of the occurrences of the definite articles have been found

[27] In the graffiti from Ḥimā, the juxtaposition of personal names to indicate a patronym or family affiliation is preferred.

[28] The author thanks Ahmad Al-Jallad for calling her attention to this point.

[29] While it is certain that etymological /s³/ merged with /s¹/, following a phenomenon that is also visible in the Sabaic corpus from Najrān and the northern Yemenite Jawf (Stein 2007: 26), it is extremely difficult to decide whether /ẓ/ merged with /ṣ/, as in some areas of southern Yemen (Prioletta 2018: 133, 139–141) and in Taymanitic (Kootstra 2016: 67–140), or with /ḍ/, as in Sabaic and in some Arabic dialects (Behnstedt & Woidich 2005: 11). The latter phenomenon has interesting implications in Sabaic as far as orthography and script register are concerned. The glyph *ẓ* is regularly replaced by that representing *ḍ* in the minuscule script from the palaeographic phase IIIa onwards. Since this occurs in all kind of documents (letters as well as contracts etc. originating from various places of ancient Yemen), Peter Stein observes that it could not be a regional phenomenon limited to al-Jawf (where the only archive of minuscule texts known so far is located, at the site of al-Sawdāʾ, ancient Nashshān). Moreover, the fact that the formal inscriptions have retained the two separate glyphs might be a graphic archaism or, alternatively, the sign of a gap between the language used in formal inscriptions and the spoken language of everyday life (Stein 2013: 43).

[30] See the graffito reproduced in Robin & Gorea 2016: pl. 2 and reading: *nmrt ḏ fḏlmnt*. Indeed, in the corpus of graffiti in the ASA script there is only one example of the pronoun *z* instead of *ḏ*. Nothing can be said on the provenance of the author, however, and therefore this example adds little to this point.

[31] In the case of the latter pair of names, however, it should be noted that both are attested in ANA: *mġwy* in Hismaic (CH.07-0001-04.2; CH.07-0022-06) and *mʿwy* in Safaitic (LP 810; C 5074); see OCIANA (accessed 11 October 2017).

[32] For the theonyms most often used in compound personal names from Ḥimā, see the note by C.J. Robin at the end of this paper.

[33] It should be noted, however, that the Thamudic B, C, and D inscriptions have not yet been entered into OCIANA.

[34] There is also a fair number of names with quite bizarre structures and no parallel elsewhere (e.g. *btt*, *nnt*, *ṯṯʿ*).

[35] 'L'article, dans la langue locale serait bien *hal-/al-*, mais, appartenant à une langue sans prestige, il serait remplacé dans l'onomastique par l'article sabaʾique -ān' (Robin & Gorea 2016: 327). The definite article *hl-* has also been found in graffiti carved in the ASA script (*hl-ʾs¹d*).

Figure 6. *A two-line graffito carved to the left of a drawing of a lion and reading:* ywyṯᶜ yqr lbʾ *'Ywyṯᶜ carved the lion' (©MAFSN).*

in personal names,[36] it is not possible to infer whether the Himaitic graffiti had a mixed situation — comparable to Safaitic or Dadanitic — or lacked any visible morphological marker for definiteness, like Hismaic.[37]

As for bound forms, we now have one example of construct-genitive in one graffito, next to a drawing of a camel with its hunter or herder, which reads: *gml ᶜmydᶜ* 'the camel of ᶜmydᶜ' (Fig. 7).

Evidence for the pronominal system is restricted to the determinative *ḏ* mentioned earlier and to two occurrences of the phrase *wqr h*, in which the element *h* could be the deictic demonstrative 'this' or the clitic pronoun 'it' (see Fig. 5).

Verbal morphology is somewhat better represented, thanks to the discovery of new verbal forms. Of many of these verbs, which are to be analysed syntactically as third masculine singular forms of the suffix conjugation,[38] the feminine singular form — ending with the expected *-t* — is now also known (*wddt*, *wqrt*, *wrbt*, and *ḏkrt*). Moreover, one of these I-w verbs, *wqr*, very often seems to exhibit the by-form *yqr*. Since the two forms appear in identical contexts[39] where the formula requires a preterite verb, I am inclined to consider both the forms to be in the suffix conjugation. The alternation of the initial glide in weak roots is known from Sabaic as a regional phenomenon (Stein 2003: 30) but here, for the present, it cannot be proved to be either a dialectal or a chronological variation.

On the other hand, the single example found so far of the by-form *ydd* instead of *wdd* is not only syntactically interesting but could also provide a further argument in favour of this point (Fig. 8). If the interpretation of the phrase offered here is correct, we would have PN *w ydd* PN. Assuming that the geminate root with the two consonants kept apart is in the D-stem (cf. Classical Arabic *waddada*), *ydd* would reflect the third masculine singular of the suffix conjugation better than that of the prefix conjugation, since the latter would have retained the initial glide (*/yuwaddid/).[40]

[36] There might also be an example of the article *h-*, in a graffito carved in the ASA script (KhShB198) that has been read by Risa Tokunaga as: *^{1}l-qs^{1}r mrn ^{2}h-rqd* 'Belongs to Qs^{1}r (son of) Mrn this inscription' (Kawatoko, Tokunaga & Iizuka 2005: 89). Robin, who rightly does not consider the name *mrn* (written in the Himaitic script) as part of the graffito, wonders whether 'ce *h-* n'est pas l'article *hl-* avec assimilation du *l*' (Robin & Gorea 2016: 329).

[37] It should be remembered that it remains 'an open question whether Hismaic employed a form of determination which does not show up in the script (e.g., a final vowel, as in the Aramaic "determinate state"), or had no definite article (as, in effect, in Syriac)' (Macdonald 2008: 209). For a summary of the present situation concerning the different forms of the definite article found in the ANA inscriptions and a reappraisal of its weight for the classification of these languages vis-à-vis Arabic, see Al-Jallad, forthcoming.

[38] See the next section for the different constructions in which these verbs have been found.

[39] Texts with a PN *yqr*, and *yqr* PN, occur along with texts in which the form is *wqr*. The verb *yqr* has also been found by itself (Robin & Gorea 2016: 325–326).

[40] The form *ydd* could also reflect the suffix conjugation of the G-stem

Figure 7. *A graffito carved in the lower part of the camel's body and reading:* gml ᶜmydᶜ *'the camel of ᶜmydᶜ'; above, two other graffiti: the upper one reading from left to right* wᶜḥmy, *and the lower one reading from right to left* qs¹rm *(©MAFSN).*

Figure 8. *A graffito reading from right to left:* yhḏkr w ydd ᶜklb *'yhḏkr and he greeted [or: loved?] ᶜklb'; after the* b *of* ᶜklb *a continuation of the text, or another graffito, of which only one letter,* m, *is readable (©MAFSN).*

Finally, three T-stem forms are now attested: *tqr*, which could reflect the infix *-t-* stem with the assimilation of the first radical /w/ (*/Vttaqara/);[41] and the prefix T-stem verbs *ts²wq* and *twdd*.[42] It is not clear whether *tqr* and *twdd* should have a reflexive or a passive meaning.

Syntax and formulae

This last section lists very briefly the new data from the lexicon and the syntactic arrangement of the most recurrent formulae. The Ḥimā region bears witness to an astonishing concentration not only of graffiti but also of rock drawings depicting many kinds of human figures, animals and, more rarely, flora. The link between text and drawing cannot always be determined, but the artists very often stated their authorship by adding their name and the verb *wqr* 'to carve'. The lexical choice of *wqr* is interesting, since this form is unknown in the authorship formulae of ANA graffiti — where words such as *ẖṭṭ* are preferred — but it is found in formal ASA inscriptions, where it has the sense of 'inscribed stone' (Beeston et al. 1982: 161).[43]

As in Hismaic, the preferred order of the components of the texts from Ḥimā is PN *wqr* — even though there are several examples where this order is reversed — but there is no example of *w* PN *wqr*, namely with the introductory conjunction *w*. This would favour the hypothesis that the form *wqr* should be interpreted as a verb and that the subject-verb order results from topicalization, following a practice found not only in the incipit formulae of ASA and Dadanitic formal inscriptions, but also in the ANA graffiti.[44]

It seems that in this case the relationship between text and drawing could play a role more immediate than syntax, and that the engraver often made his choice on the basis of the available space on the rock, the outline of the drawing, or even whimsy, as in Figure 9 where the name *bnᶜṯtr* is written in three places around the camel and the verb *wqr* is carved between the animal's hind legs. More rarely, *wqr* is replaced by *fᶜl* 'he made' (Fig. 10, top), and we also have one example of the verb *s¹ṭr* 'to write' (Fig. 11). On the other hand, unlike the graffiti in most of the ANA corpora, the authorship particle *lam auctōris* is only rarely found; in a few instances the formula *l* PN seems to be associated with the drawing of a mounted horse charging (see the photograph in Robin & Gorea 2016: pl. 18).

Besides the authorship statements, the range of textual formulae so far attested is very poor compared to that of other ANA corpora. The most common one is that with the word *wdd*, which is found in several varieties of Thamudic.[45] In Himaitic it appears in sequences, such as PN *wdd* PN, PN *wdd*, or *wdd* PN (Robin & Gorea 2016: 326). This verb can be associated in longer sequences with other verbs, such as *ḏkr* 'to remember' and *wrb l-*. The latter often appears in the place of *wdd* or even alone with no direct object. The meaning of *wrb l-* remains uncertain. The only Semitic parallel seems to be Arabic *wariba*, which has the negative meaning of swindling someone by speaking or acting ambiguously.[46] It could

(*yadad < *wadad), although this would mean that geminate roots in Himaitic were conjugated like strong roots and so behaved differently from Arabic or Sabaic, but compared to some ANA languages such as Safaitic where, for example, a geminated root like *ḥll* 'to camp' is spelled occasionally as *ḥl*, there is, so far, no example of *wd* in Himaitic. And even in Safaitic, although the meaning fits much better with the G-Form in Arabic than with the D-Form, there is no agreed opinion on whether *ḥll* reflects a base stem (as in Macdonald 2008: 202), or 'innovations based on analogy with strong roots, or, perhaps most likely, the use of the D in place of the G' (Al-Jallad 2015: 122).

[41] See the graffito reading: *zhrm tqr* (Robin & Gorea 2016: 325–326, pl. 8). Here, the editors maintain the possibility that *tqr* might instead be the third person feminine singular of the prefix conjugation.

[42] One example of *twdd* in a graffito in ASA script is particularly relevant, since it exhibits two names coordinated by the conjunction *w* and followed by the verb (*¹ṣḥbt ²w-ḥrṯt twdd*). The verb would therefore be in the unmarked dual.

[43] In legal contexts, in formulae such as *b-ḥg ḏn wqrn* 'according to this inscribed stone', the noun clearly undergoes a metonymic process by which it denotes in fact the actual decree that is inscribed on the stone (see e.g. MṢM 3640/6 on DASI, accessed 1 October 2017). The proposed translation of 'carving' is based on one very restricted sense of *wqr* in Arabic (see Biberstein Kazimirski 1860: 1582, 'fendre, crevasser, fêler'). The special use of *wqr* in the ASA legal contexts, however, might suggest that in the graffiti of Ḥimā it has a semantic implication that transcends the simple practical act of carving the rock, to become indeed a statement of the ownership of the text. The author owes this suggestion to Giovanni Mazzini.

[44] Geraldine King maintained that in the Hismaic formulae *w* PN *ẖṭṭ* or *l* PN *w* PN *ẖṭṭ*, the form *ẖṭṭ* was not a verb but 'a participle *ẖāṭiṭ* or the noun *ẖaṭṭāṭ*' (King 1990: 4 A.2). This analysis could be confirmed by comparison with the Safaitic context of C 1185: *w-mt[y] h-ẖṭ{ṭ}* 'and *Mty* is the writer' (OCIANA, accessed 1 October 2017; Al-Jallad 2015: 169). This single occurrence remains uncertain, however, as the text is known only from a dubious copy. In the most common formula *l* PN *w h-ẖṭṭ*, the latter word is interpreted as a noun 'and the carving [is his]'. The author owes this remark to Michael Macdonald.

[45] On the different formulae containing the word *wdd* and the interpretations proposed, see Tsafrir 1996: 142–143 and recently Al-Jallad, in preparation. One interesting inscription in an unclassified Thamudic script from northern Jordan also has the formula PN *wdd* PN (Stokes 2016: 33–44).

[46] Lane, 2933c: 'he was corrupt' (G stem); 'he expressed himself equivocally' (D stem); 'he strove to outwit' (L stem).

Figure 9. *A drawing of a camel with the name* bn^{c}ṯr *written three times around it, and the verb* wqr *'he carved' written between the animal's hind legs (©MAFSN).*

Figure 10. *A graffito carved above three human figures; reading from right to left:* yṯ^{c} f^{c}l, *'Yṯ^{c} made'; on the lower left side, another graffito reading from right to left:* ᵓbl^{c}n *(©MAFSN).*

therefore be assumed that the verb introduces a sort of curse formula, although this is less plausible when the verb is employed alone. Another explanation is that the root in Arabic is used in a narrow, pejorative sense and that in the Ḥimā formula the verb simply states something like 'to celebrate, pay respects to someone'.[47]

Finally, the verb *ts*^{2}*wq* 'he longed for' mentioned above, as of now has been found only once (Fig. 12). It is not clear on the stone if the verb stands alone or if the name carved below it belongs to the same text and, moreover, if it is preceded by the particle *l*, which would produce a construction similar to that found in Safaitic (Al-Jallad 2015: 220).[48]

---

[47] J. Ryckmans (1960: 204), on the other hand, compared *wrb* to *wqr/yqr* and was of the opinion that the two formulae 'auraient un sens similaire (de salutation)'.

[48] Beside *ts*^{2}*wq* used alone, the most recurrent formula in Safaitic is *ts*^{2}*wq* *ᵓl* (equivalent to Arabic *ishtāqa ilā*). Al-Jallad (2015: 43) explains the few occurrences of *ts*^{2}*wq l* either as a graphic mistake or as a spelling reflecting the loss of the ᵓ of the preposition in the utterance ('it may have coalesced in pronunciation with the co-articulated glottal stop of a glottalic *q*'). Michael Macdonald reminded the author, however, that of all the examples of *ts*^{2}*wq* in Safaitic and Hismaic, 15% (i.e. 23 out of 154) are followed by *l*, rather than *ᵓl*, and that this is far too high a percentage to assume either a graphic mistake or the reflex of an assimilation in pronunciation. See also Norris (this volume): 83, n. 41.

Figure 11. *A drawing of a camel accompanied by a two-line graffito reading from right to left:* s^{1}ṭr ^{c}bdyġṯ, *'^{c}bdyġṯ wrote' (©MAFSN).*

Figure 12. *A graffito carved over a bovid and reading from right to left:* grwt ts^{2}wq *'Grwt longed'; above, another graffito reading from right to left:* flʾn *(©MAFSN).*

Who wrote the Ancient South Arabian and Himaitic inscriptions?[49]

A note by Christian J. Robin

The pre-Islamic scripts found at Ḥimā are (in descending order of the numbers found): Himaitic, ASA, Nabataean-Aramaic, Greek, and Palaeo-Arabic. The great majority of the graffiti belong to the Himaitic and ASA groups, and they are the ones that interest us here, as we ask ourselves the same question as our predecessors: who were the people who engraved these texts?

Former hypotheses

Jacques Ryckmans (1956: 13; 1969: 246–247) maintained that the variation in writing implied a linguistic, chronological, and ethnic difference. Moreover, he observed that the graffiti in each of two scripts at Ḥimā were not the same. His conclusion was that two populations should be distinguished: the local people who wrote in Himaitic and the 'invaders' from Yemen (after the third century AD) who wrote in ASA.

In his customary vehement tone, Albert Jamme (1965: 7; 1966: 10; 1971) criticized this view, assuming that all the texts of Ḥimā were the product of a single population using either the monumental variety or the cursive variety of the same script that he called 'Sabaic'. According to him, the peculiarities of the 'cursive Sabaic' of Ḥimā that made it resemble 'Thamudic' were to be explained by geography. The only two scholars who were interested in the classification of the texts of Ḥimā thus arrived at significantly different conclusions concerning the production of the Himaitic and ASA texts: two different populations according to Ryckmans; and two varieties of the same script and therefore the same population — with no further precision — according to Jamme.

Regarding their conclusions, however, we must bear in mind that they were drawn up at a date — the 1950s and 1960s — when ASA studies had not yet undergone the extraordinary advancement which took place in the following decades. Hence, they used chronological benchmarks and terminology which are now outdated. Jamme, moreover, never went to Ḥimā and only studied a very small number of graffiti from this area on photographs that were sent to him: his conclusions are not based on a study of the local epigraphic material but are only assumptions.

The tools of investigation

The vast majority of the texts found in Ḥimā consist only of personal names; only a small percentage mention an action, and a handful of them — fewer than 100 — give an indication of the author's status or origin. Those containing context are fewer than twenty in all, and fewer than five if we do not include the inscriptions left by the Himyarites, who besieged Najrān in AD 523, and which have a different character from the rest of the documentation.[50]

To identify the origin of the authors of the texts from Ḥimā, one can rely on direct and indirect evidence. The direct data are: the tribal or communal origin explicitly mentioned by a *nisbah*, adjective of relationship; certain functions that imply an origin; lineage names; and the mention of commercial activities that imply the movement of individuals. All these direct data, without exception, have been found in inscriptions in the ASA script. If the authors of the graffiti in Himaitic did not specify their tribal affiliation and origin, it is probably because they did not consider this important, as they were 'at home'.

It is notable that only one third of the total instances of *nisbah* adjectives refers to tribes from Najrān and Qaryat al-Fāw; on the other hand, references to these cities constitute the great majority of the names of lineages and functions. Since, as we have said, the *nisbah* adjective is added to the onomastic formula only when the concerned individual is away from his place of origin, these percentages prove that, in all probability, the majority of ASA texts were carved by people from Najrān and Qaryat al-Fāw.

Indirect data are also significant. These are the orthographic rules (the presence/absence of particular letters, the presence/absence of mimation and diphthongs), language (the form of the definite article and the lexicon), and the deities which appear in the theophoric personal names.[51]

From these elements, it appears that the ASA inscriptions have, with slight differences, the same characteristics as those written in Himaitic, namely:

[49] The subject of this note has been developed at much greater length in Robin, forthcoming, especially chapter 3: 'Les auteurs des inscriptions en écriture sudarabique et en écriture ḥimāʾite'.

[50] For a summary of these events and the inscriptions from Ḥimā referring to them, see Robin, Al-Ghabban & Al-Saʿīd 2014: 1057–1060 (the section: 'Nouveaux textes relatifs au blocus de Najrān en juin et juillet 523').

[51] It should be remembered, however, that most of these indirect data have been found in the onomasticon.

twenty-seven letters, with the s^3 and *ẓ* found only in the inscriptions of people from Yemen; a similar onomasticon, with names bearing mimation, showing the reduction of diphthongs, forms of the article such as *hl-* and *ᵓl-* (the latter often reduced to *l-*), and a similar set of theonyms used in theophoric personal names; and similar lexicon and formulae.

Concerning the theophoric names, it is remarkable that deities from central Arabia,[52] such as Allāh, Allāt, Kahal, Manāt, Shams, al-ᶜUzzā, Wadd, and Yaghūth are much more common than more usual ASA theonyms such as ᶜAmm and ᶜAthtar (the latter also attested in central and eastern Arabia according to the Arab-Muslim tradition). Surprisingly, there is not a single theophoric name at Ḥimā referring to Almaqah, the great god of Sabaᵓ.

Conclusions

Inevitably, our conclusions are remarkably different from those of our predecessors, even if they agree with all the observations made by J. Ryckmans, and support (accidentally) one of Jamme's hypotheses:

- The Himaitic graffiti were engraved by the local population.
- The ASA texts were carved by passers-by.
- The population of Ḥimā was influenced by certain orthographic rules of Sabaic but their language is probably a form of Old Arabic.
- Their deities are those of the populations of north-west Arabia.
- Passers-by who wrote in the ASA script follow more strictly the orthographic rules of Sabaic, but their language was probably the same as that of the people of Ḥimā, as were the deities they venerated.

We can therefore conclude that, for the most part, the authors of these two categories of inscription belonged to the same population, living in the area between Najrān, Qaryat al-Fāw, and Tathlīth. This population had remarkable characteristics: its language was a form of Old Arabic; its orthographic rules were strongly influenced by Sabaic; the great majority of its deities were the same as those of north-west Arabia. In short, these people were North Arabian in their language and religion, but South Arabian in their culture.

The choice of script depended on the social level of the author, which in turn would depend on his way of life. Those who wrote in ASA were settled people, residing in cities, participating in exchange networks and wishing to show their full integration into the ASA civilization. Those who wrote in Himaitic inhabited the steppe and the desert, from which they derived their subsistence. They manifested their specificity and, occasionally, their spirit of dissent. It is not surprising that, as several authors have already pointed out (Jamme 1965: 5), there is no clear border between the Himaitic and ASA scripts since all intermediate states are found.

J. Ryckmans (1956: 15) based his reconstruction on the opinion that the Himaitic graffiti preceded the 'Himyaritic' ones (themselves dated from the third to the fifth century AD), but this idea has proved to be unfounded: there are very few texts in the ASA script from the earliest period; they are very numerous in the last centuries before the Christian era, and again are copious in the fourth to fifth centuries AD.[53] Concerning the Himaitic graffiti, we cannot be as precise, although we have proof that they were carved up to the late period (see above: Chronology).

These conclusions are not without consequences for the categories we use.

- The civilization of southern Arabia developed throughout Yemen as well as in what is now southern Saudi Arabia. There were nearly twenty successive South Arabian kingdoms and political entities, of which those which inhabited the area of Ḥimā were: Muhaᵓmirum, then Amīrum in Najrān; Dhakirum, Qaḥṭān and Madhīgum, Kiddat (= Kinda) and Madhḥigum in Qaryat al-Fāw.
- The languages written by subjects of these kingdoms and political entities are now known to be five in number: Sabaic, Qatabanic, Hadramitic, Minaic, and a form of Old Arabic, which borrows much from Sabaic, in Najrān, Qaryat al-Fāw, and the Yemeni Jawf.
- The category of 'North Arabian' now includes populations which wrote in the ASA script. Moreover, it is becoming increasingly clear that, among the languages written in the ASA script, we must count Old Arabic from Najrān, Qaryat al-Fāw, and the Jawf. The existing definitions and terminology therefore need to be revised.

[52] For an inventory of the deities of north-west Arabia, see Nehmé, forthcoming. To her list, the gods Wadd (attested at Dadan) and Yaghūth (ᵓmrᵓyᶜwt, see Cantineau 1930–1932, ii: 64, 104) should be added.

[53] Compared to the Himaitic graffiti, at least one quarter of the ASA inscriptions and graffiti can be dated with a small margin of error, on the basis of their internal data or script style.

Acknowledgements

I would like to express my gratitude to Ahmad Al-Jallad, who read an earlier version of this paper, and to Michael Macdonald, who edited the article. Both of them contributed significantly to its improvement. Advice given by Giovanni Mazzini has also been of great help for the drafting of the text presented during the Seminar for Arabian Studies Special Session.

Sigla

DASI	Digital Archive for the Study of pre-Islamic Arabian Inscriptions http://dasi.humnet.unipi.it/
KhShB	Inscriptions in Kawatoko, Tokunaga & Iizuka 2005.
Lane	Lane 1863–1893.
MṢM	Military Museum of Ṣanᶜāᵓ.
OCIANA	The Online Corpus of the Inscriptions of Ancient North Arabia http://krcfm.orient.ox.ac.uk/fmi/webd#ociana

References

Anati E. 1968a. *Rock art in central Arabia*. i. *The 'oval-headed' people of Arabia*. (Bibliothèque du Muséon, 50. Expédition Philby-Ryckmans-Lippens en Arabie, Ière partie. Géographie et archéologie, 3). Louvain: Institut Orientaliste.

Anati E. 1968b. *Rock art in central Arabia*. ii. *Part One: Fat-tailed sheep in Arabia; Part Two: The realistic-dynamic style of rock-art in the Jabal Qara*. (Bibliothèque du Muséon, 50. Expédition Philby-Ryckmans-Lippens en Arabie, Ière partie. Géographie et archéologie, 3). Louvain: Institut Orientaliste.

Anati E. 1972. *Rock art in central Arabia*. iii. (Publications de l'Institut orientaliste de Louvain, 4). Louvain: Institut Orientaliste.

Anati E. 1974. *Rock art in central Arabia*. iv. (Publications de l'Institut orientaliste de Louvain, 6). Louvain: Institut Orientaliste.

Arbach M., Charloux G., Dridi H., Gajda I., Āl Murayḥ Ṣ.M., Robin C.J. ... Ṭayrān S. 2015. Results of four seasons of survey in the province of Najrān (Saudi Arabia) — 2007–2010. Pages 11–46 in I. Gerlach (ed.), *South Arabia and its neighbours. Phenomena of intercultural contacts. 14th Rencontres Sabéennes*. (Archäologische Berichte aus dem Yemen, 14). Wiesbaden: Reichert.

Beeston A.F.L., Al-Ghūl M.ᶜA., Müller W.W. & Ryckmans J. 1982. *Sabaic Dictionary (English-French-Arabic). Dictionnaire sabéen (anglais-français-arabe)*. Louvain-la-Neuve: Éditions Peeters/Beirut: Librairie du Liban.

Behnstedt P. & Woidich M. 2005. *Arabische Dialektgeographie. Eine Einführung*. (Handbook of Oriental Studies. 1: The Near and Middle East, 78). Leiden: Brill.

Biberstein Kazimirski A. de 1860. *Dictionnaire Arabe-Français, contenant toutes les racines de la langue arabe, leurs dérivés, tant dans l'idiome vulgaire que dans l'idiome littéral, ainsi que les dialectes d'Alger et de Maroc*. Paris: Maisonneuve.

Cantineau J. 1930–1932. *Le nabatéen*. (2 volumes). Paris: Leroux.

Donner F. (ed.). (forthcoming). *Script and scripture*. Chicago: University of Chicago Press.

Grohmann A. 1962. *Arabic inscriptions*. (Expédition Philby-Ryckmans-Lippens en Arabie, 2. Textes épigraphiques, 1). Louvain: Institut Orientaliste.

Al-Jallad A. 2015. *An outline of the grammar of the Safaitic inscriptions*. (Studies in Semitic Languages and Linguistics, 80). Leiden: Brill.

Al-Jallad A. (forthcoming). What is Ancient North Arabian? In N. Pat-El & D. Birnstiel (eds), *Re-engaging comparative Semitic and Arabic studies*. Wiesbaden: Harrassowitz.

Al-Jallad A. (in preparation). The Thamudic C (*wdd f*) inscriptions. Paper presented during the 44th NACAL conference in Austin Texas in February 2016.

Al-Jallad A. & Al-Manaser A. 2015. A Thamudic B abecedary in the South Semitic letter order. Pages 1–15 in A.M. Butts (ed.), *Semitic languages in contact*. (Studies in Semitic Languages and Linguistics, 82). Leiden: Brill.

Jamme A. 1965. *Research on Sabaean rock inscriptions from southwestern Saudi Arabia*. Washington, D.C. [Privately printed].

Jamme A. 1966. *Sabaean and Ḥasaean inscriptions from Saudi Arabia*. (Studi Semitici, 23). Rome: Università di Roma, Istituto di Studi del Vicino Oriente.

Jamme A. 1971. Les graffites sabéens de l'Arabie saoudite méridionale. Pages 110–121 in F. Altheim & R. Stiehl, *Christentum am Roten Meer*. i. Berlin: De Gruyter.

Kabāwī ᶜA.B., Khān M.K.Ḥ.K., Al-Zahrānī ᶜA.ᶜA., Al-Mubārak ᶜA.Y., Al-Samīr M.Ḥ. & Al-Shawāṭī M.ᶜA.

1999. Al-Mawsim al-sādis/ḥaṣr wa-tasjīl al-rusūm wa-ʾl-nuqūsh al-ṣakhriya 1411h/1999m 'Wādī ʾl-Dawāsir — Najrān'. *Atlal* 14: 45–61, 55–72 (English section), pls 24–32.

Kawatoko M., Tokunaga R. & Iizuka M. 2005. *Ancient and Islamic rock inscriptions of southwest Saudi Arabia*. i. *Wādī Khushayba*. Tokyo: The Middle Eastern Culture Center in Japan and Research Institute for Languages and Cultures of Asia and Africa, Tokyo University of Foreign Studies.

King G.M.H. 1990. Early North Arabian Ḥismaic. A preliminary description based on a new corpus of inscriptions from the Ḥismā desert of southern Jordan and published material. PhD thesis, School of Oriental and African Studies, London. Available at http://krc2.orient.ox.ac.uk/ociana/index.php/hismaic

Kootstra F. 2016. The language of the Taymanitic inscriptions and its classification. *Arabian Epigraphic Notes* 2: 67–140.

Lane E.W. 1863–1893. *An English-Arabic lexicon. Derived from the best and most copious Eastern sources*. London: Williams & Norgate.

Lippens P. 1956. *Expédition en Arabie centrale.* Paris: Adrien-Maisonneuve.

Macdonald M.C.A. 2000. Reflections on the linguistic map of pre-Islamic Arabia. *Arabian Archaeology and Epigraphy* 11: 28–79. [Reprinted with addenda and corrigenda as article III in Macdonald 2009].

Macdonald M.C.A. 2008. Ancient North Arabian. Pages: 179–224 in R.D. Woodard (ed.), *The ancient languages of Syria-Palestine and Arabia*. Cambridge: Cambridge University Press.

Macdonald M.C.A. 2009. *Literacy and identity in pre-Islamic Arabia*. (Variorum Collected Studies, CS906). Farnham: Ashgate.

Macdonald M.C.A. 2015. On the uses of writing in ancient Arabia and the role of palaeography in studying them. *Arabian Epigraphic Notes* 1: 1–50.

Macdonald M.C.A. (this volume). Towards a re-assessment of the Ancient North Arabian alphabets used in the oasis of al-ʿUlā. Pages 1–19 in M.C.A. Macdonald (ed.), *Languages, scripts and their uses in ancient North Arabia*. (Supplement to volume 48 of the Proceedings of the Seminar for Arabian Studies). Oxford: Archaeopress, 2018.

Macdonald M.C.A. & King G.M.H. 2000. Thamudic. Pages 436–438 in *Encyclopaedia of Islam* (New Edition). x. Leiden: Brill.

Nehmé L. (forthcoming). The pantheon of Northwest Arabia as reflected in the Nabataean, Nabataeo-Arabic, and pre-Islamic Arabic inscriptions. Paper presented at the conference 'Scripts and Scripture: Writing and Religion in Arabia, 500–700 C.E.' held at the University of Chicago on the 18th–20th of May 2017. To be published in Donner (forthcoming).

Norris J. (this volume). A survey of the Ancient North Arabian inscriptions from the Dūmat al-Jandal area (Saudi Arabia). Pages 71–93 in M.C.A. Macdonald (ed.), *Languages, scripts and their uses in ancient North Arabia*. (Supplement to volume 48 of the Proceedings of the Seminar for Arabian Studies). Oxford: Archaeopress, 2018.

Philby H.St.J.B. 1952. *Arabian highlands*. Ithaca, NY: Cornell University Press.

Prioletta A. 2018. Ancient South Arabian graffiti from Shabathān (Governorate of al-Bayḍāʾ, Yemen). Pages 116–153 in L. Nehmé & A. Al-Jallad (eds), *To the Madbar and back again. Studies in the languages, archaeology, and cultures of Arabia dedicated to Michael C.A. Macdonald*. (Studies in Semitic Languages and Linguistics, 92). Leiden: Brill.

Al-Qaḥṭanī S.H. 2007. *Nuqūsh jibāl al-Quna fī muḥāfaẓat Tathlīth. Dirasāt taḥlīliyya muqārina*. Riyadh: Al-mamlakah al-ʿarabiyah al-saʿūdiyah, wizārat al-tarbiya wa-ʾl-taʿlīm, wikālat al-athār wa-ʾl-matāḥif.

Robin C.J. (forthcoming). Langues, écritures, tribus et religions à Najrān à la veille de l'islam. Paper presented at the conference 'Scripts and Scripture: Writing and Religion in Arabia, 500–700 C.E.' held at the University of Chicago on the 18th–20th of May 2017. To be published in Donner (forthcoming).

Robin C.J. & Gorea M. 2016. L'alphabet de Ḥimà (Arabie séoudite). Pages 310–375 in I. Finkelstein, C.J. Robin & T. Römer (eds), *Alphabets, texts and artifacts in the ancient Near East. Studies presented to Benjamin Sass*. Paris: Van Dieren.

Robin C.J., Al-Ghabbān A.I. & Al-Saʿīd S.F. 2014. Inscriptions antiques récemment découvertes à Najran (Arabie séoudite méridionale): Nouveaux jalons pour l'histoire de l'oasis et celle de l'écriture et de la langue arabes. *Comptes rendus de l'Académie des Inscriptions et Belles-Lettres*: 1033–1127.

Robin C.J., Al-Saʿīd S.F., Arbach M., Charloux G., Dridi H. & Schiettecatte J. (in preparation). Une halte dans le désert. Les gravures rupestres de ʿĀn Jamal près de Ḥimà (région de Najrān, Arabie saoudite méridionale). (Mission archéologique franco-saʿūdienne de Najrān. Inventaire des gravures rupestres de Ḥimà, Arabie saʿūdite, 1).

Ryckmans G. 1957. Graffites sabéens relevés en Arabie saᶜudite. *Rivista degli Studi orientali* 32 (Scritti in onore di Giuseppe Furlani): 557–563.

Ryckmans J. 1956. Aspects nouveaux du problème thamoudéen. *Studia Islamica* 5: 5–17.

Ryckmans J. 1960. Review of van den Branden A. *Les textes thamoudéens de Philby*, i. *Inscriptions du Sud*; ii. *Inscriptions du Nord*. (Bibliothèque du Muséon, 39 et 41), Louvain, 1956. *Bibliotheca Orientalis* 17: 199–204.

Ryckmans J. 1969. Review of A. Jamme, *Sabaean and Ḥasaean inscriptions from Saudi Arabia*, Rome, 1966. *Bibliotheca Orientalis* 26: 246–249.

Al-Saᶜīd S.F. (in preparation). A new Ancient South Arabian abecedary from Qaryat al-Fāw.

Stein P. 2003. *Untersuchungen zur Phonologie und Morphologie des Sabäischen* (Epigraphische Forschungen auf der Arabischen Halbinsel, 3). Rahden Westfalen: Leidorf.

Stein P. 2007. Materialien zur sabäischen Dialektologie: Das Problem des amiritischen ('haramischen') Dialektes. *Zeitschrift der Deutschen Morgenländischen Gesellschaft* 157: 13–47.

Stein P. 2013. *Lehrbuch der sabäischen Sprache. 1. Teil: Grammatik*. (Subsidia et Instrumenta Linguarum Orientis (SILO), 4/1). Wiesbaden: Harrassowitz.

Stokes P.W. 2016. A new and unique Thamudic inscription from northeast Jordan. *Arabian Epigraphic Notes* 2: 33–44.

Al-Theeb [Al-Dhiyīb] S.A. 1421a/2000. *Dirāsah li-nuqūsh thamūdiyyah min Jubbah bi-Ḥāʾil*. Riyadh: maktabat al-malik Fahd al-waṭaniyyah.

Al-Theeb [Al-Dhiyīb] S.A. 1421b/2000. *Nuqūsh qārā ʾl-thamūdiyyah bi-minṭaqat al-Jawf bi-ʾl-mamlakah al-ᶜarabiyyah al-saᶜūdiyyah*. Riyadh: Muʾassasat ᶜAbd al-Raḥmān al-Sudayrī al-khayriyyah.

Al-Theeb [Al-Dhiyīb] S.A. 1422/2002. *Nuqūsh thamūdiyyah min Sakākā (Qāᶜ Furaykhah, wa-ʾl-Ṭuwayr, wa-ʾl-Qudayr) al-mamlakah al-ᶜarabiyyah al-saᶜūdiyyah*. Riyadh: maktabat al-malik Fahd al-waṭaniyyah.

Tsafrir N. 1996. New Thamudic inscriptions from the Negev. *Le Muséon* 109: 79–93.

van den Branden A. 1956. *Les textes thamoudéens de Philby*. i. *Inscriptions du Sud*. (Bibliothèque du Muséon, 39). Louvain: Institut Orientaliste.

Authors' addresses

Alessia Prioletta, CNRS – UMR 8167 Orient & Méditerranée, 27 rue Paul Bert, 94204 Ivry-sur-Seine cedex, France.
e-mail alessia.prioletta@cnrs.fr

Christian Robin, CNRS – UMR 8167 Orient & Méditerranée, 27 rue Paul Bert, 94204 Ivry-sur-Seine cedex, France.
e-mail christian.robin@cnrs.fr

M.C.A. Macdonald (ed.), *Languages, scripts and their uses in ancient North Arabia.* (Supplement to volume 48 of the Proceedings of the Seminar for Arabian Studies). Oxford: Archaeopress, 2018: 71–93

A survey of the Ancient North Arabian inscriptions from the Dūmat al-Jandal area (Saudi Arabia)

Jérôme Norris

Summary

This study aims to present an overview of the Ancient North Arabian (ANA) material from the Dūmat al-Jandal area (modern al-Jawf, north-west Saudi Arabia), taking into account the texts published since the late nineteenth century and those collected during the 2010–2017 seasons of the joint Saudi-Italian-French project at Dūmat al-Jandal (DaJAP). At present, the total number of known inscriptions in that region has reached 812, of which 379 are so far unpublished. Among the latter, there is a small set of texts sharing some characteristics with the three 'Dumaitic' inscriptions discovered by Winnett in 1962, which could perhaps support the theory that the inhabitants of Dūmah had indeed developed their own North Arabian script, as did the communities of Taymāʾ and Dadan. A special focus is given to the so-called 'Mixed Safaitic-Hismaic' (MSH) inscriptions, which are by far the largest group of ANA texts found around Dūmah, representing approximately 57% of the total corpus. The genres of these mixed texts, their linguistic features, and the connections of their authors with the Nabataeans are the various points raised in the discussion. Some alternative interpretations of previously known inscriptions are suggested in the paper alongside the presentation of new documents, among which is a partial bilingual Nabataean/MSH text dated to AD 125.

Keywords: Dūmat al-Jandal, Ancient North Arabian, Thamudic, Safaitic, North-West Arabia

Introduction

Located about 50 km south-west of Sakākā, Dūmat al-Jandal, the *Adummatu* of the Akkadian sources, is one of the largest oases in north-west Arabia. It lies in a vast depression (Arabic *jawf*) at the southern end of the long Wādī Sirhān corridor, which is delimited by the steppe-like limestone plateau of the *ḥamād* in the north and by the great sand-desert of the Nafūd in the south (Figs 1 and 2). The site has some good water resources and enjoys a strategic geographical position, standing at the intersection of several caravan routes connecting the Arabian Peninsula to Mesopotamia and the Levant. This largely explains why it played a major role throughout the pre-Islamic period, having been an important centre for the Qedarite Arabs after which it was occupied by the Nabataeans, the Romans, and then by one or more rulers from the tribe of Kinda on the eve of Islam.[1] Since 2010, a joint Saudi-Italian-French project directed by Guillaume Charloux (CNRS, UMR 8167, Orient & Méditerranée) and Romolo Loreto (Università degli Studi di Napoli 'L'Orientale') has been involved in excavating the historical settlement of Dūmah and surveying a large number of archaeological and epigraphic sites in the whole Sakākā basin. The latter operations have resulted in the recording of hundreds of rock inscriptions, which include some Ancient North Arabian (ANA), Nabataean, Nabataeo-Arabic, pre-Islamic Arabic, and Kufic texts.[2]

Taking the opportunity of a Special Session on 'Languages, scripts and their uses in ancient North Arabia', this study aims to set out the present state of knowledge on the ANA material from the Dūmah area, by taking into account the texts already published and the new ones discovered during recent surveys. In addition to making new material available to the scholarly community, the present contribution is motivated by two more general issues. First, the 'Dumaitic' question: since the 1960s, the idea has emerged that the inhabitants of Dūmah developed their own North Arabian script, as did the inhabitants of

[1] For a historical overview, see Al-Sudairi 1995; Charloux & Loreto 2011: 908–912; 2014: 25–51.

[2] Editorial conventions and abbreviations: { } enclose letters and words of which the reading is doubtful; {/} indicates alternative interpretations or readings of the same letter; [ ] enclose letters or words which are restored; < > enclose additional letters inscribed in error; ---- represents a passage in which one or more letters are completely destroyed; / indicates a word-divider; * marks reconstructed forms; */ / enclose proposed vocalizations; DN: divine name; N: name; PN: personal name; ANA: Ancient North Arabian; ASA: Ancient South Arabian; MSH: Mixed Safaitic-Hismaic; ONA: Oasis North Arabian; DaJAP: Dūmat al-Jandal archaeological project.

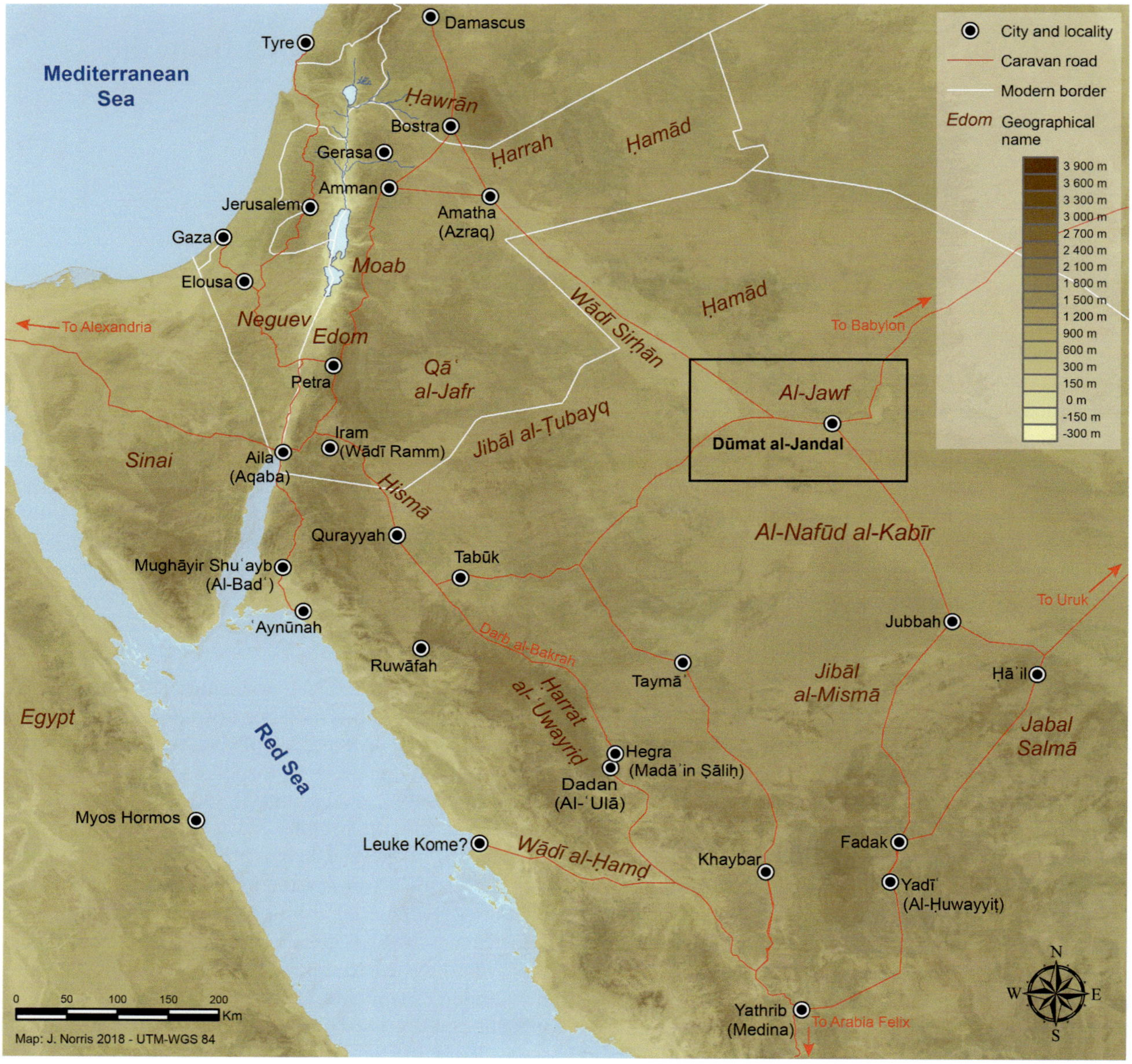

Figure 1. *A map of north-west Arabia and the southern Levant with the location of the Dūmat al-Jandal area and the main caravan routes (©J. Norris).*

the two other regional oases, Taymāʾ and Dadan (modern al-ʿUlā). The evidence on which this theory is based is, however, very fragmentary and so it seems appropriate to consider whether or not the latest discoveries can elucidate this question. Second, despite the publication of several ANA inscriptions from the Jawf area since the end of the nineteenth century, no attempt has been made so far to offer a general classification of these texts, most of which have been simply and indiscriminately labelled as 'Thamudic' by their editors. The question of the types of ANA scripts used in the Dūmah area has become of particular interest since Ahmad Al-Jallad has recently drawn attention to a Safaitic graffito from Wādī Salmā in north-eastern Jordan whose author identifies himself as

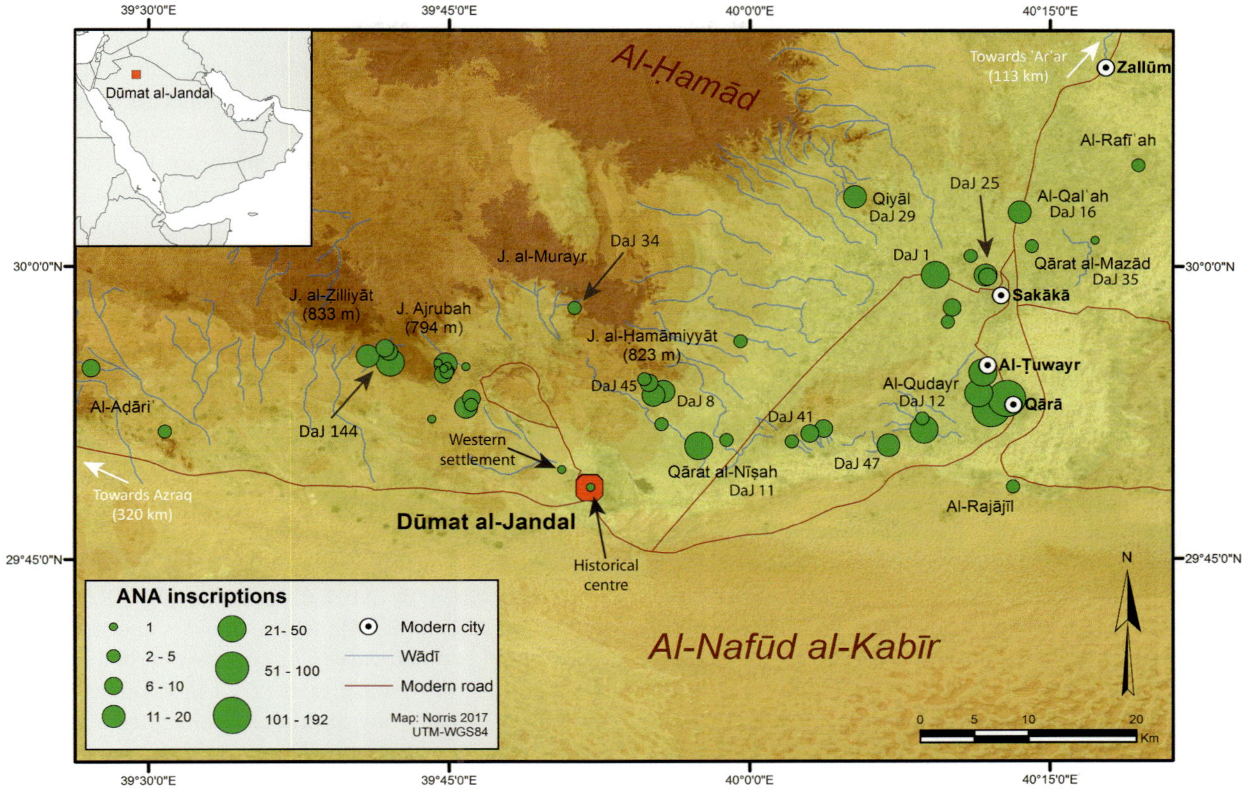

FIGURE 2. *A regional map of the area of Dūmat al-Jandal showing the distribution and numbers of Ancient North Arabian inscriptions (©DaJAP, J. Norris).*

'the Dumaean' while addressing a prayer to *Ṣlm* 'the god of Dūmat' (KRS 30).[3]

History of the discoveries

It was at Sakākā on January 11 1879 that the English travellers Lady Anne and Wilfrid S. Blunt made the first copy of an ancient inscription in the Dūmat al-Jandal area. They ingeniously interpreted two of its characters as the Greek letters Π and H (Blunt 1881, i: 148), but one can hypothesize that they were in fact dealing with an ANA graffito since its third letter, which they were not able to decipher, looks very like a South Semitic *y*.[4] Four years later, Charles Huber and Julius Euting crossed the area on their way to Ḥāʾil and copied seventeen ANA texts next to the *qaṣr* of al-Ṭuwayr (HU 1–17 = Eut 1–17) and two on a boulder at Qārā (HU 18–19 = Eut 18–19).[5] Unfortunately, the copies they produced were so inaccurate that it was virtually impossible to tell anything about these 'Thamudic' texts, despite van den Branden's desperate attempt to interpret them (1950: 44–50). It was not until eighty years later that new inscriptions came to light with the first major epigraphic survey of the area in May 1962 by Winnett and Reed, who collected fifty-seven ANA graffiti at four different sites around Dūmah. Published in *Ancient Records from North Arabia* (Winnett & Reed 1970), eleven of these were discovered at Qalʿah

[3] KRS 30: *l ʾbn bn ʿnhlh h-dmy w ḫrṣ f h ṣlm ʾlh dmt rwḥ* 'By ʾbn son of ʿnhlh the Dumaean and he kept watch so, O Ṣlm, god of Dūmat, let there be ease' (Al-Jallad 2015a: 20). So far, the only known document attesting to the worship of *Ṣlm* at Dūmah was a Latin inscription from the oasis dated from the third century AD that is dedicated to the emperors, Jupiter Hammon, and *Sancto Sulmo*, 'Saint Sulmus', by a centurion of *Legio III Cyrenaica* (Bauzou 1996: 24).

[4] If so, the text would probably consist of the letters *y*, *{ḏ/z}*, and *b*.

[5] See Huber 1891: 44–47. As noted by van den Branden (1950: 51), HU 20 = Eut 20, which is also from Qārā, is certainly not a text but a group of *wusūm*.

(WTI 1–11), twelve on a hill near the Saysarā well at akākā (WTI 12–23), thirty-three on a rock formation located 5 km west of Sakākā (WTI 25–56), and one on the megalithic site of al-Rajājīl (WTI 24).

In the frame of the Comprehensive Archaeological Survey Program, the Saudi Arabian Department of Antiquities carried out two surveys in the Dūmah region in 1976 (Adams et al. 1977: 33, 38–39) and 1977 (Parr et al. 1978: 33–34, 48) during which several inscriptions are said to have been discovered. Alongside this programme, a specialized survey on epigraphy started in 1984, the Comprehensive Rock Art and Epigraphic Survey. The Jawf region was explored in 1985, leading to the recording of '967 Thamudic inscriptions' (Khan, Al-Kabawi & Al-Zahrani 1986: 93). As far as I know, this material has remained unstudied and only one photograph of an inscribed panel from al-Qudayr was published in the report, although without a reading or comment on the texts (1986: pl. 91, A). During the same period, V.A. Clark published two Safaitic texts from a private collection that are said to have come from Sakākā (CSA 1.1–2) but unfortunately, he gave no information about the exact place and year of their discovery (Clark 1984–1985: 14).

From 1986 onwards, two Saudi scholars, Kh. Al-Muaikel and S. Al-Theeb, started some intensive surveys throughout the area which were to result in the collection of a large number of ANA graffiti, virtually all new (see Al-Muaikel 1994: xxi; Al-Theeb 1994: 33). The study of this material was undertaken by Al-Theeb who published it in three successive books: *Nuqūsh Qārā al-thamūdiyyah* (ThNQT) in which he deals with 192 texts from Qārā (2000a);[6] *Nuqūsh thamūdiyyah min Sakākā* (ThNTS) which is an edition of 117 texts from three sites located south-west of Sakākā (2002a);[7] and *Nuqūsh thamūdiyyah jadīdah min al-Jawf* (ThNTJ) in which he studied fifty-three texts from eight sites scattered around Sakākā (2003).[8] Finally, the recent surveys conducted by the DaJAP between 2010 and 2017 in a zone of about 80 x 40 km around the Dūmah oasis[9] have resulted in the recording of 456 texts, of which 379 are new.

[6] This collection includes the two graffiti from Qārā previously discovered by Huber and Euting (ThNQT 162, 164 = HU 18, 19 = Eut 18, 19).

[7] ThNTS 92–95 from al-Qudayr are the texts which appear on the photograph published in Khan, Al-Kabawi & Al-Zahrani 1986: pl. 91, A.

[8] Among these are four texts from al-Ṭuwayr already known from the copies of Huber and Euting (ThNTJ 14– 17 = HU 2a, 2b, 4, 7 = Eut 2a, 2b, 4, 7).

[9] See the report of the 2011 survey with a description of the sites DaJ 1 to DaJ 16 (Arbach et al. 2016: 79–92).

Number and classification

By adding the texts published since the end of the nineteenth century to the new ones collected since 2010, one obtains a total of 812 known ANA inscriptions (Fig. 2). This represents by far the most numerous type of ancient Semitic inscription in the Dūmah region, given that about 163 Nabataean texts, two Ancient South Arabian, and a single Imperial Aramaic inscription have been identified so far. In terms of scripts, we are dealing here with a remarkable epigraphic diversity, with the representation of eleven different ANA categories and the presence of thirty-three texts which cannot be assigned at present to a specific group (Fig. 3). Alongside the well-defined categories, the label 'Jubbaitic' is used here to refer to a single inscription written in a type of script otherwise exclusively attested in the Jubbah area, at the other extremity of the Nafūd desert.[10] Interestingly, the combination of the name and the patronym in this graffito recurs several times at Jubbah (Al-Saud, Khan & Al-Hadlaq 2005: pl. 7.8.d; Olsen & Bryant 2013: 62–63), which could suggest that the same individual had carved inscriptions on both sides of the Nafūd. A provisional label '*Dgn* inscriptions' is also employed to name the specimens belonging to a little-known category of 'Thamudic' inscriptions mostly found in the Ḥāʾil area, that consist almost entirely of prayers to the deity *Dgn/Dṯn*.[11]

Given this diversity, it is important to note that only two categories are represented in large numbers. These are the MSH inscriptions and the Thamudic C^1 texts.[12] The former are by far the most common type of ANA graffiti found around Dūmah with a total of 462 items, while there are approximately 176 of the latter, representing 57% and 22% respectively of the total corpus. The other scripts are

[10] DaJ163ANA4 = HU 4 = Eut 4 = ThNTJ 16: *l ʾẖyt bn ḏhbn* 'By ʾẖyt son of Ḏhbn. These inscriptions from Jubbah show an interesting combination of Thamudic B and Thamudic C^2 features, in terms of script, direction of writing, and content. They consist mainly of prayers to *Rḍw*, *wd(d) f*-formulae and artists' signatures. To date, the published texts belonging to this group are spread across the copies of Huber and Euting (HU 21–81; Eut 21–98) and a collection edited by Al-Theeb (2000b). Note that many new inscriptions have recently come to light in the surveys conducted by rock art specialists on Jabal Umm Salmān.

[11] Ahmad Al-Jallad has recently drawn attention to these texts and suggested the rereading of the divine name as *Dgn* instead of *Dṯn* in a conference presentation 'The Thamudic C (*wdd f*) inscriptions' at Austin, Texas, on 14 February 2016. These '*Dgn* inscriptions' were previously thought to be either Thamudic B or Thamudic C, but it now seems clear that they should be treated as a specific group since they present a number of singular characteristics in terms of their script, language, and content.

[12] On the need to distinguish two different groups among the Thamudic C inscriptions, the C^1 and the C^2, see King 1990: 36, n. 105; Macdonald & King 1999: 469.

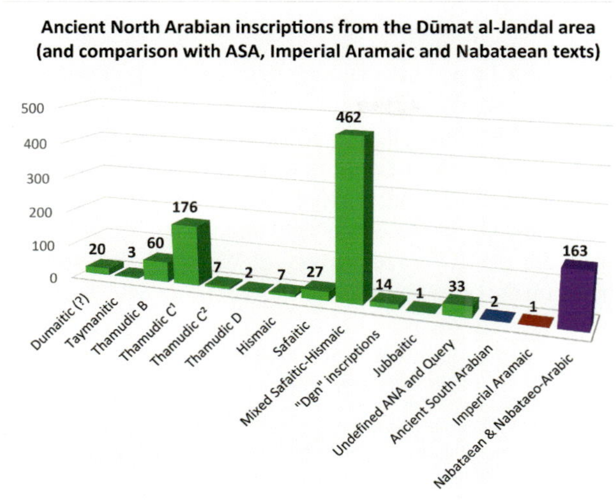

Figure 3. *A diagram showing the number of inscriptions from the Dūmat al-Jandal area in each ANA script (©DaJAP, J. Norris).*

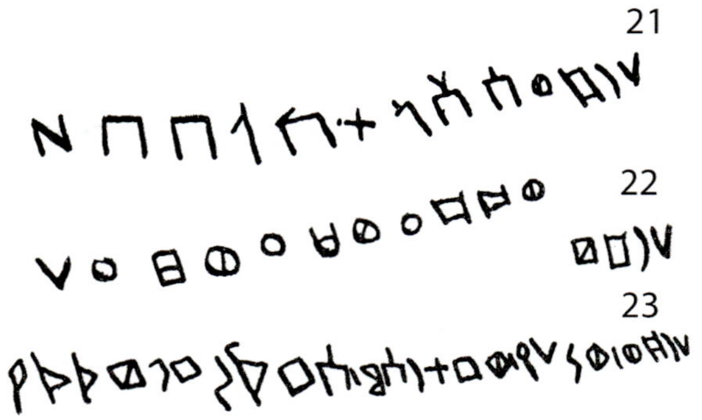

Figure 4. *The Dumaitic inscriptions WTI 21–23 (Winnett & Reed 1970: 207, pl. 3).*

represented as follows: Thamudic B (60), Safaitic (27),[13] the supposed 'Dumaitic' (20), the '*Dgn* inscriptions' (14), Hismaic (7), Thamudic C² (7), Taymanitic (3), and Thamudic D (2) along with the single 'Jubbaitic' graffito mentioned above. In general, these various inscriptions conform in terms of their content to some very basic structural formulae specific to the categories to which they belong. This is especially the case of the Thamudic C¹ and C² graffiti, which are virtually all *wdd f*-compositions, or the Thamudic B graffiti that are essentially invocations to *Rḍw*. Only two of these categories of texts will be discussed below, as they appear to be the most informative from both a linguistic and a historical point of view. These are the Dumaitic and the MSH texts.

Dumaitic

About three texts from Sakākā

During his survey of the Dūmah area in 1962, Winnett discovered three religious graffiti written in a script never encountered before which is close to, but distinct from, Dadanitic and Taymanitic (Fig. 4). He identified it as a local alphabet used in ancient Dūmah for which he invented the label 'Jawfian', assuming from its similarities with Taymanitic that it should date from the same period (1970: 69, 73, 80–81).

WTI 21

h rḍw s¹ʾlt klb bz

'O Rḍw, the petition of Klb is here'

WTI 22

h rḍw wdd ʿw{ṣ} ʿw{ḏ} ʿh

'O Rḍw, let there be love, ʿw{ṣ} ʿw{ḏ} ʿh (?)[14]

WTI 23

h rḍw / w nhy / w ʿtrs¹m / s¹ʿd-n ʿl-wdd-y

'O Rḍw / and Nhy / and ʿtrs¹m / help me in the matter of my love'

Winnett's view was further developed by Macdonald who suggested considering this script together with Taymanitic and Dadanitic as three related alphabets, the 'Oasis North Arabian' (ONA) scripts, which would have been developed and used by the settled communities of the three major oasis-towns of North Arabia, Dūmah, Taymāʾ, and Dadan, around the middle of the first millennium BC. In order to harmonize and improve the epigraphic nomenclature, in the meantime Macdonald proposed the new name of 'Dumaitic' to replace 'Jawfian' (Macdonald 2000: 29, 33, 65, n. 31; 2004: 490).

[13] Since there are relatively few 'pure' Safaitic inscriptions in the Dūmah area, we may deduce that the Dumaean who carved KRS 30 in Wādī Salmā did not carve his composition in his 'own' script, but instead used the local alphabet of the *ḥarrah* where he was staying, or perhaps that someone carved the text for him.

[14] None of the interpretations of this text so far suggested are satisfactory (see Winnett 1970: 80 and OCIANA), but I am at present unable to propose a viable alternative.

This hypothesis is supported by the identity of the deities invoked in the texts, *Rḍw*, *Nhy*, and *ʿtrs^{1}m*, who were three of the local gods worshipped in the oasis during the seventh century BC, as evidenced by the Assyrian annals that refer to them as *Ru-ul-da-a-au*, *Nu-ẖa-a-a*, and *A-tar-sa-ma-a-a-in* (see Winnett 1970: 76, 80–81; Knauf 1985: 81–88). Besides the resemblance of their letter-forms to those of Dadanitic and Taymanitic, one can also note the consistent direction of writing from right to left of the three texts and the use of word-dividers in WTI 23. This may indeed suggest that Dumaitic had a formal register and that it is not just yet another example of a Desert North Arabian script. Although likely, one has to admit the highly speculative aspect of this theory, being so far based on the identification of only three brief texts which are, moreover, not 'monumental' inscriptions, but graffiti.

New finds

From the large collection of inscriptions published by Al-Theeb, only one could be related to the three texts published by Winnett. It is so short, however, that it is in fact impossible to assign it to a specific category with any certainty (ThNTS 42: *b-nms^1* 'By Nms^1' [?]) (Fig. 5/a). Unfortunately, the recent surveys undertaken by the DaJAP have not led to the rediscovery of Winnett's texts.[15] They have, on the other hand, led to the recording of sixteen new

[15] According to the notes in Winnett & Reed 1970: 11, the texts WTI 21–23 were discovered on the ridge which stands to the west of the Saysarā well at Sakākā. This zone, which is nowadays located in the immediate proximity of a residential area and a modern road, was given the site number of DaJ 25 and surveyed several times by the DaJAP team. Only six ANA graffiti were recorded there and all are new. Nevertheless, epigraphic surveys are very difficult to carry out comprehensively in the Jawf area and we can therefore still hope that these texts will be found in the near future.

Figure 5. a. *ThNTS 42 (Al-Theeb 2002a: 160);* **b.** *DaJ0ANA1 (©DaJAP, P. Siméon);* **c.** *DaJ144ANA27;* **d.** *DaJ144ANA5 (©DaJAP, C. Poliakoff).*

Figure 6. a. *DaJ45ANA6;* **b.** *DaJ41ANA5;* **c.** *DaJ41ANA4 (©DaJAP, G. Charloux).*

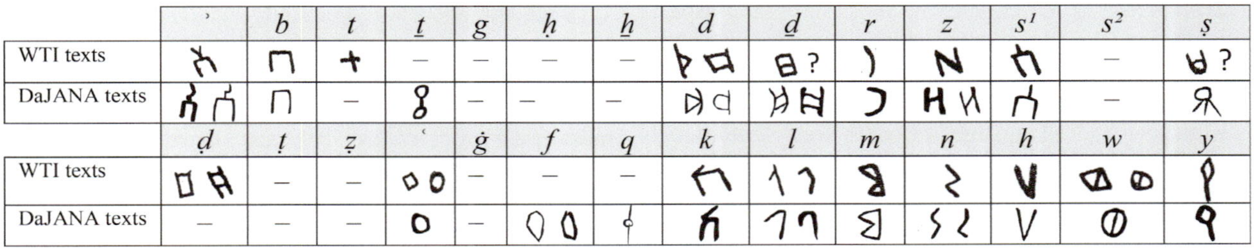

Figure 7. *A script table of the 'Dumaitic' inscriptions comparing the letter-forms of Winnett's texts with those of the new finds; the dashes indicate the non-attested letters.*

inscriptions which may well be 'Dumaitic'. Clearly written in a form of ONA, they make use of word-dividers and exhibit the same V-form of the *h* as in WTI 21, 22, and 23 (DaJ26ANA1, DaJ41ANA4, DaJ144ANA27) (Figs 5/b–d & 6/a–c). Two texts contain a *z* (DaJ144ANA4, 5), which has a shape comparable to the one in WTI 21, being formed by two parallel vertical bars that are joined by a diagonal line. Nevertheless, they differ from Winnett's texts in the representation of ʾ, *ḏ*, and *ṣ* (Fig. 7).[16] The first two letters are formed as their equivalents in the ASA formal script whereas the sign for /ṣ/ appears identical to the Dadanitic one.[17] Despite this, it is certainly not necessary to distinguish this new material from Winnett's texts, given that a single script can show considerable variations in the representation of a particular letter, as exemplified by the Dadanitic inscriptions from al-ʿUlā (Farès-Drappeau 2005: 100-111; Macdonald, this volume).

Two of these new texts are very interesting because of their provenance, having been discovered inside the oasis during the excavation of the western settlement and the historical centre at the foot of Mārid Castle (DaJ0ANA1 and Loreto 2018). Deeply and regularly carved, their engraving technique may suggest that they could have been public inscriptions, but they are unfortunately very badly preserved.[18] All the other finds are graffiti carved on various rock formations outside the settlement area. Leaving aside four texts too damaged to be satisfactorily interpreted (DaJ11ANA2, 3, 5; DaJ144ANA3), they

[16] It should be emphasized, however, that the Dumaitic glyphs for *ḏ* and *ṣ* that appear on the script-tables in Winnett & Reed 1970: 205 and in Macdonald 2000: 34; 2004: 496 are only based on WTI 22, the reading of which is completely uncertain.

[17] For ʾ, see DaJ41ANA3 and DaJ144ANA4, 5; for *ḏ*, DaJ26ANA1, DaJ41ANA4, and DaJ144ANA5; for *ṣ*, DaJ41ANA3 and DaJ45ANA6.

[18] On the archaeological context of DaJ0ANA1 (Fig. 5/b), which is carved on a block found in a reused position in wall M2023 of structure L 2018, see Charloux et al. 2016a: 211–212. The block is very badly preserved and only two glyphs of the text have survived …*b {ṭ/ḍ/w}*…, identified as some ANA letters by Christian Robin (see Charloux et al. 2016a: 211, n. 18).

can be divided into two groups: simple authorship texts ('signatures') and invocations.

Signatures

From the first group, one graffito from Jabal al-Ẓilliyāt (19 km north-west of Dūmah) reads *l ṯwb h-kbr* 'By Ṯwb the kabīr' (DaJ144ANA27) (Fig. 5/c, inscription on the left).[19] From a historical point of view, this short text appears to be of great interest since it provides a first insight into the socio-political organization of the local population, revealing the existence of a kabirate institution inside their society. Nevertheless, it is impossible to tell whether this title was that of a chieftain, a provincial governor, or an administrative head of any other kind.[20] A second text from the same site (Fig. 5/d) is particularly intriguing, reading *w{q}{ḏ}n / bn yʿzbʾ{l} / dmy*^{n} 'W{q}{ḏ}n / son of Yʿzbʾ{l} / the Dumaean' (?) (DaJ144ANA5).[21] Of course, the most surprising aspect is the form of the adjective by which the author identifies himself, which seems to be the *nisbah* (gentilic adjective) of Dūmah whose determination is marked with *nūnation* as in the Sayhadic languages of south-west Arabia, and not with a prefixed article as would be expected in the north.[22] Another possibility would be to take this word as a CVCCān adjective of the root √dmy 'to draw, produce an image', but this interpretation appears unlikely for two reasons. First, because the text is not associated with a rock drawing, which would normally have been the case since the root √dmy refers specifically to the production of an image, not to the action of carving in general. Second, because the adjective would appear without any definite marking. An attempt may then be made to solve this problem by taking the twelfth letter as a reversed *h*. The word division of the text, however, rules out a reading as *h- / dmyn* since the article would be separated from its attached noun by a word-divider.[23] Although surprising, 'the Dumaean' seems therefore to be the most appropriate translation. If this is correct, it should be noted that the *-n* suffix would not be the usual mark of definiteness in Dumaitic given that the previous text clearly uses a *h*-definite article, which is also the case with another inscription reading *ṣdq h-yfʿ* 'Ṣdq the young man' (DaJ45ANA6) (Fig. 6/a).[24]

Since the author was apparently a native, as he indicates himself, we can only speculate why he used an ASA *nisbah* form. One could propose that he did so for reasons of prestige, but this is purely a suggestion.[25] Whatever the answer, this must result from contact between Dūmah and southern Arabia. Although poorly documented, the existence of such relationships is obvious when one takes into account the position of the oasis on the trade route towards Mesopotamia and the famous report of the governor of Sūḫu that refers to a Sabaean and Taymanite caravan crossing the middle Euphrates region in the mid-eighth century BC (Cavigneaux & Ismail 1990: 351). While this document suggests, together with the inscriptions of Tiglath-Pileser III and Job 6: 19 (see Robin 1996: 1117; Macdonald 1997: 337), that the Sabaeans and the Taymanites were trading together inside a sort of commercial union during the first half of the first millennium

[19] I have interpreted what stands before *l ṯwb* as a separate text (DaJ144ANA26), which could be an invocation to *Dgn*. Of course, a reading *l ṯwb hkbr* 'By Ṯwb (son of) Hkbr' (?) remains possible, although the absence of *bn* and the rarity of the name *Hkbr*, for which there is only one doubtful example in Safaitic (SIJ 356), makes this interpretation less likely.

[20] Besides the Minaeans of al-ʿUlā whose leader is known as the *kbr mʿn b-ddn* 'kabīr of Maʿīn in Dadan' (Ja 2288), JSLih 72 (= D 53) may indicate that the title of *kbr* was also borne by some Dadanite chiefs (see Farès-Drappeau 2005: 100). This was until now the only known example of a kabirate institution among a North Arabian community.

[21] Although most of the inscription is clear, there are two difficulties in reading it. The first relates to the author's name, the second and third letters of which are unclear. These could be a crude *q* and a *ḏ*, although the vertical line of the *q* would be slightly wavy, which is unusual. An alternative interpretation is to read a *s*^{2}, but this does not really help since the following glyph would then be completely illegible. If correctly read, *W{q}{ḏ}n* has not been found before, although √wqḏ, is an attested root in Arabic. The second problem concerns the last letter of the patronym, which I have taken as a *l* bonded to a word-divider. At first sight, one may be tempted to read a *z* with a shape comparable to the one in WTI 21, but the letter would be very different from the *z* which stands earlier in the text, between ʿ and *b*. Moreover, the name produced by such a reading would be difficult to explain whereas *Yʿzbʾl*, although not previously attested, is a perfectly possible theophoric name, 'may ʾ*l* make [him] go away' (cf. Classical Arabic *aʿzaba-hu allāh*; Lane, 2033b).

[22] The ASA *nisbah* form *dmy*^{n} would indeed be the exact equivalent of the Safaitic *h-dmy* (KRS 30) and the Classical Arabic *al-dūmī* (Ibn al-Athīr [n.d.], i: 515: *al-dūmī [...] hadhihi al-nisbah ilā dūmat al-jandal*).

[23] Compare the position of the definite article in relation to the word-dividers in the following Taymanitic and Dadanitic inscriptions: Esk A 31: *ʾs*^{1} *b dmg / l ʾṣr / h-ḍbʾ / {h-}{r}{ʿ}{y}* 'ʾs^1 son of Dmg / for ʾṣr / the soldier / {the chief', (Kootstra 2016: 88); WTay 3: *znk rfty / h-rkb* 'this is Rfty / the riding camel' (Kootstra 2016: 97); JSLih 54: *h-mqdr / w hn-ʿnk* 'the dimension / and the base'; JSLih 63: *ʾdq / {l}-ḏġ{b}t / hn-ʾṣl[m]* 'he offered / {for} {Ḏġbt} / the {statues}' JSLih 64: *l bhny / hn-ʾfklt* 'By Bhny / the priestess'; etc.

[24] Cf. Classical Arabic *yafaʿ* and *yāfiʿ* 'a boy grown-up' (Lane, 3063c).

[25] Another possibility could be to identify the carver as a South Arabian installed in Dūmah who would have carved his inscription in his own language but with the local alphabet, a situation attested at Dadan (see Kootstra, this volume). The example of the Minaeans of Dadan, however, makes this hypothesis debatable since it appears that these South Arabians living in a foreign milieu usually identify themselves according to their tribal groups and not according to their place of residence. See, for instance, M 354: *ʾws*^{1}*ʾl bn ʾlwhb ḏ-yfʿn ḏ-mwt b-ddn* 'ʾws^{1}ʾl son of ʾlwhb of the [group] of Yfʿn, who died in Ddn', and M 360 in which the adjectives *ddny* and *[m]ʿnyt* are precisely used to differentiate a local man from a Minaean woman.

BC, it must be recognized that Dūmah could also have been a trading post of the Sabaeans since it represents an inevitable point of passage between Taymāʾ and Babylonia, see Figure 1.[26]

b-s^{1}mh inscriptions

Five other texts recorded during the surveys seem to be religious invocations, the interpretation of which is delicate since they appear very different from the Dumaitic prayers published by Winnett. Three of them are composed with the same formula, *b*-N^1 + N^2 + *w ḏ wd(d)* (DaJ26ANA1; DaJ41ANA4, 5) (Fig. 6/b–c). From an examination of the ANA corpora, one can note that a very similar formula occurs several times in the *Dgn* religious texts (e.g. Esk A 176: *b-dgn ntn w z wdd*; HU 337: *b-dgn ns^1{b/q} w z wd*),[27] which supports the identification of our texts as invocations of some kind. The first thing that stands out is that the texts to *Dgn* have *z* before *wd(d)* while those of Dūmah have *ḏ*. It seems clear that these elements are equivalent and it can therefore be assumed that the interdental fricative /ḏ/ has certainly shifted to /z/ in the language of the inscriptions invoking *Dgn*. Certainly, the most natural interpretation of this element is to take it as the masculine singular form of the relative pronoun. If so, the preceding noun is more likely to represent a personal name than a substantive, which seems likely as this element differs from one text to another both in the *Dgn* inscriptions and in the 'Dumaitic' ones. A probable interpretation of the complete formula could therefore be 'May be with DN PN and the one whom he loved'.[28]

The divine name is difficult to read in one text (DaJ26ANA1), but it clearly occurs as *S^{1}mh* in the other two graffiti: */ b-s^{1}mh / mrd / w ḏ wd / ndb /* 'May be with S^{1}mh / Mrd / and the one whom he loved / Ndb /' (DaJ41ANA4);[29] */ b-s^{1}mh / --- / w ḏ wd /* 'May be with S^{1}mh / --- / and the one whom he loved' (DaJ41ANA5). An explanation of this theonym, which is so far unknown in the Arabian Peninsula, could be to infer that it is derived from an original *s^{1}my* 'sky', being presumably the name of a celestial deity such as *bʿls^{1}mn* (variant *bʿls^{1}my*), *ʿtrs^{1}m*, and *ḏ-s^{1}mwy* (variant *ḏ-s^{1}my*).[30] The invocation WTI 23 dedicated to *ʿtrs^{1}m* shows that the final */āy/ of the word *s^{1}my* has contracted to /ā/ in the Dumaitic language, thus */samā/. Consequently, it seems a possible assumption that *s^{1}mh* represents an orthographic variant of *s^{1}m* with the employment of *h* as a *mater lectionis* for the final /ā/, exactly as in Dadanitic (Farès-Drappeau 2005: 62). Compare also the Minaic spelling of the word 'sky', which occurs precisely as *s^{1}mh* (M 85, 197). No deities named *S^{1}my* or *S^{1}m* have so far been noted in any of the ANA inscriptions, but Laïla Nehmé has recently drawn attention to a god *Šmyʾ* invoked in two Nabataean inscriptions from Madāʾin Ṣāliḥ.[31] If the interpretation suggested above is correct, then these deities in Ḥegrā and Dūmah would probably be connected.

The 'Mixed Safaitic-Hismaic' inscriptions

Definition and script

In his study of the inscriptions from al-Jawf, Winnett classified many of these as 'Tabuki/Thamudic E' (1970:

[26] Relationships between Dūmah and the Minaeans, who succeeded the Sabaeans as conveyors of South Arabian goods towards the north in the second half of the first millennium BC, are more difficult to grasp. Having their trading colony at Dadan, not Taymāʾ, the Minaeans appear to have privileged the western road running towards Gaza via Tabūk (see Fig. 1). It should, moreover, be pointed out that the identification of one text from Dūmah as Minaic by Winnett (WMin 1) is very uncertain as it could well also be an ANA graffito (Dumaitic?). We can of course think back to the references of the Qedarite women in the *Hierodulenlisten* from Maʿīn (M 392 B–C), but it is not certain whether this tribe was still located around Dūmah in the Achaemenid period, knowing that these documents ignore both Dūmah and Taymāʾ as place names. Similarly, if the Minaic text Riyāḍ 302F8 clearly indicates that Minaean caravans were reaching Mesopotamia (*Nhr*) and Seleucia on the Tigris (*S^{1}lky*), the fact that this text comes from Qaryat al-Fāw suggests that this was certainly by using the route connecting South Arabia to Mesopotamia through the Najd and not through Dūmah.

[27] Interestingly, this formula also occurs in the *Dgn* inscriptions from Dūmah: ThNTJ 29 (= DaJ11ANA16): *b-dgn ḥyw w z wdd*; ThNTJ 31a (= DaJ11ANA14): *b-dgn ʿzr w z wdd*; ThNTJ 43 (= DaJ8ANA11): *b-dgn wkl w z wdd*.

[28] In support of this explanation, note the following variants in the *Dgn* inscriptions: *b-dgn ʿbs^1 w wdd-h rm{ʿ}* 'may be with Dgn ʿbs^1 and his beloved/friend, Rm{ʿ}' (HU 395b = Eut 588); *b-dgn lḥdʾ w wdd-h* 'may be with Dgn Lḥdʾ and his beloved/friend' (Esk B 209). On the interpretation of the 'Thamudic' invocations of the type *b-DN + PN* as 'may PN be with DN', see Norris 2017: 202.

[29] *Ndb* is certainly a personal name (cf. the Arab name *al-Nadab*, CIK, ii: 440, 1). Otherwise, it could represent an active participle 'wailing, weeping' describing *Mrd*'s state or even a passive participle 'desired' that would refer to the beloved person. The occurrence of the name *Mrd* in this text is of interest as it immediately brings to mind the name of the fortress dominating the oasis of Dūmat al-Jandal, the well-known Qaṣr Mārid. Nevertheless, this is undoubtedly pure coincidence with no historical implication, especially as it is unknown when the fort was built and if it already had this name before the thirteenth century; see Charloux 2012: 44–45.

[30] A completely different way of interpreting these texts would be to read *b-s^{1}m-h* 'in his name', although the comparison with the *Dgn* inscriptions leads us to take the element after *b-* as a proper noun.

[31] This was in a paper entitled 'Les panthéons de Pétra et de Hégra' delivered at the conference *Épigraphie et histoire de la Jordanie antique et médiévale* in Lyon, 15 June 2017. On this occasion, L. Nehmé presented a new Nabataean inscription dedicated to *Šmyʾ* and recalled that this deity was already known from *CIS* ii 236 as reread by Milik (1972: 409–410).

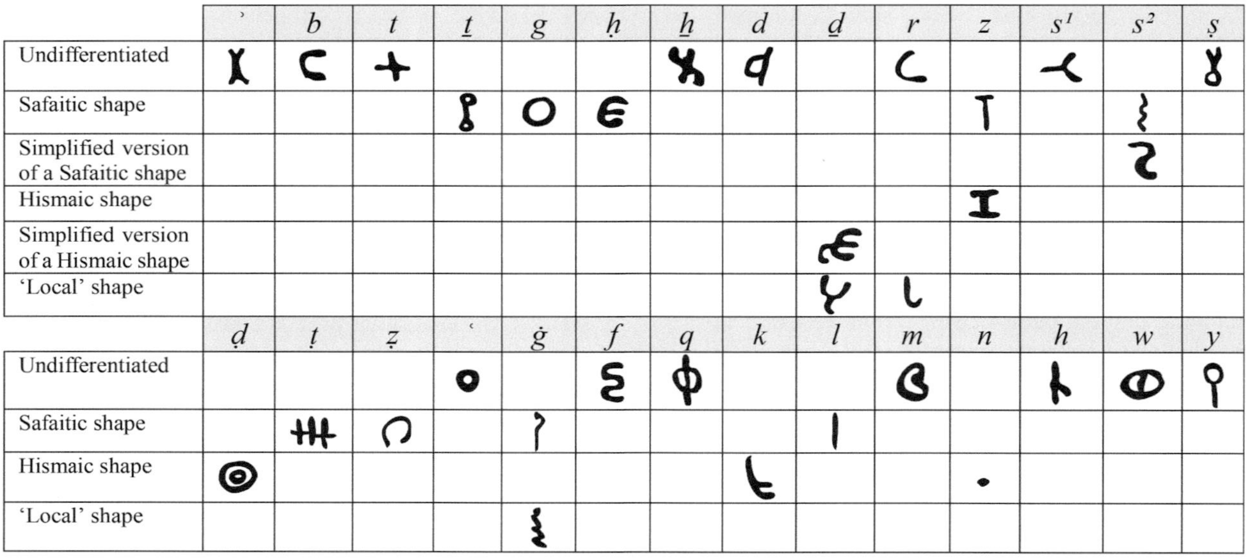

Figure 8. *Letter-forms of the Mixed Safaitic-Hismaic (MSH) inscriptions from the Dūmat al-Jandal area.*

73), the script nowadays labelled 'Hismaic'. G. King, however, has rightly demonstrated that only one text in Winnett's collection can really be identified as Hismaic (WTI 11),[32] whereas all the others are better defined as 'Mixed Safaitic-Hismaic' inscriptions since they combine letter shapes from both the scripts (King 1990: 34–35). Graffiti exhibiting a mixture of Hismaic and Safaitic features were identified long ago in the various areas where the Safaitic and the Hismaic scripts meet from Transjordan to Ḥāʾil in Saudi Arabia (see Harding 1972: 5; Macdonald 1980: 188; King 1990: 34–35; Al-Salameen 2011: 215; Al-Jallad 2015a: 28). From one place to another, however, the mixture of features in these inscriptions can differ considerably,[33] which makes it clear that there are actually several categories of inscriptions to which the labels of 'Mixed Safaitic-Hismaic' could be applied, the classification of which remains to be made. Regarding the texts found around Dūmah, their main characteristics can be defined as follows (Fig. 8):

- the occurrence of *ṯ*, *g*, *ḥ*, *ṭ*, *ẓ*, *ġ* and *l* with the Safaitic letter-forms;
- the occurrence of *ḍ*, *k*, and *n* with the Hismaic letter-forms;[34]
- a variation in the representation of *z* which occurs most often with the Safaitic shape (WTI 47; ThNQT 6; DaJ46ANA3, etc.) and sometimes with the Hismaic form (WTI 33; ThNQT 128; DaJ47ANA20);
- the occurrence of s^2 with a simplified version of the Safaitic form which is reduced to two undulations; there are, however, a few examples where the letter takes the 'common' Safaitic form (DaJ46ANA3);

[32] From the available corpus of 812 known texts, it now seems clear that Hismaic inscriptions are extremely rare in the Jawf area. From the texts recently collected by the Dūmat al-Jandal project, only six exhibit diagnostic letter shapes identifying them as Hismaic (i.e. *ṯ*, *g*, *ḥ*, s^2, *ṭ*, *ġ*, *l*), whereas none of those published by Al-Theeb do. This scarcity of Hismaic inscriptions may appear surprising in view of the relative proximity of Dūmah to Tabūk, the Jabal Ṭubayq, and the south-eastern Jordanian Bādiyah where many Hismaic graffiti are found.

[33] Note, for instance, the poetic text KRS 2453 from north-eastern Jordan studied by Al-Jallad (2015b) which exhibits the Hismaic forms of the *g*, *ẓ*, and *ṭ*, whereas these glyphs always have their Safaitic forms in the mixed texts from Saudi Arabia. See also the text published by Al-Salameen (2011) from al-Ḥusaynīyah (north of Maʿān, Jordan) which presents a singular situation with the use of the Safaitic shapes for most of the letters, except for *ḏ* and *ṯ* which are Hismaic.

[34] As noted by Della Puppa (in her paper at the Special Session), the letters *ḍ*, *k* and, at times, *n*, also take the 'Hismaic' shapes in the Safaitic square-script inscriptions. This could perhaps suggest a relationship between the MSH and the Safaitic square-script texts, as these two groups also exhibit some comparable letter-forms for *ḏ* and s^2. As pointed out to me by M.C.A. Macdonald, it remains true, however, that the *n* is not really diagnostic since it appears as a dot in numerous clearly Safaitic inscriptions from the Syro-Jordanian *ḥarrah* desert. Furthermore, I note that *n* can occasionally occur as a short vertical line (i.e. with the 'Safaitic' form) in some 'pure' Hismaic inscriptions from the Wādī Ramm area (KJA 32, KJC 418).

Figure 9. a. *DaJ12ANA120;* **b.** *ThNTS 77 = DaJ12ANA91;* **c.** *DaJ47ANA20 (©DaJAP, G. Charloux);* **d.** *ThNTS 99 (Al-Theeb 2002a: 205).*

- the occurrence of *ḏ* with a simplified version of the Hismaic shape, consisting of a trident with a tail that is hooked at its end;
- the development of some unique or 'local' shapes which alternate either with those described above or with their basic South Semitic forms. These include the *r* which frequently occurs as a stroke with a hook at one end (WTI 14, 55; ThNQT 1, 17); the *ġ* which can appear as a wavy line identical to the Safaitic *s*^{2} (ThNQT 94, 153; DaJ8ANA9); the *ḏ* whose tail is not dissecting the half-circle in a number of cases (WTI 14, DaJ8ANA9, DaJ46ANA3); and the *s*^{1} which can be represented with a hooked tail (WTI 14; DaJ8ANA8, 9).

Genres and content of the texts

The vast majority of these texts consist of simple signatures introduced by the *lām auctoris*. Most often, they are restricted to the author's name and patronym, but a few contain some detailed genealogies and affiliations to a social group by the characteristic expression *ḏ-ʾl* 'of the lineage of'. The other texts which are very frequent, with about ninety-six examples, are those expressing yearning with the verb *ts*^{2}*wq*, for example, *l ʿmr bn ʿlyn w ts*^{2}*wq ʾl-ḥmyt* 'By ʿmr son of ʿlyn and he longed for Ḥmyt' (DaJ12ANA120) (Fig. 9/a). On five occasions, the formula does not take a direct object and instead is followed by the phrase *f ktm* 'but he concealed', namely the name(s) of the person(s) from whom the author was separated: *l rgmn w ts*^{2}*wq f ktm* 'By Rgmn and he longed but he concealed' (DaJ12ANA122; see also ThNQT 9, 27, 39, 126). Two published texts from al-Qudayr, which their editor has interpreted as prayers to the Palmyrene deity *ʾšr*, appear to be completed by the sentence *w s*^{1}*ʾl b-s*^{1}*lm-k* 'and he inquired about your welfare'.[35] This formula has no parallel in the ANA corpora, although it echoes the North-West Semitic epistolary greeting *šʾl (b)-šlm-k* (Cunchillos 1983: 61–66).

There are about fifteen texts expressing grief with the common expression *wgm ʿl* 'he grieved for'. It is interesting to note that the persons grieved for are most often the writers' close relatives, as shown by the different kinship terms identifying them as the *ʾḫ* 'brother' (ThNQT

[35] The *editio princeps* reads these texts as follows: *l ḥmy bn s*^{1}*my w ts*^{2}*wq l-s*^{1}*ʿdt w ʾs*^{2}*r s*^{1}*lmh* 'By Ḥmy son of S^{1}my and he longed for S^{1}ʿdt and, [O] ʾs^{2}r, peace!' (ThNTS 101); *l ḥn bn bkr w ts*^{2}*wq l-s*^{1}*ʿdt w h ʾs*^{2}*r s*^{1}*lmh* 'By Ḥn son of Bkr and he longed for S^{1}ʿdt and, O ʾs^{2}r, peace!' (ThNTS 103). There are several problems with these interpretations. First, the glyph following *s*^{1}*ʿdt w* is clearly a *s*^{1} and not a *h*. Compare the *s*^{1} in *s*^{1}*ʿdt*, *s*^{1}*lm*, and *s*^{1}*my*. Note, moreover, that *h* is never written horizontally in this script, which excludes reading the sign as the vocative particle. The second problem relates to the value of the second letter in the alleged theonym which consists of a straight vertical line. This is unlikely to be a Hismaic *s*^{2} since the *s*^{2} in *ts*^{2}*wq* is clearly represented by the wavy glyph. It is thus a *l*. Thirdly, the final letter of both texts is undoubtedly a *k* and not a *h*, certainly representing the clitic pronoun of the second person singular, even though the use of the second person is surprising. I would therefore suggest the following reinterpretations: *l ḥmy bn s*^{1}*my w ts*^{2}*wq l-s*^{1}*ʿdt w s*^{1}*ʾl b-s*^{1}*lm-k* 'By Ḥmy son of S^{1}my and he longed for S^{1}ʿdt and he inquired about your welfare' (ThNTS 101); *l ḥn bn bkr w ts*^{2}*wq ʾ[l]-s*^{1}*ʿdt w s*^{1}*ʾl b-s*^{1}*lm-k* 'By Ḥn son of Bkr and he longed {for} S^{1}ʿdt and he inquired about your welfare' (ThNTS 103).

24), *ʾẖt* 'sister' (ThNQT 138), *ʾb* 'father' (ThNTS 11), *dd* 'paternal uncle' (ThNQT 134), or *ẖl* 'maternal uncle' (DaJ12ANA140) of the authors. Among these texts is ThNTS 77 (= DaJ12ANA91) from al-Qudayr. The *editio princeps* interpreted its last section as a prayer to Ruḍā,[36] but the new photographs allow us to reconsider the passage as a variant of the Safaitic expression *rġmn mny*, here expressed by a finite verb in the passive, */ruġimū/ (Fig. 9/b).[37]

> *l ʾmt bn khln w wgm ʿl-mḥrb w ʿl-mḥbb w ʿl-ʾmt kl-hm rġm mny*
> 'By ʾmt son of Khln and he grieved for Mḥrb and for Mḥbb and for ʾmt, all of them who were struck down by Fate'.

Also to be noted is a text from Qārat Duwayfinah, between Dūmah and Qārā, which contains the verb *ṣwy* after the expression of grieving, *l ʾs^{1}wd bn zġbr bn ẖzn bn nhḍ w wgm ʿl-ls^{2}ms^1 w ṣwy* (DaJ47ANA20) (Fig. 9/c). From the context, it is almost certain that this refers to the building of a funerary cairn for the dead person (cf. Classical Arabic *ṣawwā*; see Lane, 1739b), and not to the lack of rain. Thus, 'By ʾs^{1}wd son of Zġbr son of Ḫzn son of Nhḍ and he grieved for Ls^{2}ms^1 while he built a cairn'.[38] Only a few texts deal with religious matters, among which fifteen invocations stand out — mostly of the type *ḏkr(t) DN PN* 'may DN be mindful of PN' and *w ndw DN* 'he called out to DN' (see below)[39] — and two graffiti that mention the building of a sacred structure (DaJ29ANA5, 6). One may consider the occurrence of both the *ts^{2}wq*-compositions and the *ḏkr(t)*-prayers in these texts as a second reason, in addition to the script, to think in terms of a 'mixed' category, since the former formula is more a characteristic of the Safaitic group whereas the latter is, in ANA, specific to Hismaic.

The references to pasturing activities and travels suggest that these graffiti were, at least in part, carved by nomadic groups (see DaJ8ANA9 and DaJ144ANA35, below). On the other hand, there is one text which raises the question of whether the inhabitants of the local settlements could equally have been involved in their production. This is WTI 13, which comes from the area of the Saysarā well at Sakākā and reads *ḏkrt ʾlt kll s^{1}kkt* 'May ʾlt be mindful of all S^{1}kkt'. As the editor of this text in OCIANA notes, the name *s^{1}kkt* is likely to stand for the toponym Sakākā, exactly where the text was discovered. According to Yāqūt, the ancient spelling of this village was *Sukākah* (1977, ii: 487; iii: 229), which would indeed appear in ANA as *s^{1}kkt.* Although no architectural remains from the pre-Islamic period have been identified so far at Sakākā, its occupation by a settled population in antiquity appears probable according to Al-Muaikel, who says that he recorded 'pre-Islamic' sherds around the Zaʿbal castle and argues in favour of an early dating of the Saysarā well (1994: 124, 301–302). Therefore, WTI 13 should be considered for future research in order to test Al-Muaikel's theory.

Finally, there are two texts, possibly three, that refer vaguely to military activities, which could lead us to ascribe another part of these MSH graffiti to men patrolling around Dūmah on behalf of the Nabataeans or the Romans, although we cannot know whether they were drawn from nomadic or settled communities. See DaJ34ANA3/DaJ34Nab4 (below), and ThNTS 99 which I would reread as *l ʿḏr w ts^{2}wq ʾl-tbn w ẖls^1 b-gs^2 mḥrb* 'By ʿḏr and he longed for Tbn because he was carried off among a troop which was plundered' (Fig. 9/d).[40] Although the evidence is extremely limited, this assumption deserves to be considered since many of the Nabataean graffiti scattered around Dūmah are signed by military men, some *pršyʾ* 'cavalrymen', and other soldiers (Nehmé 2017).

Linguistic features

General

These MSH texts are also interesting from a linguistic point of view. One of their peculiar features is the interchangeability of the prepositions *ʾl-* and *l-*, in

[36] *l ʾmt bn y{ṯ}drt w wgm ʿl mḥrb w ʿl mḥbb w ʿl ʾmt kl-hm s^{1}lm mn {r}{ḍ}* 'By ʾmt son of {Yṯdrt } and he grieved for Mḥrb and for Mḥbb and for [the lineage of] ʾmt, all of them, peace from [the deity] {Rḍ}'.

[37] I have not taken the dot occurring between the two *m*s in the last line as a *n* (thus producing plural passive participle *rġmn mny*, the more common form of this expression when referring to a plural subject) because of its position, standing very high in comparison with the other letters, especially as compared with the *n* in *mny* that stands on the median axis of the text as expected. A reading *rġmn* cannot be completely excluded, however, even though this position of the *n* would be very unusual, since, even in the case of an omission, there was sufficient space for the author to have inserted the *n* afterwards.

[38] *Zġbr* is a new name. In Classical Arabic, the word *zaghbar* refers to the 'nap of a piece of cloth' (Lane, 1234c). Note also the place name *Zaghbār*, a small Syrian town south of Damascus.

[39] Of the *ḏkr(t)* type: WTI 13, 14; DaJ144ANA20, DaJ8ANA5; of the *ndw* type: ThNTS 75a, 80 (= DaJ12ANA97); ThNQT 29, 32, 57, 178 (?); DaJ12ANA21.

[40] See also ThNTJ 35 (= DaJ156ANA1), *l ʿbdl bn ẖrzt w qṣṣ* 'By ʿbdl son of Ḫrzt and he patrolled', but the reading is not totally clear since a third *ṣ* seems to follow *qṣṣ*. Nevertheless, it is interesting to note that this graffito, which comes from Qārat al-Mazād, is carved immediately next to ten Nabataean texts written by cavalrymen (Al-Theeb 1992: nos. 4–7, 14, 16–17, 20–22).

Figure 10. a. *ThNTS 80 = DaJ12ANA97 (©DaJAP, G. Charloux);* **b.** *ThNQT 29 (Al-Theeb 2000a: 187);* **c.** *ThNQT 57 (Al-Theeb 2000a: 163).*

particular in the *ts^{2}wq*-inscriptions, fifty-one of which occur as *ts^{2}wq ʾl-* and twenty-three as *ts^{2}wq l-*. This is a significant difference from the Safaitic inscriptions, as Al-Jallad observes that *ʾl* and *l* do not have an equal distribution in Safaitic and that the verb *ts^{2}wq* almost always takes the former preposition (2015a: 144; 2017: 80).[41] The word-final triphthongs of the weak verbs are always preserved, for example, *rʿy* 'he pastured' (WTI 55), *bny* 'he built' (DaJ29ANA5), *ʾtw* 'he came' (ThNTS 80), *ndw* 'he called out' (ThNQT 29), with one possible exception in ThNQT 178 where the final */awa/ of *ndw* could have collapsed to a long vowel, *nd* (on the verb *ndw*, see below). The passive participle of the G-stem is formed on the characteristic Arabic *mafʿūl* pattern, *mḥrb* */maḥrūb/ 'plundered' (ThNTS 99). If, on the other hand, the word *rġm* in ThNTS 77 is a passive participle with an assimilation of the final *n* to the following consonant, one would have to admit the existence of a *faʿīl* pattern used alongside the *mafʿūl* one. One may also note the adversative function of the conjunction *f* 'but' (DaJ12ANA122) and the occurrence of the quantifier 'all' as both *kll* */kalīl/ (WTI 13; DaJ8ANA5, DaJ144ANA20) and *kl* */kull/ (ThNTS 77). One text contains the masculine plural form of the relative pronoun that occurs, as expected, as *ḏw* (DaJ8ANA9).

An ʾl- *definite article?*

Two published texts from Qārā and one from al-Qudayr have been interpreted by their editor as using the *ʾl-* definite article in the alleged phrase *w ʾlt (ʾ)l-s^{1}lm* (Fig. 10/a–c).[42] Having re-examined ThNTS 80 (DaJ12ANA97) with the aid of new photographs, it seems that these texts are capable of alternative interpretations. Instead of reading their common element as *nd w ʾlt*, I would suggest that the *w* before *ʾlt* is more likely to be the third radical of the verb than the coordinating conjunction 'and'. The verb *ndw* has so far not been found in ANA, although it could well be

[41] Although a minority, the 23 examples of *ts^{2}wq l-* in the MSH texts from Dūmah represent too high a proportion (about 31%) of the total to be explained as an accidental omission of the glottal stop of the preposition *ʾl-*, especially in view of the fact that the construction *ts^{2}wq l-* also occurs in four Hismaic and about twenty 'pure' Safaitic texts in the OCIANA corpus. While Ahmad al-Jallad has rightly suggested that the phrase *ts^{2}wq l-* could be explained by a coalescence of the glottal stop in the preposition *ʾl-* with that of the glottalic *q* of *ts^{2}wq* (2015a: 43), consideration of the MSH material points instead to the variation between *ts^{2}wq ʾl-* and *ts^{2}wq l-* being dialectal differences: certain dialects admitting an interchangeability of *ʾl-* and *l-* and others not. The fact that the prepositions *ʾl-* and *l-* also appear to be interchangeable in the MSH phrase *ndw ʾlt ʾl-s^{1}lm / l-s^{1}lm* 'he called out to ʾlt for security' (see below) — where nothing would explain an elision or coalescence of ʾ — may support this view. See also Prioletta (this volume): 63, n. 48.

[42] According to the *editio princeps*, these texts read: *l s^{2}ms^1 bn ms^{1}lm {b}n s^{1}ʿdlh bn whblh w ndw {ʾ}{l}t l-s^{1}lm* 'By S^{2}ms^1 son of Ms^{1}lm {son} of S^{1}ʿdlh son of Whblh and he travelled and, [O] ʾlt, the peace!' (ThNQT 29); *l s^{2}ms^{1}y bn ms^{1}lmt w ts^{2}wq ʾl-ʾys^1 ʾḫ-h b-ʾṣ f nqr w nd w ʾlt ʾl-s^{1}lm* 'By S^{2}ms^{1}y son of Ms^{1}lmt and he longed for ʾys^1 his brother at ʾṣ and so he wrote (this text) and he travelled and, [O] ʾlt, the peace!' (ThNQT 57); *l s^{2}ms^{1}y bn ms^{1}lmt w ts^{2}wq ʾl-ʾḫ-h b-ʾṣ f nqr w ʾt wld-h w nd w ʾlt ʾl-s^{1}lm w lʿnt mhlkt-h* 'By S^{2}ms^{1}y son of Ms^{1}lmt and he longed for his brother at ʾṣ and so he wrote [this text] and he visited his children, after which he departed; and, [O] ʾlt, the peace! And may she [ʾlt] curse the destroyer of it [the text]' (ThNTS 80 = DaJ12ANA97).

equivalent to Classical Arabic *nādā* (Form III of the root √ndw) which means 'to call out to' (Lane, 3030b). This interpretation is especially suitable in a religious context and one may compare the phrase *ndw ʾlt* with Quranic *nādā rabba-hu* 'he called to his Lord' (21. 83, 89; 38. 41).

Regarding the elements *l* in ThNQT 29 and *ʾl* in ThNQT 57 and 80 (Fig. 10), there are reasons to doubt that they represent the definite article. This is not because we would expect an assimilation of the /l/ to the following coronal, but rather because the word *s*^{1}*lm* 'security' never takes the article when occurring as the object of a request to deities.[43] A second reason is that the elision of the article's onset after *ʾlt* in ThNQT 29 is highly unlikely. Another way to interpret these elements could therefore be to take them as the prepositions *l* and *ʾl*, which would presumably be used with a dative function 'for, to'. As noted above, these two prepositions seem to be interchangeable in the language of these inscriptions, which supports this interpretation. If the aforementioned remarks are correct, these texts can thus be reread as follows:

ThNQT 29 (Fig. 10/b)

l s^{2}*ms*^{1} *bn ms*^{1}*lm {b}{n} s*^{1c}*dlh bn whblh w ndw {ʾ}{l} t l-s*^{1}*lm*
'By S^{2}ms^{1} son of Ms^{1}lm {son of} S^{1c}dlh son of Whblh and he called out to {ʾlt} for security'

ThNQT 57 (Fig. 10/c)

l s^{2}*ms*^{1}*y bn ms*^{1}*lmt w ts*^{2}*wq ʾl-ʾys*^{1} *ʾḫ-h bʾṣ f nqr w ndw ʾlt ʾl-s*^{1}*lm*
'By S^{2}ms^{1}y son of Ms^{1}lmt and he longed in distress for ʾys^{1} his brother and so he wrote and called out to ʾlt for security'[44]

ThNTS 80 =DaJ12ANA97 (Fig. 10/a)

l s^{2}*ms*^{1}*y bn ms*^{1}*lmt w ts*^{2}*wq ʾl-ʾḫ-h bʾṣ f nqr w ʾtw l-dn-h w ndw ʾlt ʾl-s*^{1}*lm w lʿnt m hlk-nh*
'By S^{2}ms^{1}y son of Ms^{1}lmt and he longed in distress for his brother and so he engraved and came in order to be closer to him and called out to ʾlt for security and may she curse whosoever would destroy it [the inscription]'[45]

In support of these interpretations, note a fourth text from Qārā, ThNQT 32, in which *s*^{1}*lm* appears directly after the divine name as an existential clause: *l grm bn hrm w ts*^{2}*wq ʾl-s*^{1}*lmt w ndw ʾlt s*^{1}*lm* 'By Grm son of Hrm and he longed for S^{1}lmt and he called out to ʾlt in order that there be security'.[46] In actual fact, there is no secure attestation of a definite article of any form within the approximately 462 MSH texts from the Dūmah area.[47] This raises the question, whether the language that they express could simply have no visible mark for definition, exactly as in Hismaic. This hypothesis appears probable in view of the four following texts, which lack the definite article where one would expect it (Fig. 11/a–d):

DaJ1ANA19 (Fig. 11/a)

l ʿṯ wqʿ
'By ʿṯ is [the] inscription'[48]

ThNQT 129 (Fig. 11/b)

l grs^{2c} *bn ʿs*^{1}*n w ʾḫḏ ṯʿl*
'By Grs^{2c} son of ʿs^{1}n and he caught [the/a] fox'[49]

---

[43] There are two apparent cases in Safaitic, KRS 25 and BSWSA 52. In KRS 25, however, I would follow Al-Jallad (2015a: 254) in interpreting *f h lt qbll **h** s*^{1}*lm* as *qbll-h s*^{1}*lm* 'O Lt, reunite him with loved ones safely', and in BSWSA 52 I would interpret *f h lt ʾqbl **h** s*^{1}*lm* as *ʾqbl-h s*^{1}*lm* 'and, O Lt, may his kinsmen be secure'.

[44] Already known from Safaitic, the word *bʾṣ* appears to be a misspelling of the original *bʾs*^{1} (Al-Jallad 2015a: 44, 306). I suggest that here it represents a masculine singular active participle 'distressed, who is in want, in a state of affliction' (cf. Classical Arabic *bāʾis*; Lane, 147a) used adverbially to refer to the author's state rather than that of his brother. The term *nqr* occurs in Safaitic (ISB 107) and Taymanitic (Esk A 288) as a substantive 'inscription, writing', although ThNQT 57 and 80 remain so far the only examples of its attestation as a suffix-conjugated verb (cf. Classical Arabic *naqara fī ḥajar*^{in} 'he wrote upon a stone'; Lane, 2837c).

[45] Written by the same author, this text is a simple variant of ThNQT 57. The element following the verb *ʾtw* is open to several interpretations. I have taken it as a purpose clause formed with the preposition *l-* and the infinitive of the root √dnw 'to become near, approach' (cf. Classical Arabic *danā*; Lane, 920b-c, 921a). Note the abstract noun *dnwt* 'closeness' which occurs in the prayer to Lt in a MSH text from ʿArʿar (JaS 73). As Al-Jallad notes, this may refer to the closeness to kin or loved ones (2015a: 310). The non-representation of the final glide *w* before the pronominal suffix could be because it was realized as a diphthong */danāw/ and interpreted as word internal by the writer. On the *nh*-form of the 3rd person masculine singular pronominal suffix, see Al-Jallad 2015a: 97–98.

[46] *Editio princeps*: *l grm bn hrm w ts*^{2}*wq ʾl-s*^{1}*lmt w nd {w} {ʾ}{l}t s*^{1}*lm* 'By Grm son of Hrm and he longed for S^{1}lmt and he travelled {and}, [O] {ʾlt}, [the] peace!'.

[47] According to Al-Theeb, there would be some attestations of the *h*-definite article in ThNTS 56: *l {z}dn h-{g}[ml]*; ThNTJ 4: *h-{b}{k}{r}{t}* and ThNTJ 9: *h-n{q}{t}*. From the photographs, these readings seem to me very doubtful.

[48] Compare this with Hismaic *l ʾʿbdt bn s*^{1}*yr ḫṭṭ* 'By ʾʿbdt son of S^{1}yr is [the] carving' (KJB 90).

[49] In this case, the substantive *ṯʿl* could well be undefined, referring to 'a fox'. In Safaitic, however, the animal name usually takes the article in this type of text, e.g. *w ʾḫḏ h-frs*^{1} (WH 865); *ʾḫḏ grm h-frs*^{1} (KhS 2); *w ʾḫḏ h-ʾs*^{1}*d* (HaNSB 333); *w ʾḫḏ h-bkrt* (AWS 245). But some of these inscriptions are actually accompanied by a drawing of the animal, so the *h-* can simply be used here as a proximal demonstrative 'this'. I therefore admit that the example of ThNQT 129 is not really enlightening in terms

Figure 11. a. *DaJ1ANA19 (©DaJAP, G. Charloux);* **b.** *ThNQT 129 (Al-Theeb 2000a: 229);* **c.** *DaJ8ANA9;* **d.** *DaJ144ANA35 (©DaJAP, C. Poliakoff).*

DaJ8ANA9 (Fig. 11/c)

l mṣrẖ w mṭy w s^{1}lm l-ʾġr <ḏ> ḏw wld gml

'By Mṣrẖ and he journeyed and may [the] young camels which were born during [the acronical rising of] Gemini [mid-December] have security' (?)[50]

DaJ144ANA35 (Fig. 11/d)

l brḥ bn blqt bn bgt ḏ-ʾl ʾṣr w tnẓr ġrt f h ds^{2}r s^{1c}d w s^{1}lm l-mn blġ ʾrḍ t kll-h

'By Brḥ son of Blqt son of Bgt of the lineage of ʾṣr and he waited for abundance so, O Ds^{2}r, may whosoever arrives in this whole land have good fortune and security'[51]

of definiteness in the MSH texts from Dūmah.

[50] The text, although fairly clearly written, is not easy to interpret. I have taken the word *ʾġr* as a ʾCCC broken plural of an unattested **ġrw* on the basis of Classical Arabic *gharā* (pl. *aghrāʾ*), which, among a variety of meanings, is applied to the 'young camel when just born' (Lane, 2254a). The absence of the final glide, however, is problematic as a form *ʾġrw would be expected to correspond to Classical Arabic *aghrāʾ*. So far, we have no evidence of an /āw/ > /ā/ sound change in Safaitic and Hismaic, so the only way to defend this interpretation is to posit a writing error. This is not impossible in view of the dittography of *ḏ* immediately after *ʾġr*. I suggest that the following word, *ḏw*, represents the masculine plural form of the relative pronoun that is already known from three Safaitic texts (see the references in Al-Jallad 2015a: 87 to which should be added KRS 1482). But again, this is not without problem since non-human plurals are usually treated as feminine singular. As several varieties of Arabic attest exceptions to this rule, however, I would say that this solution deserves to be considered. Whereas it may be tempting to translate the last word *gml* as 'camels' and to take it as the agent of the verb *wld*, one has to renounce this idea since the word *gml* has the meaning of 'male camel' and would be unlikely to be used as a collective noun within the birth context with which we seem to be dealing here. I am most grateful to M.C.A. Macdonald for pointing this out to me. I would therefore tentatively suggest that this refers to the constellation *gml*, recently identified as Gemini by Al-Jallad (2014: 224–225). If this is correct, then this would signal the acronical rising of Gemini that takes place in mid-December since it is during the winter and early spring that camels calve in northern Arabia. Note that the author's name, *mṣrẖ*, is not previously attested. It is possible that it represents an active participle of the C-stem, cf. Arabic *muṣrikh* 'one who comes to the rescue in response to a cry for help' (Badawi & Haleem 2008: 521).

[51] Here, the use of the post-positive feminine demonstrative *t* normally requires its head, the common noun *ʾrḍ* 'land', to be preceded by the definite article, as is the case in C 2953, AbaNS 906, and a third Safaitic

If these examples are representative of a linguistic reality, then the language of these texts would share an interesting feature with the one expressed in the Hismaic inscriptions that are found in great concentrations a few hundred kilometres further west. Although this may be seen as a further argument to justify the label of 'Mixed Safaitic-Hismaic', it should be kept in mind that the absence of a visible definite article does not seem to be restricted to Hismaic, as Al-Jallad has recently identified some Safaitic varieties that apparently lack the article as well (2015a: 17).

Dating and connections with the Nabataeans

As is always the case with the ANA material, the chronology of these inscriptions is difficult to establish. Nevertheless, three clues indicate that some of them were clearly produced during the Nabataean and Roman periods.[52] Firstly, the element *s¹lm* that appears at the end of twelve inscriptions, including some signatures (ThNTS 92, 98; ThNQT 47, 124, 125, 142, 168; DaJ29ANA2), texts of yearning (ThNQT 20, 54, 60), and one text of grieving (ThNQT 138). As Chiara della Puppa convincingly argued at the Special Session,[53] this element, which is also attested in the 'Safaitic square-script' inscriptions from north-eastern Jordan, is likely to be a calque of the Nabataean *šlm* PN formula 'May PN be secure, safe and sound'. Secondly, the onomasticon of the authors. Although few in number, there are three texts whose carvers bear the basiliophoric names *ᶜbdḥrṯt* 'servant of Aretas' (ThNQT 106) and *ᶜbdmk* 'servant of Malichos' (ThNQT 74, ThNQT 182). Equally remarkable is the occurrence of several personal names ending with a non-etymological *-w*, which can only be imitations of Nabataean spellings with a representation of *wāwation* (e.g. ThNQT 59, 63, 74, 185). Note, in particular, ThNQT 47 which contains, on the one hand, the formula *s¹lm* and, on the other, *wāwation* on the triptotic names but not on the diptotic *ʾḥwḍ*,[54] suggesting that the author was fully aware of the Nabataean Arabic case system.[55] Thirdly, the surveys conducted by the members of the DaJAP on the top of the Jīlān al-Murayr ridge, 16 km north of Dūmah, led to the exciting discovery of a partial bilingual Nabataean/MSH text which is, very fortunately, dated.[56] The inscription is carefully written inside a cartouche on the lateral half of a split block which provides a flat and circular-shaped panel very suitable for carving (Fig. 12). Running from right to left on three lines, it begins in MSH after which it continues in Nabataean without interruption:

DaJ34ANA3 (MSH section)

l nṣr{l}{h} bn dmṣy
'By {Nṣrlh} son of Dmṣy'

DaJ34Nab4 (Nabataean section)

dkyr nṣrʾlhy br dmsy
w grm[w] {b}{r} tymw b-ṭb l-ᶜlm nṭryʾ
šnt 10+5+4 *b-yrḥ ʾdr*
'May be commemorated Nṣrʾlhy son of Dmsy
and Grm[w] {son} of Tymw for good forever, the guards,
the year 19 in the month of Adār'

A group of modern *wusūm* and a drawing of a camel obscure the author's name in the MSH section as well as the right part of the second line, but there are sufficient traces of the letters to makes the restorations virtually certain. The only difficulties in reading are the values of the last two numerals in the date. The former is clearly bent to the left which suggests that it is more certainly 5 rather than 1, even if it lacks its upper stroke. The latter consists of a cross, which points towards 4. This numeral is usually formed as a St Andrew's cross in Nabataean, whereas it occurs here as a +. An identically shaped 4 is, however, found in the pre-Islamic Arabic graffito at Jabal Usays (see Macdonald 2010: fig. 1). If the reading 10+5+4 is correct and the date is according to the era of Provincia Arabia, as is usually the case when dates in North Arabia are encountered without the name of a Nabataean king, it would be equivalent to February/March AD 125.

This text can therefore be added to the small list of ANA inscriptions that are precisely dated. Taken with a group of other new Nabataean inscriptions from a nearby site, it highlights the early integration of Dūmah in the province

text from the OCIANA corpus that contain the phrase *h-ʾrḍ t*. All the names appearing in this new text are known. The verb *blġ* is not attested elsewhere in ANA, although it should be connected with Classical Arabic *balagha* 'he reached, arrived at' (Lane, 250b–c).

[52] In addition to the inscriptions, the Nabataean presence at Dūmah is now evidenced by strong archaeological data. See Loreto 2012: 166, 174–176; Charloux et al. 2016b.

[53] Her paper is not published in this volume since it will form part of her Ph.D. thesis.

[54] ThNQT 47: *l ʾḥwḍ bn s¹lmw bn qbrw s¹lm* 'By ʾḥwḍ son of S¹lmw son of Qbrw, may he be secure'.

[55] For a comprehensive study of Nabataean *wāwation* with a reassessment of the available data, see Al-Jallad, forthcoming.

[56] I am most grateful to L. Nehmé for generously allowing me to publish this inscription and for her invaluable observations on its reading. On the bilingual Nabataean/ANA texts in general, see Hayajneh 2009.

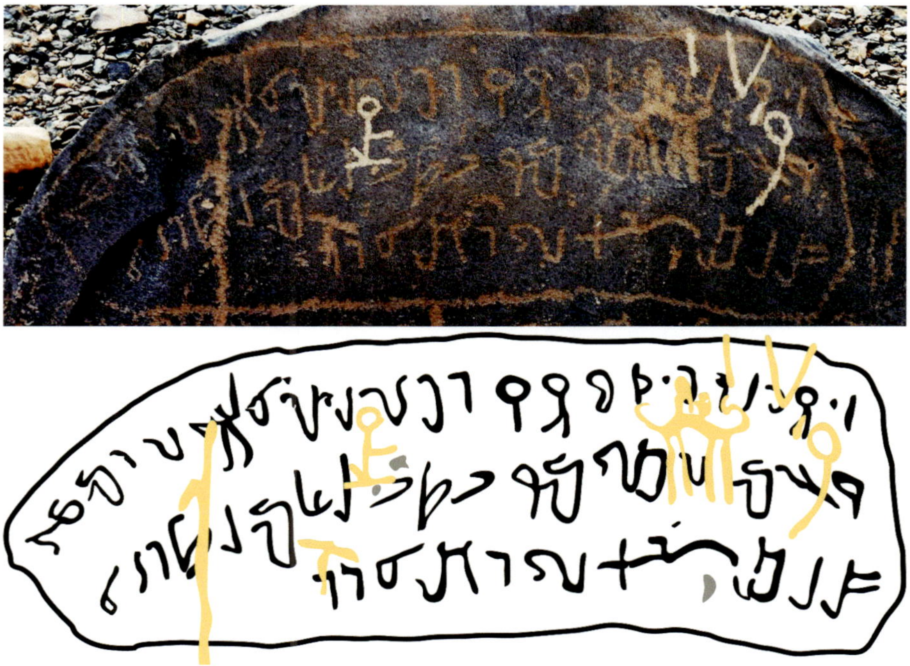

Figure 12. *The partial bilingual Nabataean/MSH inscription DaJ34ANA3/DaJ34Nab4 (©DaJAP, P. Siméon; tracing J. Norris).*

of Arabia and the enrolment of Nabataean soldiers within the Roman army to ensure the control of the region (Nehmé 2017).[57] The text is also of great interest since it confirms, for the first time, the hypothesis formulated long ago about the possible equivalence of ANA *Dmṣy* with Nabataean *Dmsy*, the latter being generally taken as a hypocoristic of the Greek name Δαμάσιππος.[58] Only one person of the name *Dmsy* is so far known in Nabataean, namely the famous son of the *strategos Rbybʾl* (JSNab 84), who is thought to have led a rebellion in AD 71, according to some Safaitic evidence (Winnett 1973: 54–57). In view of this, it is worth considering that the author of our inscription could be the son of this same *Dmsy*, which would make him the great-grandson of Damasippos (Fig. 13). There are at least two members of this well-known Nabataean family who were active in the Dūmah area during the first century AD. They are the father of *Dmsy*, who wrote ARNA.Nab 3 at al-Qalʿah, and his uncle, *ʿnmw*, who is mentioned as *rb mšrytʾ* 'camp commander' at Dūmah in a text from AD 44–45.[59] As this family appears to have been in charge of military affairs at Dūmah during the first century AD, it could well be assumed that this continued for some time in the aftermath of the Roman annexation. Nevertheless, the example of a Safaitic square-script inscription left by a member of the *ʿmrt* tribe, whose father also bears the name *Dmṣy* (SIAM 36), shows that such a suggestion should be treated with great caution. As noted by Macdonald thirty-eight years ago, several individuals living in the *ḥarrah* may well have been named after the leader of the rebellion mentioned in SIJ 287 and 823 (Macdonald 1980: 186), and a comparable scenario could well be applied to the father of the author of our bilingual text.

[57] The word *nṭryʾ* 'guards' that occurs in line 2 was already known from one Nabataean inscription from Maqʿad al-Jundī, where it occurs as a masculine plural in the absolute state within a curious construction, *pršyʾ nṭryn* 'the cavalrymen-guards' (?) (JSNab 245–246). The text is not dated so it is impossible to tell whether this military title was used in both the Nabataean and the Roman periods.

[58] See Milik & Starcky 1970: 142; Winnett 1973: 54–55. Some doubts about the interpretation of the Safaitic *Dmṣy* as a Greek name were expressed by Macdonald (1980: 186; 1993: 360), who rightly noted that it could just as well be derived from the Arabic root √dmṣ. This bilingual inscription allows us to set aside these doubts and we can now be sure that both *dmsy* and *dmṣy* transcribe a foreign name since the ANA has *ṣ* where the Nabataean has *s*. This obviously points towards a Greek *sigma* or a Latin *s*.

[59] If the identification of *Wtrw* (ARNA.Nab 1, 4, 14) and *Gryšw* (ARNA. Nab 4) as the nephews of *Rbybʾl* is correct (see Milik & Starcky 1970: 142), two other members of Damasippos' family would have thus been active at Dūmah.

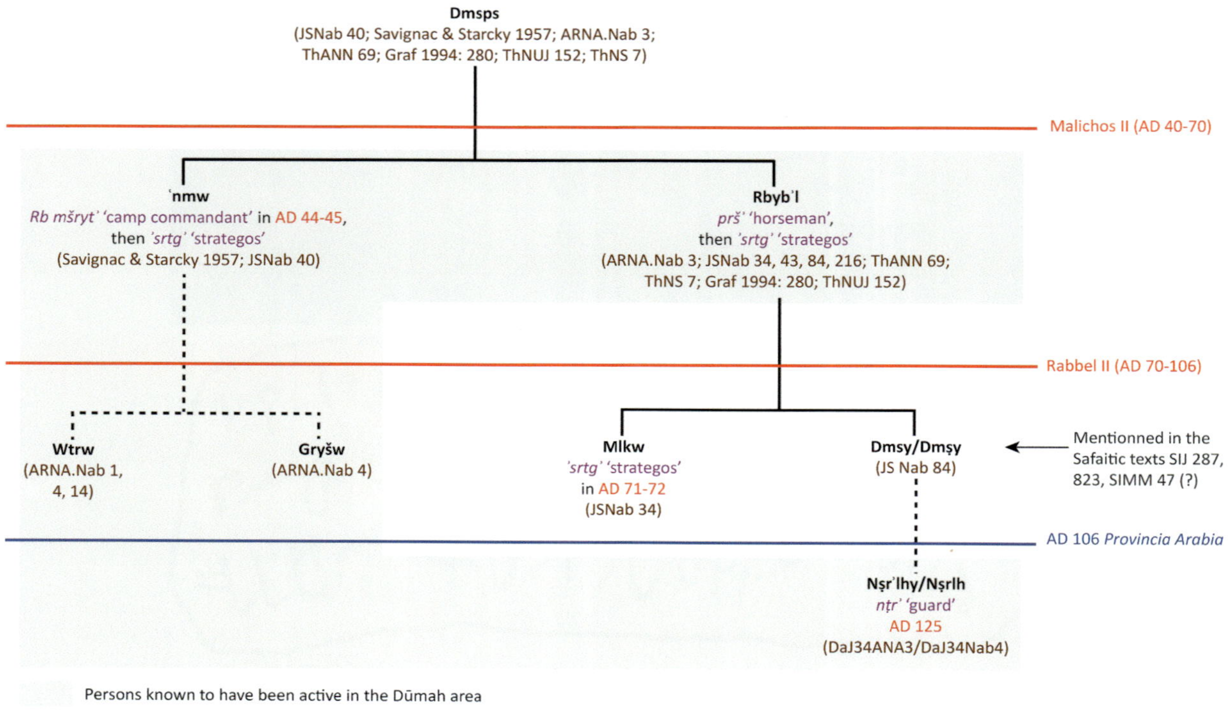

Figure 13. *Hypothetical addition to the genealogy of Damasippos (after Graf 1988: 199 and Healey 1993: 223).*

Conclusion

Given the impossibility of carrying out any systematic survey in such a large area as that of the basin of Sakākā, I should emphasize that our present understanding of the ANA material from this region can only be fragmentary and partial, knowing that new inscriptions will almost certainly come to light in the near future. Nevertheless, the available corpus of 812 known texts provides a picture that can be considered as representative of the regional epigraphic situation.

A remarkable diversity of script characterizes the Dūmah area, with the presence of inscriptions written in eleven different ANA scripts. This is easily explained by Dūmah's geographical location between central Arabia and the Syrian desert, its key role in the trans-Arabian trade and the attractiveness of its oasis, which has always been a specific point of contact between different tribes as well as between the nomads and the settled populations.

The discovery of new texts sharing some features with WTI 21–23 reinforces the hypothesis of the existence of a local Oasis North Arabian script used at Dūmah during the first millennium BC, especially since the author of one of the texts seems to be described as a 'Dumaean'. Nevertheless, these recent finds remain very small, badly preserved, and difficult to interpret with any certainty. On the other hand, if the documents presented above are read correctly, then we must underline the use of an ASA *nisbah* form, the title of *kbr*, and the spelling of *s^1mh*, which could attest to contact between Dūmah and southern Arabia.

The mixed Safaitic-Hismaic inscriptions are by far the most numerous group of texts found in the region. Though often brief, these interesting documents reveal a little about the language and lifestyle of their authors who seem to have been culturally close to the Nabataeans and to include perhaps both nomads and sedentary peoples. The discovery of a partial bilingual Nabataean/MSH text dated to AD 125 provides a rare fixed chronological point for attempting to date these texts while giving further evidence on the early integration of Dūmah within *Provincia Arabia*. If the attribution of this text to a member of the Damasippos family is correct, it would moreover illustrate an interesting example of the use of an ANA alphabet by someone whom we would call a 'Nabataean' in a political or ethnic sense.

Acknowledgements

I wish to express my deep gratitude to Michael C.A. Macdonald for inviting me to read a paper at the special session of the Seminar for Arabian Studies 2017 and for having been, as the editor of the *Supplement*, very accommodating to make this text ready for publication and for reviewing and correcting it so carefully. This contribution owes a great deal to Guillaume Charloux to whom I am most grateful for putting all the French component's project material at my disposal and for the numerous extremely positive discussions I had with him on the subject matter developed here. My thanks also go to him for his thorough reading of this paper and his most valuable input. I am also greatly indebted to Laïla Nehmé for her permission to publish DaJ34Nab4 and her observations on its reading, and to Ahmad Al-Jallad and Chiara della Puppa for their insightful remarks on the paper I gave at the Seminar. All errors are my own.

Sigla

AbaNS	Safaitic inscriptions in Ababneh 2005.
ARNA.Nab	Nabataean inscriptions published in Milik & Starcky 1970.
AWS	Safaitic inscriptions in ᶜAlūlū 1996.
BSWSA	Safaitic inscriptions recorded by the Badia Epigraphic Survey in Wādī Suwayᶜid, north-eastern Jordan and published in OCIANA.
CIS ii	Imperial Aramaic, Nabataean, and Palmyrene inscriptions in *Corpus Inscriptionum Semiticarum. Pars II. Inscriptiones aramaicas continens.* Paris: Imprimerie nationale, 1889–1954.
C	Safaitic inscriptions in *Corpus Inscriptionum Semiticarum. Pars V. Inscriptiones Saracenicae continens. Tomus 1. Inscriptiones Safaiticae*. Paris: Imprimerie nationale. (2 volumes). 1950–1951.
CIK	Caskel 1966.
CSA	Safaitic inscriptions published in Clark 1984–1985.
D	Dadanitic inscriptions as numbered in Farès-Drappeau 2005.
DaJ ANA	Ancient North Arabian inscriptions recorded during the 2010–2017 seasons of the Dūmat al-Jandal archaeological project.
DaJ Nab	Nabataean inscriptions recorded during the 2010–2017 seasons of the Dūmat al-Jandal archaeological project.
Esk A	Ancient North Arabian inscriptions in Eskoubi 1999.
Esk B	Ancient North Arabian inscriptions published by Eskoubi 2007.
Eut	Thamudic inscriptions recorded by Julius Euting, published in van den Branden 1950 and Jamme 1974.
HaNSB	Safaitic inscriptions in Ḥarāḥishah 2010.
HU	Thamudic inscriptions copied by Charles Huber, published and renumbered in van den Branden 1950.
ISB	Safaitic inscriptions in Oxtoby 1968.
Ja	Ancient South Arabian inscriptions in Jamme 1974.
JaS	Safaitic, Hismaic, and mixed inscriptions published by A. Jamme. JaS 44–176 are in Jamme 1971.
JSLih	Dadanitic inscriptions in Jaussen & Savignac 1909–1922.
JSNab	Nabataean inscriptions in Jaussen & Savignac 1909–1922.
KhS	Safaitic inscriptions in Al-Khraysheh 2007.
KJA, KJB, KJC	Hismaic inscriptions from sites A, B, and C in King 1990.
KRS	Safaitic inscriptions recorded by G.M.H. King during the Basalt Desert Rescue Survey and published in OCIANA.
Lane	Lane 1863–1893.
M	Minaic/Madhabic inscriptions in Garbini & Capuzzi 1974.
OCIANA	Online Corpus of the Inscriptions of Ancient North Arabia. http://krc.orient.ox.ac.uk/ociana/index.php
Riyāḍ 302F8	Minaic inscription published in Robin 2010: 324.
SIAM	Safaitic inscriptions in Macdonald 1980.
SIJ	Safaitic inscriptions in Winnett 1957.
SIMM	Safaitic inscriptions from the Mafraq Museum published in OCIANA.
ThANN	Nabataean inscriptions in Al-Theeb 1993.
ThNQT	Thamudic inscriptions in Al-Theeb 2000a.
ThNS	Nabataean inscriptions in Al-Theeb 2014.

ThNTJ	Thamudic inscriptions in Al-Theeb 2003.
ThNTS	Thamudic inscriptions in Al-Theeb 2002a.
ThNUJ	Nabataean inscriptions in Al-Theeb 2002b.
WH	Safaitic inscriptions in Winnett & Harding 1978.
WMin	Minaic/Madhabic inscriptions published in Winnett 1970.
WTay	Taymanitic inscriptions published in Winnett 1970.
WTI	Thamudic inscriptions in Winnett 1970.

References

Ababneh M.I. 2005. *Neue safaitische Inschriften und deren bildliche Darstellungen.* (Semitica et Semitohamitica Berolinensia, 6). Aachen: Shaker.

Adams R.M., Parr P.J., Ibrāhim M. & Al-Mughannum A.S. 1977. Saudi Arabian Archaeological Reconnaissance 1976. The preliminary report on the first phase of the Comprehensive Archaeological Survey Program. *Atlal* 1: 21–40.

ᶜAlūlū Gh.M.Y. 1996. Dirāsah nuqūsh ṣafawiyyah jadīdah min Wādī al-Sūᶜ janūb Sūriyah. M.A. thesis, Yarmouk University. [Unpublished].

Arbach M., Charloux G., Al-Malki T.A., Al-Marshd A.M.N., Morel Q., Al-Qeyaed A.A. ... Al-Traad A.K. 2016. The Archaeological and Epigraphic Survey. Pages 61–92 in Charloux & Loreto 2016.

Badawi E.M. & Abdel Haleem M. 2008. *Arabic-English dictionary of Qurᵓanic usage*. (Handbook of Oriental Studies, 1; The Near and Middle East, 85). Leiden/Boston: Brill.

Bauzou T. 1996. La Praetensio de Bostra à Dumata (El-Jowf). *Syria* 73: 23–35.

Blunt A. 1881. *A pilgrimage to Nejd: The cradle of the Arab race.* (2 volumes). London: Murray.

Caskel W. (ed.). 1966. *Ǧamharat an-Nasab. Das genealogische Werk des Hišām ibn Muḥammad al-Kalbī.* (2 volumes). Leiden: Brill.

Cavigneaux A. & Ismail B.Kh. 1990. Die Statthalter von Suḫu und Mari im 8. Jh. v. Chr. anhand neuer Texte aus den irakischen Grabungen im Staugebiet des Qadissiya-Damms. *Baghdader Mitteilungen* 21: 321–456.

Charloux G. 2012. Known and unknown archaeological monuments in the Dūmat al-Jandal oasis in Saudi Arabia: A review. *Proceedings of the Seminar for Arabian Studies* 42: 41–55.

Charloux G. & Loreto R. 2011. Dûmat al-Jandal (Arabie Saoudite). Premières explorations de l'oasis antique par la mission archéologique italo-franco-saoudienne. *Comptes-rendus de l'Académie des Inscriptions et Belles-Lettres* 155/2: 905–919.

Charloux G. & Loreto R. 2014. Historical overview. Pages 25–56 in G. Charloux & R. Loreto (eds.), *Dûma 1: 2010 Report of the Saudi–Italian–French archaeological project at Dûmat al-Jandal, Saudi Arabia*. Riyadh: Saudi Commission for Tourism and Antiquities.

Charloux G. & Loreto R. (eds). 2016. *Dûma 2: The 2011 report of the Saudi–Italian–French archaeological project at Dumat al-Jandal*. Riyadh: Saudi Commission for Tourism and National Heritage.

Charloux G., Al-Traad A.K., Al-Qeyaed A.A. & Morel Q. 2016a. The Western Settlement, Sector C. Pages 183–226 in Charloux & Loreto 2016.

Charloux G., Bouchaud C., Durand C., Monchot H. & Thomas A. 2016b. Banqueting in a Northern Arabian oasis: A Nabaṭaean triclinium at Dûmat al-Jandal, Saudi Arabia. *Bulletin of the American Schools of Oriental Research* 375: 13–34.

Clark V.A. 1984–1985. New Safaitic inscriptions from Sakaka and Azraq. *Abr-Nahrain* 23: 14–21.

Cunchillos J.L. 1983. Une formule inédite de salutation en ugaritique: *bᶜl yšᵓul šlmk* 'que Baal s'occupe de ton bien-être' RS 17.117. Ses parallèles akkadien, hébreu et araméen. *Aula Orientalis* 1: 61–66.

Eskoubi [Askūbī] Kh.M. 1999. *Dirāsah taḥlīliyyah muqārinah li-nuqūsh min minṭaqat (Rum) janūb gharb Taymāᵓ*. Riyadh: Wizārat al-maᶜārif wakālat al-āthār wa-ᵓl-matāḥif.

Eskoubi [Askūbī] Kh.M. 2007. *Dirāsah taḥlīliyyah muqārinah li-nuqūsh thamūdiyyah min minṭaqat Rum bayna Thulaythuwāt wa Qīᶜān al-Ṣanīᶜ janūb gharb Taymāᵓ*. (Silsilat al-rasāᵓil al-jāmiᶜiyyah, 26). Riyadh: Dārat al-malik ᶜAbd al-ᶜAzīz.

Farès-Drappeau S. 2005. *Dédan et Liḥyān. Histoire des Arabes aux confins des pouvoirs perse et hellénistique (IVᵉ–IIᵉ s. avant l'ère chrétienne)*. (Travaux de la Maison de l'Orient et de la Méditerranée, 42). Lyon: Maison de l'Orient et de la Méditerranée.

Garbini G. & Capuzzi A. 1974. *Iscrizioni sudarabiche 1. Iscrizioni minee.* (Istituto Universitario Orientale di Napoli; Ricerche, 10). Naples: Istituto Universitario Orientale.

Al-Ghabban A.I., André-Salvini B., Demange F., Juvin C. & Cotty M. (eds). 2010. *Routes d'Arabie: Archéologie et histoire du royaume d'Arabie Saoudite*. Paris: Musée du Louvre/Somogy Éditions d'Art.

Graf D.F. 1988. Qurā ᶜArabiyya and Provincia Arabia. Pages 171–211 in P.L. Gatier, B. Helly & J.P. Rey-Coquais (eds), *Géographie historique au Proche-Orient: Syrie, Phénicie, Arabie, grecques, romaines, byzantines. Actes de la table ronde de Valbonne, 16–18 septembre 1985*. (Notes et Monographies Techniques, 23). Paris: Éditions du CNRS.

Ḥarāḥishah R.M.A. 2010. *Nuqūsh ṣafāʾiyyah min al-bādiyat al-Urduniyyah al-shamāliyyah al-sharqiyyah, dirāsah wa taḥlīl*. Amman: Ward Books.

Harding G.L. 1972. Safaitic inscriptions from Tapline in Jordan. *Annual of the Department of Antiquities of Jordan* 17: 5–14.

Hayajneh H. 2009. Ancient North Arabian-Nabataean bilingual inscriptions from southern Jordan. *Proceedings of the Seminar for Arabian Studies* 39: 203–222.

Healey J.F. 1993. *The Nabataean tomb inscriptions of Madaʾin Salih. Edited with introduction, translation and commentary*. (Journal of Semitic Studies, Supplement, 1). Oxford: Oxford University Press.

Huber C. 1891. *Journal d'un voyage en Arabie (1883–1884)*. Paris: Imprimerie nationale.

Ibn al-Athīr, ᶜIzz al-Dīn/ed. Anon. [n.d.]. *Al-Lubāb fī tahdhīb al-ansāb*. (3 volumes). Baghdad: Maktabat al-Muthannā.

Al-Jallad A. 2014. An ancient Arabian zodiac. The constellations in the Safaitic inscriptions, Part I. *Arabian Archaeology and Epigraphy* 25: 214–230.

Al-Jallad A. 2015a. *An outline of the grammar of the Safaitic inscriptions*. (Studies in Semitic Languages and Linguistics, 80). Leiden/Boston: Brill.

Al-Jallad A. 2015b. Echoes of the Baal cycle in a Safaito-Hismaic inscription. *Journal of Ancient Near Eastern Religions* 15: 5–19.

Al-Jallad A. 2017. Marginal notes on and additions to *An outline of the grammar of the Safaitic inscriptions* (Studies in Semitic Languages and Linguistics, 80. Leiden: Brill, 2015), with a supplement to the dictionary. *Arabian Epigraphic Notes* 3: 75–96.

Al-Jallad A. (forthcoming). One *wāw* to rule them all: The origins and fate of wawation in Arabic and its orthography.

Jamme A. 1971. Safaitic inscriptions from the country of ᶜArᶜar and Raʾs al-ᶜAnānīyah. Pages 41–109, 609–637 in F. Altheim & R. Stiehl (eds), *Christentum am Roten Meer*. i. Berlin: De Gruyter.

Jamme A. 1974. *Miscellanées d'ancient* [sic] *arabe*. vii. Washington. [Privately printed].

Jaussen A. & Savignac R. 1909–1922. *Mission archéologique en Arabie*. (5 volumes). Paris: Leroux/Geuthner.

Khan M., Al-Kabawi A.R. & Al-Zahrani A.R. 1986. Preliminary report on the second phase of the Comprehensive Rock Art and Epigraphic Survey of Northern Province 1405/1985. *Atlal* 10: 82–93, pls 86–93.

Al-Khraysheh F.H. 2007. Al-ṣayd ᶜinda ʾl-ᶜarab al-ṣafāʾiyyin qabla ʾl-islām. *Journal of Epigraphy and Rock Drawings* 1: 9–28.

King G.M.H. 1990. Early North Arabian Thamudic E. A preliminary description based on a new corpus of inscriptions from the Ḥismā desert of southern Jordan and published material. PhD thesis, School of Oriental and African Studies, University of London. [Unpublished].

Knauf E.A. 1985. *Ismael. Untersuchungen zur Geschichte Palästinas und Nordarabiens im 1. Jahrtausend v. Chr.* (Abhandlungen des Deutschen Palästinavereins). Wiesbaden: Harrassowitz.

Kootstra F. 2016. The language of the Taymanitic inscriptions and its classification. *Arabian Epigraphic Notes* 2: 67–140.

Kootstra F. (this volume). Scribal practices in contact: two Minaic/Dadanitic mixed texts. Pages 21–30 in M.C.A. Macdonald (ed.), *Languages, scripts and their uses in ancient North Arabia*. (Supplement to volume 48 of the Proceedings of the Seminar for Arabian Studies). Oxford: Archaeopress, 2018.

Lane E.W. 1863–1893. *An Arabic-English lexicon, derived from the best and most copious Eastern sources*. London: Williams & Norgate.

Loreto R. 2012. The Saudi-Italian-French Archaeological Mission at Dūmat al-Jandal (ancient Adumatu). *Proceedings of the Seminar for Arabian Studies* 42: 165–182.

Loreto R. 2018. Results from the 2009–2016 excavation seasons in the historical core of Dūmat al-Jandal, ancient Adummatu. *Proceedings of the Seminar for Arabian Studies* 48: 151–164.

Macdonald M.C.A. 1980. Safaitic inscriptions in the Amman Museum and other collections II. *Annual of the Department of Antiquities of Jordan* 24: 185–208.

Macdonald M.C.A. 1993. Nomads and the Hawran in the late Hellenistic and Roman periods: A reassessment of the epigraphic evidence. *Syria* 70: 303–403. [Reprinted with addenda and corrigenda as article II in Macdonald 2009].

Macdonald M.C.A. 1997. Trade routes and trade goods at the northern end of the 'incense road' in the first millennium B.C. Pages 333–349 in A. Avanzini (ed.), *Profumi d'Arabia: atti del convegno*. (Saggi di storia antica, 11). Rome: 'L'Erma' di Bretschneider. [Reprinted with addenda and corrigenda as article IX in Macdonald 2009].

Macdonald M.C.A. 2000. Reflections on the linguistic map of pre-Islamic Arabia. *Arabian Archaeology and Epigraphy* 11: 28–79. [Reprinted with addenda and corrigenda as article III in Macdonald 2009].

Macdonald M.C.A. 2004. Ancient North Arabian. Pages 488–533 in R.D. Woodard (ed.), *The Cambridge Encyclopedia of the World's Ancient Languages*. Cambridge: Cambridge University Press.

Macdonald M.C.A. 2009. *Literacy and identity in pre-Islamic Arabia.* (Variorum Collected Studies, CS906). Farnham: Ashgate.

Macdonald M.C.A. 2010. The Old Arabic graffito at Jabal Usays: A new reading of line 1. Pages 141–143 in M.C.A. Macdonald (ed.), *The development of Arabic as a written language.* (Supplement to volume 40 of the Proceedings of the Seminar for Arabian Studies). Oxford: Archaeopress.

Macdonald, M.C.A. (this volume). Towards a reassessment of the Ancient North Arabian alphabets used in the oasis of al-ᶜUlā. Pages 1-19 in M.C.A. Macdonald (ed.), *Languages, scripts and their uses in ancient North Arabia* (Supplement to volume 48 of the Proceedings of the Seminar for Arabian Studies). Oxford: Archaeopress, 2018.

Macdonald M.C.A. & King G.M.H. 1999. Thamoudique. Pages 467–469 in *Encyclopédie de l'Islam (Nouvelle Édition).* x. Leiden: Brill/Paris: Maisonneuve & Larose.

Milik J.T. 1972. *Recherches d'épigraphie proche-orientale I. Dédicaces faites par des dieux (Palmyre, Hatra, Tyr) et des thiases sémitiques à l'époque romaine*. (Bibliothèque archéologique et historique, 92). Paris: Geuthner.

Milik J.T. & Starcky J. 1970. Inscriptions nabatéennes. Pages 141–160 in Winnett & Reed 1970.

Al-Muaikel Kh.I. 1994. *Study of the Archaeology of the Jawf Region, Saudi Arabia*. Riyadh: King Fahd National Library.

Nehmé L. 2017. New dated inscriptions (Nabataean and pre-Islamic Arabic) from a site near al-Jawf, ancient Dūmah, Saudi Arabia. *Arabian Epigraphic Notes* 3: 121–164.

Norris J. 2017. The expression *h-rhwy* in Thamudic B inscriptions from north-west Arabia. *Proceedings of the Seminar for Arabian Studies* 47: 193–208.

Olsen S.L. & Bryant R.T. 2013. *Stories in the rocks. Exploring Saudi Arabian rock art*. Pittsburgh, PA: Carnegie Museum of Natural History.

Oxtoby W.G. 1968. *Some inscriptions of the Safaitic Bedouin*. (American Oriental Series, 50). New Haven, CT: American Oriental Society.

Parr P.J., Zarins J., Ibrāhim M., Waechter J., Garrard A., Clarke C. ... Al-Badr H. 1978. Preliminary report on the second phase of the Northern Province Survey 1397/1977. *Atlal* 2: 29–50.

Prioletta A. (this volume). New research on the 'Thamudic' graffiti from the region of Ḥimā (Najrān, Saudi Arabia). Pages 53–69 in M.C.A. Macdonald (ed.), *Languages, scripts and their uses in ancient North Arabia.* (Supplement to volume 48 of the Proceedings of the Seminar for Arabian Studies). Oxford: Archaeopress, 2018.

Robin C.J. 1996. Sheba. II. Dans les inscriptions de l'Arabie du Sud. Cols 1047–1254 in J. Briend & É. Cothenet (eds), *Supplément au Dictionnaire de la Bible.* Fasc. 70. Paris: Letouzey & Ané.

Robin C.J. 2010. 136. Plaque inscrite ornée de bouquetins. Page 324 in A.I. Al-Ghabban et al. (eds). 2010.

Al-Salameen Z. 2011. A new Ancient North Arabian inscription with a reference to the Nabataean king Aretas. *Arabian Archaeology and Epigraphy* 22: 215–218.

Al-Saud A.S., Khan M. & Al-Hadlaq A. 2005. Report on the Rock Art Survey at Jubbah. *Atlal* 18: 39–42.

Savignac R. & Starcky J. 1957: Une inscription nabatéenne provenant du Djôf. *Revue Biblique* 64: 196–217.

Al-Sudairi A. 1995. *The desert frontier of Arabia: Al-Jawf through the ages.* London: Stacey International.

Al-Theeb [Al-Dhiyīb] S.A. 1992. Nuqūsh nabaṭiyyah jadīdah min Qārat al-Mazād Sakākā, al-Jawf, al-mamlakah al-ᶜarabiyyah al-saᶜūdiyyah. *al-ᶜUṣūr* 7: 217–254.

Al-Theeb S.A. 1993. *Aramaic and Nabataean inscriptions from North-West Saudi Arabia*. Riyadh: King Fahd National Library.

Al-Theeb S.A. 1994. Two new Nabataean inscriptions from al-Jawf. *Journal of Semitic Studies* 39: 33–40.

Al-Theeb [Al-Dhiyīb] S.A. 2000a. *Nuqūsh Qārā al-thamūdiyyah bi-minṭaqat al-Jawf bi-ᵓl-mamlakah al-ᶜarabiyyah al-saᶜūdiyyah*. Riyadh: Muᵓassasat ᶜAbd al-Raḥmān al-Sudayrī ᵓl-khayrīyah bi-ᵓl-Jawf.

Al-Theeb [Al-Dhiyīb] S.A. 2000b. *Dirāsah li-nuqūsh thamūdiyyah min Jubbah bi-Ḥāᵓil*. Riyadh: Maktabat al-malik Fahd al-waṭaniyyah.

Al-Theeb [Al-Dhiyīb] S.A. 2002a. *Nuqūsh thamūdiyyah min Sakākā (Qāᶜ Furayḥah wa-ʾl-Ṭuwayr wa-ʾl-Qudayr). Al-mamlakah al-ᶜarabiyyah al-saᶜūdiyyah.* Riyadh: Maktabat al-malik Fahd al-waṭaniyyah.

Al-Theeb [Al-Dhiyīb] S.A. 2002b. *Nuqūsh Jabal Umm Jadhāyidh al-nabaṭiyyah.* Riyadh: Maktabat al-malik Fahd al-waṭaniyyah.

Al-Theeb [Al-Dhiyīb] S.A. 2003. *Nuqūsh thamūdiyyah jadīdah min al-Jawf, al-mamlakah al-ᶜarabiyyah al-saᶜūdiyyah.* Riyadh: Maktabat al-malik Fahd al-waṭaniyyah.

Al-Theeb [Al-Dhiyīb] S.A. 2014. *Nuqūsh mawqiᶜ Sarmadāʾ muḥāfaẓat Taymāʾ.* (Dirāsāt āthāriyyah, 12). Riyadh: Fahrasah maktabat al-malik Fahd al-waṭaniyyah/Jāmiᶜat al-malik Saᶜūd, kullīyat al-siyāḥah wa-ʾl-āthār.

van den Branden A. 1950. *Les inscriptions thamoudéennes.* (Bibliothèque du Muséon, 25). Louvain: Institut Orientaliste de l'Université de Louvain.

Winnett F.V. 1957. *Safaitic inscriptions from Jordan.* (Near and Middle East Series, 2). Toronto: University of Toronto Press.

Winnett F.V. 1970. The Arabian inscriptions. Pages 67–138 in Winnett & Reed 1970.

Winnett F.V. 1973. The revolt of Damasī: Safaitic and Nabataean evidence. *Bulletin of the American Schools of Oriental Research* 211: 54–57.

Winnett F.V. & Harding G.L. 1978. *Inscriptions from fifty Safaitic cairns.* (Near and Middle East Series, 9). Toronto: University of Toronto Press.

Winnett F.V. & Reed W.L. 1970. *Ancient records from North Arabia.* (Near and Middle East Series, 6) Toronto: University of Toronto Press.

Yāqūt/ed. Anon. 1977. *Kitāb muᶜjam al-buldān.* (5 volumes). Beirut: Dār Ṣādir.

Author's address

Jérôme Norris, HISCANT-MA (EA 1132), Université de Lorraine, Salle A 020, 23 Boulevard Albert 1er, BP 13 397, 54015 Nancy cedex, France.
e-mail norris.jerome@gmail.com

M.C.A. Macdonald (ed.), *Languages, scripts and their uses in ancient North Arabia.* (Supplement to volume 48 of the Proceedings of the Seminar for Arabian Studies). Oxford: Archaeopress, 2018: 95–100

A preliminary investigation of an Ancient North Arabian invocation from the Madaba region of central Jordan

Hani Hayajneh

Summary

This paper will edit and discuss two hitherto unpublished Ancient North Arabian (ANA) inscriptions from the Madaba region of central Jordan. They were found during the surveys of the Wādī al-Thamad Project in northern Moab (TT-5-WT Site WT-48) under the direction of Prof. M. Daviau. The inscriptions (consisting of one line and twenty lines respectively) are carved in the Hismaic script on a horizontal shelf of bedrock near a spillway in a curve of Wādī al-Thamad, which flows south-west into Wādī Mūjib. A decipherment of the inscriptions based on fresh photographs and photogrammetry is provided.

Keywords: Ancient North Arabian epigraphy, Wādī al-Thamad, Hismaic, Madaba, central Jordan

Introduction

This paper deals with an inscribed rock discovered during the archaeological surveys led by Prof. Michèle Daviau of Wilfrid Laurier University, Canada, and her team in Wādī al-Thamad in the Madaba area of central Jordan.

This survey yielded Ancient North Arabian (ANA) inscriptions of the Hismaic type[1] that will be treated in a series of articles by the present author. In terms of the history of research, a reference should be made to the two longest inscriptions from this region published by Bikai and Al-Khraysheh (2002) and Graf and Zwettler (2004). The vast majority of inscriptions of this type are found in the Ḥismā desert of southern Jordan and northern Saudi Arabia, which is why they have been labelled 'Hismaic',[2]

[1] For recent discussions of Hismaic and other ANA scripts see Macdonald 2000; 2004; Al-Jallad 2015: 10–14; Kootstra 2016; Hayajneh 2016: 538, n. 3; 2017a.

[2] Here, one should highlight two corpora of Hismaic inscriptions from southern Jordan one recorded by Geraldine King (1990) and the other by Glenn Corbett (2010). We should keep in mind that Thamudic E is called Hismaic because the largest numbers of these texts discovered so

Figure 1. *The location of the rock in relation to Wādī al-Thamad (H. Hayajneh).*

Figure 2. *A general view of the rock (H. Hayajneh).*

Figure 3. *A photogrammetric image of the rock (George Bevan, Queen's University, Canada).*

Figure 4. *A photogrammetric image with a tracing of the inscription (Yousuf Al-Zuʿbi, Yarmouk University).*

but small numbers have also been found in the Irbid (Hayajneh 2009a) and Jerash (Hayajneh 2017b) areas of northern Jordan.

The inscriptions

The two inscriptions, consisting of one line and twenty lines respectively, are hammered on a horizontal shelf of bedrock (1.85 m in width and 2.46 m in length) near a spillway in a curve of Wādī al-Thamad (Figs 1 & 2). Inscription 2 contains over 500 letters and is, to the best of my knowledge, the longest ANA text ever discovered.

The black and white photographs provided by Michèle Daviau were partially helpful in deciphering the inscriptions. Parts of the longer text, however, were not covered by them and the low quality of such old photographs made me sceptical about the reading of many of the signs. My colleagues, Dr Glenn Corbett and Dr George Bevan,[3] suggested taking new digital photographs of the rock using photogrammetric techniques, which would enable us to take measurements and record the exact positions of surface points.[4] I am deeply appreciative of their efforts in producing an excellent image of the rock (Fig. 3), which enabled me to read the majority of the signs carved on it and to produce a good and readable tracing (Figs 4 & 5).

far are concentrated in the Ḥisma, but significantly a growing minority of them are being discovered near settled areas.

[3] Associate Professor in the Department of Geography and Planning, Queen's University, Canada.

[4] See https://en.wikipedia.org/wiki/Photogrammetry.

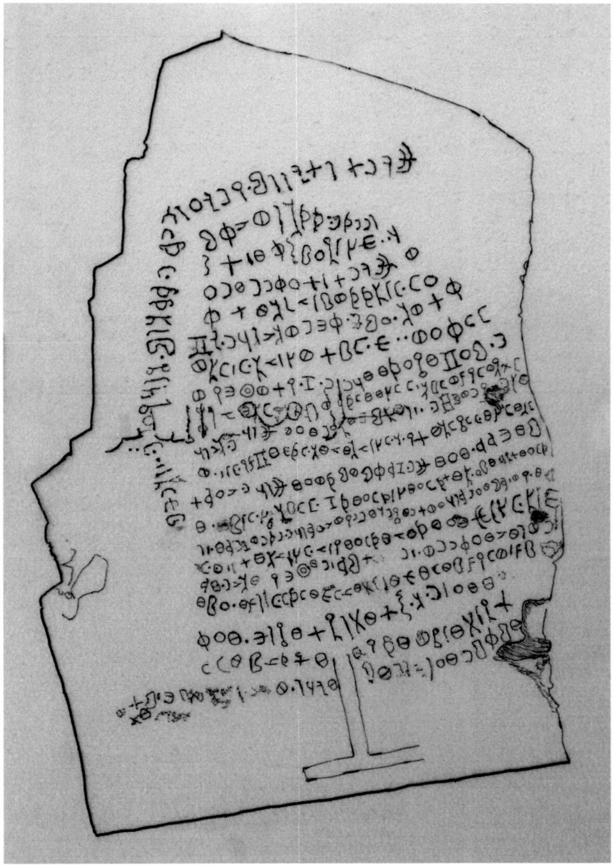

Figure 5. *A tracing of the inscription (H. Hayajneh).*

The inscriptions[5]

Inscription 1

This text runs from right to left across the upper part of the rock and then vertically down to the left of the first twelve lines of Inscription 2.

Transliteration

ḏkrt lt kll mn ybk ʿl s^{1}rd bn ddʾl m{n} {ʾ}l h{ṣ}ʿ bn ns^{2}l ʾ-rḥm [or *ʾrḥm*]

Translation

May Lt be mindful of anyone who would weep for S^{1}rd son of Ddʾl {of} {the lineage of} {Hṣʿ} son of Ns^{2}l the merciful/[the] most merciful

Commentary

ḏkrt lt, 'May Lt[6] be mindful of', is a well-known invocation found frequently in Hismaic, for example KJA 36, KJC 42, and KJC 272.

kll is known in Hismaic, for example KJA 44, KJC 42 and 641, and other ANA corpora. It has the same function as Classical Arabic *kull* 'all, each, entire, every', although the spelling with two *l*s would suggest a different pronunciation (see Al-Jallad 2015: 89). It is used here in construct with the indefinite relative pronoun *mn* 'who' (King 1990: 94). The following form of an apocopate prefix conjugation is derived from the root *b-k-y* 'to weep'. In Safaitic, the verb *bky* 'to weep' is attested several times (Al-Jallad 2015: 308).

mn ʾl 'of the lineage of' has been found once before in Hismaic (KJC 641) as a variant of the usual *ḏ ʾl* (see also Safaitic NST 3 and RWQ 346). I would suggest that it could be interpreted in two ways. First, we can identify *mn* as the indefinite relative pronoun */man/, and the phrase would thus be the exact equivalent of *ḏ ʾl*, both meaning 'he of the lineage of'. Second, we can also consider the hypothesis that *mn* represents the preposition */min/ which would be used to indicate origin.

h{ṣ}ʿ has been found once as a personal name in Safaitic (C 2891). The reading here is uncertain and it is not previously attested as a lineage name. An example of a name which begins with a *h-* is known in Hismaic *hʿtl* (TIJ 394), although the other possible examples from Hismaic, *hʾmr*, *hʾmy*, *hẖn*, *hkdn*, *hkn*, are considered by King (1990: 131) either to be doubtful readings or to be open to alternative interpretations.

ʾ-rḥm/*ʾrḥm*: this is apparently an epithet of the lineage name *h{ṣ}ʿ bn ns^{2}l* and can be interpreted in two different ways. The first is to read *ʾ* + *rḥm*. In Safaitic, *rḥm* occurs as the epithet of a deity apparently meaning 'merciful'. If we accept this interpretation, the *alif* in the present case would represent the definite article, either in the *ʾ*-form or the *ʾl*-form with an assimilation of the [l] before the [r].

[5] The editorial signs are as follows: [ ] enclose a restored letter; { } in the transliteration enclose a letter whose reading is doubtful, and in the translation enclose the whole word or name containing one or more doubtful letters; ---- indicate one or more letters that are too badly damaged to suggest a reading; - attaching one or more letters to the beginning or end of a name or word indicate a proclitic preposition or a suffixed pronoun respectively; = at the end of a line shows that a name or word has been split between two lines.

[6] For the Arabian goddess *lt*, see Krone 1992: 96.

Given that no visible definite article is used in Hismaic, however, one would have to assume that *ʾ-rḥm* was a loan epithet or name from a language/dialect which used the *ʾ-/ʾl-* definite article. The problem with this theory is that it is difficult to explain the function of a divine epithet or name in this context. On the other hand, if the reading is *ʾrḥm*, it would be the elative adjective meaning 'more merciful'. Moreover, since Hismaic has no visible definite article, *ʾrḥm* could be the equivalent of Arabic *al-arḥam* meaning 'the most merciful', but one is still faced with the problem of what function it serves in this position in the inscription.

Inscription 2

The text runs boustrophedon starting from right to left. The letter forms are Hismaic, but it should be noted that although the *ḥ* has its typical Hismaic form, the part of the central prong which extends beyond the back of the letter is extremely short in the names *ḥddn* (line 11), *ḍḥy* (line 15), *ḥbs^1* (line 16), and *ḥs^{2}mt* (line 19) and was not shown in the tracing of the inscription, thus giving the impression that it is a *ṭ*.

Transliteration

1. *l brd bn ddʾl w s^{1}qm*
2. *f ts^{2}wq {f} mʿṣ l-h ḥnn-h*
3. *w ḏkrt lt ʿqrb w bʿ=*
4. *qt w ʾls^{1}lm w ddʾl bn bʿ=*
5. *qt w ʾnʿm bn qṭb w ʾs^{1}lh bn ġṯ*
6. *w ʾrs^2 bn ʾs^{1}lh w tm bn ḥnn w ʿqrb*
7. *bn mʿṯ w gʿd w whbl bn znyt w ḍḥy w*
8. *gls^1 w ʾbn ---- w {b}dr* [?] *w whb bn ʾmr w ġyr w ṣẖb*
9. *[w] whbn {w} {ʾ}b w {ġ}ṯ* [?] *{w} bn ns^{2}l {w} ʾmr w {ṣ}ʿb w ʿwḏlh bn ʾs^{1}lh*
10. *w ns^{2}l bn yġṯ w ḥd bn ʾws^1 w ʾs^{1}lh bn hnyt w ʾbgr bn whb w hb=* [?]
11. *[..]m w {ḥ}ddn w ʿwḏ bn zdqm w md w ʿwḏlh bn s^{1}ʿdt*
12. *w n{ʿ}ml bn h{n} ʾmr* [?] *bn zd w ʿbdlh w ʿbdt w ʾnʿm w ʿṣt w ʿbd*
13. *{w} wny w ndm w ʿbdl{h} w wtr w grh* [?] *w bry w s^{1}ʿdlh bn bdr w zbd w ns^{2}l*
14. *bn ḍnlt w ʾs^{1}lh bn s^{1}ly w ʿbd w s^{1}ʿd w ʿwḏlh bn ʾl{w}* [?]
15. *[h]b* [?] *w lws^1 w ʿqrb w ns^{2}l ---- [w] tmds^{2}r w ḍ{ḥ}y w ʾs^1 bn wd*
16. *w mʿn w ẖll bn bdr w {ḥ}bs^1 w ẖ{l}l w ḥwr w mġyr w s^{2}km w*
17. *---- w wʿl bn ʾnft w ẖlṣt w glḥn w ʿq=*
18. *rb w ms^{1}dt w ---- ʿbd* [or *{q}yd* ?] *w wgl w ẖlṣt ----*
19. *w mqm b[n] wʿl ----wm---- w khln ---- w----{ḥ} s^{2}mt* [?] *w*
20. *ẖw ----*

Translation

[1]By Brd son of Ddʾl and he was ill [2] and he was full of longing, {and so} became angry {because of} his yearning [3] and may Lt be mindful of ʿqrb and Bʿ[4]qt and ʾls^{1}lm and Ddʾl son of Bʿ[5]qt and Nʿm son of Qṭb and ʾs^{1}lh son of Ġṯ [6] and ʾrs^2 son of ʾs^{1}lh and Tm son of Ḥnn and ʿqrb [7] son of Mʿṯ and Gʿd and Whbl son of Znyt and Ḍḥy and [8] Gls^1 and ʾbn ---- and {Bdr} [?] and Whb son of ʾmr and Ġyr and Ṣẖb [9] {and} Whbn {and} {ʾb} and {Ġṯ} [?] {and} the son of [?] Ns^{2}l {and} ʾmr and {Ṣʿb} and ʿwḏlh son of ʾs^{1}lh [10] and Ns^{2}l son of Yġṯ and Ḥd son of ʾws^1 and ʾs^{1}lh son of Hnyt and ʾbgr son of Whb and Hb[?][11][..]m and {Ḥddn} and ʿwḏ son of Zdqm and Md and ʿwḏlh son of S^{1}ʿdt [12] and {Nʿml} son of {Hnʾmr} [?] son of Zd and ʿbdlh and ʿbdt and ʾnʿm and ʿṣt and ʿbd [13] {and} Wny and Ndm and {ʿbdlh} and Wtr and Grh [?] and Bry and S^{1}ʿdlh son of Bdr and Zbd and Ns^{2}l [14] son of Ḍnlt and ʾs^{1}lh son of S^{1}ly and ʿbd and S^{1}ʿd and ʿwḏlh son of {ʾlw} [?] [15] [h]b [?] and Lws^1 and ʿqrb and Ns^{2}l ---- {and} Tmds^{2}r and {Ḍḥy} and ʾs^1 son of Wd [16] and Mʿn and H̱ll son of Bdr and {Ḥbs^1} and {H̱ll} and Ḥwr and Mġyr and S^{2}km and [17] ---- and Wʿl son of ʾnft and H̱lṣt and Glḥn and ʿq[18]rb and Ms^{1}dt and ---- ʿbd [or {Qyd} ?] and Wgl and H̱lṣt ----[19] and Mqm {son of} Wʿl ----wm---- and Khln ---- w----{Ḥs^{2}mt} [?] and [20] {H̱w ----}

Commentary

l + PN:

The translation of the *lām* as an introductory particle depends on the context of the inscription.[7]

s^{1}qm: a verb in the suffix conjugation which could be interpreted here as 'to be ill'. It is already known in Hismaic (see Graf & Zwettler 2004: 61) and Safaitic (Al-Jallad 2015: 343).

---

[7] In non-funerary ANA inscriptions it introduces the text indicating the person who is the subject of the inscription (see Macdonald 2006: 294f. and nn. 97–99 for details). We also encounter this situation in some Hismaic-Nabataean bilingual texts, where the introductory *l* in the ANA version is not graphically present in the Nabataean version (Hayajneh 2009b).

f ts^{2}wq 'and he longed for'.

m^{c}ṣ: this word could be understood in the light of Arabic *ma^{c}iṣa*, which has been given the meanings *ḫağila* 'be ashamed, embarrassed', and *ġaḍiba* 'be angry, annoyed' (Al-Ḥimyarī 1999: 6341 and *Lisān*, p. 4233). Other morphological variants with similar meanings can be found in Hava (1982: 727), *imta^{c}aṣa, tama^{cc}aṣa* 'to be in a rage'.

l-h 'to him'.

ḥnn is found as a verb in Safaitic meaning 'to show compassion' (e.g. C 31; and see Al-Jallad 2015: 323). In Classical Arabic, the root Ḥ-N-N means 'to be affected with grief, yearning' (Lane: 652c). Here, *ḥnn* clearly represents an abstract noun connected to Classical Arabic *ḥanīn* 'longing, yearning, desire' (Lane: 653c). This noun, which is the object of the verb *m^{c}ṣ*, bears the pronominal suffix of the third person singular, thus 'his yearning'.

The invocation is followed by a list of the names of the individuals for whom the writer invoked the 'mindfulness /remembrance' of Lt. To the best of my knowledge this is the longest chain of names listed in an individual ANA inscription. It should be noted that some of them are known from the inscription published by Graf and Zwettler (2004) from the same area: *ʾs^{1}lh*, *ʾrs^2*, *zdqm*, *qṭb*, *s^{1}ly*. The latter name could be compared with Nabataean *šlyw* (Al-Khraysheh 1986: 174). Similarly, the name *tmds^{2}r* (line 15), is known from the Nabataean onomasticon in the form *tymdwšrʾ* 'Knecht des *Ḏū Šarā*' (1986: 187). The second part of the name is, of course, the main deity worshipped by the Nabataeans and known in Safaitic as *ds^{2}r* and *ḏs^{2}r* (Al-Jallad 2015: 312). No exact historical conclusion can be drawn, however, as to whether this is an onomastic borrowing from Nabataean, but one may speculate that our text could have been composed in a Nabataean cultural context.

Concluding remarks

Both inscriptions studied here are an important addition to the previous corpus of ANA inscriptions discovered in central Jordan. More investigation and additional archaeological and epigraphical surveys are needed to understand such inscriptions in their cultural and historical contexts. One could suggest that both texts represent a linguistic and scribal community which lived in the Madaba area. The second text is the longest known ANA inscription. It provides us with a new lexical item, *m^{c}ṣ*, which presents interpretational difficulties due to the vague context of the text.

Acknowledgements

I am indebted to Prof. Daviau for asking me to publish the remaining epigraphical materials from this project. I am also deeply grateful to my colleagues, Ahmad Al-Jallad (Leiden University) and Jérôme Norris (PhD candidate at Université de Lorraine) for their comments on an early version of the reading of these inscriptions. J. Norris (personal communication, 3 October 2017) also commented on the reading of some signs in the second text.

Sigla

C	Safaitic inscriptions in *Corpus Inscriptionum Semiticarum. Pars V. Inscriptiones Saracenicas continens. Tomus 1. Inscriptiones Safaiticae*. Paris: Imprimerie nationale, 1950–1951.
KJA	Hismaic inscriptions from Wādī Judayyid Site A in King 1990 (see OCIANA).
KJC	Hismaic inscriptions from Wādī Judayyid Site C in King 1990 (see OCIANA).
Lane	Lane 1863–1893.
Lisān	Ibn Manẓūr [n.d.].
NST	Safaitic inscriptions in Harding 1951.
OCIANA	The Online Corpus of the Inscriptions of Ancient North Arabia at http://krc.orient.ox.ac.uk/ociana/index.php
RWQ	Safaitic inscriptions in Al-Rousan 2005.
TIJ	Inscriptions in Harding & Littmann 1952.

References

Bikai P. & Al-Khraysheh F. 2002. A Thamudic E Text from Mādabā. *Annual of the Department of Antiquities of Jordan* 46: 215–224.

Corbett G.J. 2010. Mapping the mute immortals: A locational and contextual analysis of Thamudic E/

Ḥismaic inscriptions and rock drawing from the Wādī Ḥafīr of southern Jordan. PhD thesis, University of Chicago. [Unpublished].

Graf D.F. & Zwettler M.J. 2004. The North Arabian 'Thamudic E' inscription from Uraynibah West. *Bulletin of the American Schools of Oriental Research* 335: 53–89.

Harding G.L. 1951. New Safaitic texts. *Annual of the Department of Antiquities of Jordan* 1: 25–29.

Harding G.L. & Littmann E. 1952. *Some Thamudic inscriptions from the Hashemite Kingdom of Jordan*. Leiden: Brill.

Hava J.G. 1982. *Al-Faraid Arabic-English dictionary*. Beirut: Dār al-mashriq.

Hayajneh H. 2009a. A fragmentary Ancient North Arabian inscription from al-Ḥuṣun-Kitim Area near Irbid, northern Jordan. *Zeitschrift des Deutschen Palästina-Vereins* 125: 176–178.

Hayajneh H. 2009b. Ancient North Arabian-Nabataean bilingual inscriptions from southern Jordan. *Proceedings of the Seminar for Arabian Studies* 39: 203–222.

Hayajneh H. 2016. Ancient North Arabian inscriptions, rock drawings, and tribal brands (*wasms*) from the Šammāḫ/ᵓAyl (ᵓĒl) region, Southern Jordan. Pages 505–541 in B. MacDonald, G.A. Clark, L.G. Herr, D.S. Quaintance, H. Hayajneh & J. Eggler, *The Shammakh to Ayl Archaeological Survey Southern Jordan (2010–2012)*. (American Schools of Oriental Research, Archaeological Reports, 24). Boston: American Schools of Oriental Research.

Hayajneh H. 2017a. Die frühnordarabischen vorislamischen Sprachformen in Südpalästina anhand epigraphischer Zeugnisse. Pages 171–230 in U. Huebner & H. Niehr (eds), *Kolloquium 2012 des Deutschen Vereins zur Erforschung Palästinas e.V. Sprachen in Palästina im 2. und 1. Jahrtausend v.Chr. DPV-Tagung 'Sprachen und Schriften in Palästina im 2. und 1. Jahrtausend v. Chr.* (Abhandlungen des Deutschen Palästinavereins, 43). Wiesbaden: Harrassowitz.

Hayajneh H. 2017b. An Ancient North Arabian inscribed *nefesh* stele from the vicinity of Jerash (north-western Jordan). *Syria* 94: 253–260.

Al-Ḥimyarī, Našwān b. Saᶜīd/ed. H. Al-ᶜAmrī, A.M. Al-Iryānī & Y.M. Abdallah. 1999. *Shams al-ᶜulum wa-dawā ᵓ kalām al-ᶜArab min al-kulum*. Beirut: Dar al-fikr al-muᶜāsir/Damascus: Dār al-fikr.

Ibn Manẓūr, Jamāl al-Dīn Abū al-Fadl Muhammad b. Mukarram al-Ansārī. [n.d.]. *Lisān al-ᶜArab*. Cairo: Dār Al-maᶜārif.

Al-Jallad A. 2015. *An outline of the grammar of the Safaitic inscriptions.* (Studies in Semitic Languages and Linguistics, 80). Leiden: Brill.

Al-Khraysheh F.H.1986. *Die Personennamen in den nabatäischen Inschriften des Corpus Inscriptionum Semiticarum.* Inaugural-Dissertation zur Erlangung der Doktorwürde des Fachbereichs Außereuropäische Sprachen und Kulturen der Philipps-Universität Marburg/Lahn.

King G.M.H. 1990. Early North Arabian Thamudic E: A preliminary description based on a new corpus of inscriptions from the Ḥismā desert of southern Jordan and published material. PhD thesis, School of Oriental and African Studies. Available at www.ancientarabia.co.uk/ (accessed June 2013).

Kootstra F. 2016. The language of the Taymanitic inscriptions and its classification. *Arabian Epigraphic Notes* 2: 67–140.

Krone S. 1992. *Die altarabische Gottheit al-Lāt*. (Heidelberger Orientalistische Studien, 23). Frankfurt am Main: Lang.

Lane E.W. 1863–1893. *An Arabic-English Lexicon: Derived from the best and the most copious Eastern sources*. London: Williams & Norgate.

Macdonald M.C.A. 2000. Reflections on the linguistic map of pre-Islamic Arabia. *Arabian Archaeology and Epigraphy* 11: 28–79. [Reprinted with addenda and corrigenda as article III in M.C.A.Macdonald, *Literacy and identity in pre-Islamic Arabia*. (Variorum Collected Studies, CS906). Farnham: Ashgate, 2009.

Macdonald M.C.A. 2004. Ancient North Arabian. Pages. 488–531 in R.D. Woodard (ed.), *The Cambridge Encyclopedia of the World's Ancient Languages*. Cambridge: Cambridge University Press.

Macdonald M.C.A. 2006. Burial between the desert and the sown. Cave-tombs and inscriptions near Dayr al-Kahf in Jordan. *Damaszener Mitteilungen* 15: 273–301.

Al-Rousan M. 2005. Nuqūsh ṣafawiyyah min Wādī Qaṣṣāb bi-ᵓl-Urdunn. PhD thesis, Ǧāmiᶜat al-malik Saᶜūd, Al-Riyāḍ. [Unpublished].

Author's address

Hani Hayajneh, Faculty of Archaeology and Anthropology, Yarmouk University, Irbid, Jordan.
e-mail hani@yu.edu.jo

M.C.A. Macdonald (ed.), *Languages, scripts and their uses in ancient North Arabia.* (Supplement to volume 48 of the Proceedings of the Seminar for Arabian Studies). Oxford: Archaeopress, 2018: 101–109

Understanding Safaitic inscriptions in their topographical context

ALI AL-MANASER

Summary

The first aim of this paper is to determine whether there is a relationship between the locations in which Safaitic inscriptions are found and the interpretation of the inscriptions themselves. The second aim is to use the results of the Badia Surveys of the OCIANA project to focus on the different shapes of the cairns (*rujūm*) on which Safaitic inscriptions are very often found and the different names used to describe them in the Arabic dialect of the local Jordanian Bedouin.

Keywords: Safaitic inscriptions, Bedouin Arabic dialect, ancient North Arabia, OCIANA, cairns

Introduction

It is important to consider context when interpreting inscriptions, and this includes understanding the geographical landscape in which they were found and any relationship between these locations and the content of the inscriptions themselves. I will examine this relationship in the case of two stones, which were found by the Badia Epigraphic Survey (BS) in 2015.[1] During this season, we made a systematic survey of an area in the Jordanian *ḥarrah* from Wādī al-Ḥašād in the west to Wādī and Biyār al-Ghuṣayn in the east (Fig. 1).

The *ḥarrah* is made up of a number of different types of landscape and the BS team found inscriptions in most of them. The spread was not even, however, and the number of inscriptions found varied considerably across the area. For example, in some locations, we discovered only one inscription, while in another we found more than 1500. Most inscriptions were found on hilltops and/or cairns, *rujūm* (sg. *rujm*). At the junction of two wadis, there was, in most cases, one or more cairns. By contrast, in areas where there were no wadis, there were generally no cairns and we found the fewest inscriptions (Fig. 2).

Examples of inscriptions whose location is important for the understanding of the text[2]

BS 1 (Fig. 3/A)

l ṯfl bn frʾ bn frd w qbr bny-h b-h-mẓr
By Ṯfl son of Frʾ son of Frd and he buried his son(s) at the lookout point.[3]

Commentary

This first example was found on the very top of a hill which is one of Tell al-ᶜAbd's *ᶜiyāl* ('dependents'). Tell al-ᶜAbd wa-ᶜiyāl-hu[4] consists of a large hill with a line of much smaller hills (the *ᶜiyāl*) running for some 12 km north-west of it (Fig. 4). Tell al-ᶜAbd itself is considered to be one of the largest hills in the Jordanian *ḥarrah*. The area on and around it has a particular abundance of inscriptions, many of which were first discovered and recorded by F.V. Winnett and his research team during his survey in 1950 (Winnett 1957: nos. 673–913). The OCIANA Team has since re-recorded some of these

[1] The team members were Michael Macdonald, Ali Al-Manaser, and Joseph O'Hara from the University of Oxford, and Chiara della Puppa from the University of Leiden. The survey was made under the auspices of the Online Corpus of the Inscriptions of Ancient North Arabia (OCIANA) at the Khalili Research Centre, University of Oxford (http://krc.orient.ox.ac.uk/ociana/index.php) and the inscriptions recorded have been published in the OCIANA database.

[2] The editorial symbols are as follows: { } in the transliteration enclose letters whose reading is doubtful; in the translations they enclose the whole name or word, one or more letters of which are marked as doubtful in the transliteration; {/} indicates alternative interpretations of the same letter; [ ] enclose letters or words which are restored; ---- indicates a damaged area of the text.

[3] Note that *bny-h* could mean 'his sons', 'his two sons', or 'his little son'. Safaitic orthography provides no means of distinguishing *baniy-uh from *banay-uh from *bunay-uh. For the pronunciation of the 3 masc. sg. enclitic pronoun, see Al-Jallad 2015: 96.

[4] Tell al-ᶜAbd lies at 32° 25' 18.31" N 37° 19' 44.12" E. It is also known as Tlāl or Tulūl al-ᶜAbd wa-ᶜiyāl-hu or Qiṭār al-ᶜAbd.

FIGURE 1. *A map of the Jordanian ḥarrah desert showing the survey area, from Wādi Al-Ḥašād in the west to Wādī al-Ghuṣayn and Biyār al-Ghuṣayn in the east.*

FIGURE 2. *A map showing the locations where numerous inscriptions were found.*

Figure 3. A. *Inscription BS 1;* **B.** *the lookout point where it was found and which is mentioned in the inscription;* **C.** *a grave possibly the one mentioned in the inscription;* **D.** *the extensive view from this lookout point.*

Figure 4. *A view from the summit of Tell al-ᶜAbd, looking north-west (photograph A. Al-Manaser).*

inscriptions with photographs and GPS points, as well as all those that Winnett did not record on the twelve members of the Tell al-ᶜAbd wa-ᶜiyāl-hu group of hills. We found BS 1 (above) on the most south-easterly of those of the *ᶜiyāl* which reach into Qāᶜ al-ᶜAbd. It was the only inscription found on this hill and was located at the very top, near a grave which may have been that of the author's son(s) (Fig. 3/B–D).

It can be seen from Figure 3/C–D that the site is aptly described in the inscription as a *mẓr*, a lookout point, and it is possible that the author's son(s) was/were killed while keeping watch up there and were buried where they died. But we also know from Arabic literature and Bedouin culture that it remains very important for families to bury their loved ones on hilltops and other high places so that the graves are easily recognizable by visitors or relatives who return to the site. One example comes from the poet Mālik son of al-Rayb (early eighth century AD) when, in his most famous poem *Marṯiyat Mālik bin al-Rayb*, he asked his friends to bury him on a high place, so that anyone who passed by it could see his grave (Al-Joulan 2010: 38–40). This is surely why almost every hilltop in the *ḥarrah* is surmounted by a cairn. Knowing the physical location of this inscription thus gives us a far more intense appreciation of its meaning and significance to the author than we would have if we simply saw it on the page or in a close-up photograph.

BS 2130 (Fig. 5)

This stone bears thirteen inscriptions of which only BS 2130 will be discussed here. Readings and translations of the remaining inscriptions, BS 2131–2142, and a description of the drawing will be found in the Appendix.

l ᶜwḏ bn rġḍ bn mfny bn s^{2}rk bn ġyrʾl w gls^{1} h- ḥrf w ẖṭṭ f hlt s^{1}lm w nqʾt b- wdd l-ḏ yᶜwr h-s^{1}fr

By ᶜwḏ son of Rġḍ son of Mfny son of S^{2}rk son of Ġyrʾl and he stopped briefly on this **ledge** [of the tell] and he carved [this inscription] so O Lt [grant] security and [inflict] ejection from the grave by a loved one on whoever scratches out the inscription.

Commentary

This example is a stone which was found at the edge of the summit of Tell al-ᶜAbd itself (Fig. 4). As noted above, it bears thirteen inscriptions and a drawing, and the author

Figure 5. *Inscriptions BS 2130–2142.*

of BS 2130 says that he stopped briefly at this ledge and carved [this inscription]. Can we really understand what the author was trying to express if we view this text in isolation? Central to our understanding is the word *ḥrf*. In Arabic, *ḥarf* can mean 'summit' in general, such as a hilltop, and this is the translation which has been proposed for the word *ḥrf* in other graffiti found in this location (see for instance SIJ 752 discussed below). Another possible meaning of *ḥarf* in Arabic, however, is 'edge' or 'corner'. For example, in Arabic *ḥarf al-jabal* means 'cliff edge', or the very edge of the summit of a mountain. Considered in isolation, the exact meaning of *ḥarf* is not clear from this inscription — the author could be referring to the summit of the hill in general, or to its very edge. I believe that if the inscription is considered in relation to the place in which it was found, the correct interpretation of the word *ḥarf* in this case is 'cliff edge' or 'ledge'.

This should also enable us to understand SIJ 752 more clearly.

SIJ 752: *l rb^{c}t bn fṣ^{c} w nẓr h- ḥrf*
By Rb^{c}t son of Fṣ^{c} and he guarded the mountain top

Winnett translated *nẓr h-ḥrf* as 'he was on the look out for comrades' but OCIANA has translated it as 'he guarded the hill-top', taking into account that it was found on top of Tell al-^{c}Abd.

Different types of cairn in the Jordanian *ḥarrah*

While working in the *ḥarrah* we found that, unsurprisingly, the local Ahl al-Jabal Bedouin have different words to describe different kinds of cairn (Fig. 6). So far, however, only one of these words has been found in the Safaitic inscriptions where *rgm* and *ṣwy* appear to be the only terms used for 'a cairn'. Nevertheless, it may be helpful to be able to give the different kinds of cairn a distinctive name.

On the tops of the hills of Tell al-^{c}Abd wa-^{c}ayāl-hu, we found cairns of two different forms (Figs 7 & 8). Judging from the shapes of A and B in Figure 8, it is possible that they could be tombs. If this is the case, then the first structure could perhaps have been built as a simple circular *rujm*, and the square structure subsequently added to enable visitors to the grave to carve inscriptions such as prayers for, or memories of, the dead person. The square structure (A) consists mostly of thick stone and the majority of the inscriptions on it are simply people's names. On the other hand, the small stones lying on the ground *inside* the square structure include long inscriptions incised with very fine, elegant characters. Generally, the inscriptions include a genealogy, a narrative, and a prayer. The last usually invokes several deities. It is possible that local people carved the inscriptions on these small stones and presented them during a religious ritual but it is, of course, impossible to prove this.

There are many well-known examples of *rujūm* that were built for one specific person, such as the Cairn of *Haniʾ* (Harding 1953) or the Cairn of Ward (AMSI 9, 10, 36, 68, 69, 96, 150–153),[5] but excavation of further examples is needed before we can confirm whether there is any significance in the differences between the square, circular, and triangular varieties of *rujm* and whether there is a relationship between the shape of the *rujm* and any religious ritual that may have been carried out there. Another interesting subject for future research would be to analyse the distribution of the verb *ḏbḥ* 'to sacrifice' (e.g. BS 891). The OCIANA team discovered twenty-three examples of this verb in one place, inscribed on

[5] See also the cairn of S^{1c}d excavated by G.L. Harding (1978) and the cairn of Ḫrg bnt Ġṯ excavated by V.A. Clark (1981).

Rujm	رجم	This is a cairn of stones piled on top of each other, sometimes in a pyramid shape and sometimes with no obvious shape (see Lane, 1048b–c).
Zmīlah	زميلة	This is the same shape as a *rujm* cairn but is found mostly in flat areas, whereas *rujm* cairns are typically found in high areas
Marqāb	مرقاب	This is derived from the verb *raqaba*, to watch over (Lane, 1132c–1133a). These are always found in high places and are always round, consisting of several courses of stones. These could be watch-towers or look-out posts (Figure 7: A)
Qaṣrīyah	قصرية	This word is derived from the word, *qaṣr* meaning 'a palace'. These are typically square in shape, although we did discover some pentagonal cairns of this class. These are built in courses, similarly to the *marqāb* (Figure 7: C)

Figure 6. *A table listing the different words for cairn among the Ahl al-Jabal in the Jordanian* ḥarrah.

Figure 7. *Different types of cairn in the* ḥarrah.

a path leading to a *rujm*. These will be published in the OCIANA database.

Conclusion

I hope to have shown that a knowledge of the topography of the location where an inscription was found can sometimes help in the interpretation of the text. In former times, the amount of film that could be carried by an expedition and kept cool meant that the number of photographs taken was severely limited and most inscriptions were recorded as hand-copies. At the same time, before the advent of GPS it was extremely difficult to provide precise records of the location of inscriptions. Now that digital photography with GPS is readily available, I hope that more attention will be paid to recording the topographic locations of inscriptions as this will greatly add to our understanding of the circumstances in which their authors carved them.

Appendix

BS 2130 shares the stone with a remarkable drawing and twelve other Safaitic inscriptions, five of which are by brothers of the author of BS2130 and 2131 and most of the others are probably by more distant relatives.

BS 2131 (Fig. 5)

l ᶜwḏ bn rġḍ bn mfny bn s^{2}rk h- ḫṭṭ
By ᶜwḏ son of Rġḍ son of Mfny son of S^{2}rk is the carving

Commentary

This is by the same author as that of BS 2130 (see above). Unfortunately, *ḫṭṭ* simply means carving and so could refer to either the inscription, or the drawing, or both. The author of BS 2139, however, attributes the drawing to *ᶜwḏ*, and so it is probable that *ᶜwḏ* intended to claim both. The drawing shows a rider with long hair standing on end, sitting on the hump of a female camel (note the curled tail, see Searight 1983: 575; Macdonald, forthcoming) which he is guiding with a single rein running from his left hand to its nose and a camel-stick held in his right. He is seated on a saddle cloth shown by criss-crossing lines and possibly two short tassels. What look like long tassels may be intended to represent the rider's legs and feet, both shown on the visible side in a common convention in Arabian rock art

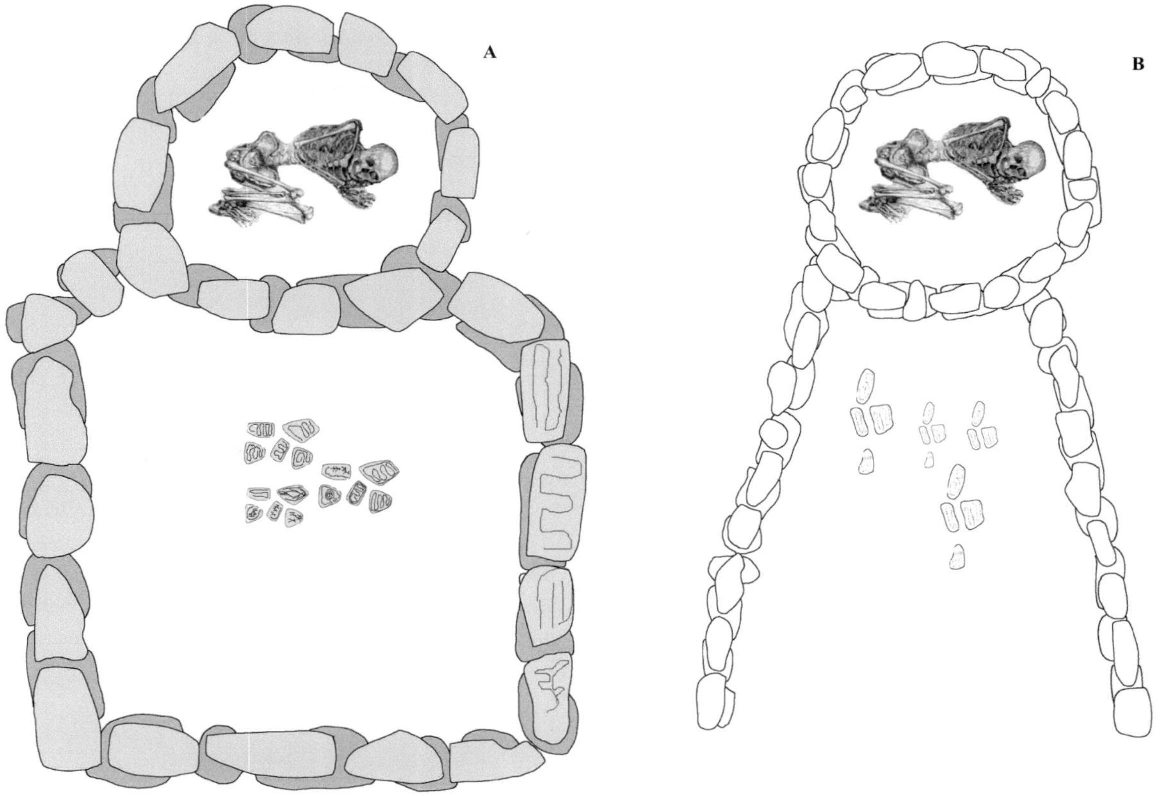

Figure 8. A. *A square enclosure, with a* rujm *beside one of its edges;*
B. *an isosceles triangle with only two sides and a circular* rujm *at one end.*

(see Macdonald 2009: 161). At the level of his thighs, rather than his waist, is what looks like a dagger, but note that the bulbous shape at the top end of it is the final letter of BS 2132 with hammering over it. There is what looks like a small hump behind the base of the camel's neck, but this is presumably a mistake in the drawing.[6] There is what might be a girth with two long tassels on it. Behind the rider is a long object ending at the top in what looks like a hand (?), which might be a bow-case and, very unusually, two lunate hilted swords. Immediately behind them is what is either a slightly misshapen shield (they are usually circular, not oval) or a water skin. A tasselled bag hangs down below this, which may be the bag that is placed over the camel's udders to prevent the calf from suckling. In front of the camel is an oryx (note the long straight horns and the hump behind the neck) drawn in the same style.

[6] It is unlikely to be a Bactrian camel as, although these are occasionally shown in Arabian rock art (e.g. LP 325 in OCIANA, and Macdonald, forthcoming), the heavier neck and large amounts of hair are always emphasized, as well as the two humps.

BS 2132 (Fig. 5)

This text starts behind the camel's hump and crosses the drawing before curling up in front of the rider. The last letter is hammered over, producing the bulbous shape at the top of the rider's dagger.

l mlk bn m{f}{n}y bn {q}dm bn mfny bn nᶜmn bn wh[b]
By Mlk son of {Mfny} son of {Qdm} son of Mfny son of Nᶜmn son of {Whb}

BS 2133 (Fig. 5). The inscription is carved on the bottom left-hand side of the face and the end has been destroyed.

l s¹lmn bn s²ḥl bn mfny bn s²rk bn ġyrʾl ----
By S¹lmn son of S²ḥl son of Mfny son of S²rk son of Ġyrʾl

BS 2134 (Fig. 5). The inscription is very thinly scratched below BS 2133.

l r{ẖ}{ʿ}l{t} bnt qdm bn q{ḏ}{y}
By {Rẖʿlt} daughter of Qdm son of {Qḏy}

BS 2135 (Fig. 5). This text begins between the camel's hind feet.

l ʾs^{1}lm bn tm bn ṯlg bn zbdy
By ʾs^{1}lm son of Tm son of Ṯlg son of Zbdy

BS 2136 (Fig. 5). This inscription begins in bold thick letters below the camel's udder-bag.

l ns^{2}l bn rġḍ bn mfny bn s^{2}rk
By Ns^{2}l son of Rġḍ son of Mfny son of S^{2}rk

BS 2137 (Fig. 5). This begins below the possible feet of the rider.

l ġṯ bn rġḍ bn mfny bn s^{2}rk bn ġyrʾl
By Ġṯ son of Rġḍ son of Mfny son of S^{2}rk son of Ġyrʾl

BS 2138 (Fig. 5). This begins just behind the camel's front legs.

l ls^{2}ms^1 bn s^{2}ḥl bn mfny bn s^{2}rk
By Ls^{2}ms^1 son of S^{2}ḥl son of Mfny son of S^{2}rk

BS 2139 (Fig. 5). This begins between the front of the camel's neck and the hind legs of the oryx.

l mfny bn s^{2}ḥl bn mfny bn s^{2}rk w wgd dmyt ʿwḏ f ts^{2}wq
By Mfny son of S^{2}ḥl son of Mfny son of S^{2}rk and he found the drawing of ʿwḏ, so he yearned [for him]

The *ʿwḏ* here refers to the author of BS 2130 and 2131 above.

BS 2140 (Fig. 5). This starts above the oryx and continues below it.

l ḫṭs^{1}t bn {q}{ḏ}{y} bn qdm bn {q}d[m] [bn] mfny
By Ḫṭs^{1}t son of {Qḏy} son of Qdm son of {Qdm} {son of} Mfny

The end of the text is confused. It is difficult to interpret the *{w}d* before *mfny*. The latter looks at first sight to be *mġny*, but on close inspection, the upper stroke of the *f* can be seen.

BS 2141 (Fig. 5). On the adjoining face of the stone, starting at the bottom and curling up to the top.

l rmzn bn qdm bn rmzn bn mfny w gls^1
By Rmzn son of Qdm son of Rmzn son of Mfny and he stopped briefly [here]

BS 2142 (Fig. 5). On the same face as BS 2141, carved vertically downwards.

l {z}{d} bn rgl
By {Zd} son of Rgl

Acknowledgements

I would like to thank the OCIANA project for allowing me to use its materials, and Lydia Ellis for her suggestions. Without the help and support received from M.C.A. Macdonald, this paper would not have been completed, and I would like to extend my gratitude to him.

Sigla

AMSI	Inscriptions recorded by Ali Al-Manaser in Wādī al-Ḥashād, Jordan in 2004 and published in OCIANA.
BS	Inscriptions recorded by the Badia Survey in north-eastern Jordan in 2015 and published in OCIANA.
LP	Safaitic inscriptions in Littmann 1943.
OCIANA	Online Corpus of the Inscriptions of Ancient North Arabia http://krc.orient.ox.ac.uk/ociana/index.php
SIJ	Safaitic inscriptions in Winnett 1957.

References

Clark V.A. 1981. Archaeological investigations at two burial cairns in the Ḥarra Region of Jordan. *Annual of the Department of Antiquities of Jordan* 25: 235–265.

Harding G.L. 1953. The cairn of Haniʾ. *Annual of the Department of Antiquities of Jordan* 2: 8–56.

Harding G.L. 1978. The cairn of Saʿd. Pages 242–249

in P.R.S. Moorey & P.J. Parr (eds), *Archaeology in the Levant: Essays for Kathleen Kenyon*. Warminster: Aris & Phillips.

Al-Jallad A. 2015. *An outline of the grammar of the Safaitic inscriptions*. (Studies in Semitic Languages and Linguistics, 80). Leiden: Brill.

Al-Joulan N.A. 2010. Aesthetic dying: The Arab's heroic encounter with death. *Canadian Social Science* 6/6: 31–44.

Littmann E. 1943. *Safaïtic inscriptions*. (Syria. Publications of the Princeton University Archaeological Expeditions to Syria in 1904–1905 and 1909. Division IV. Section C). Leiden: Brill.

Macdonald M.C.A. 2009. Wheels in a land of camels: another look at the chariot in Arabia. *Arabian Archaeology and Epigraphy* 20: 156–184.

Macdonald M.C.A. (forthcoming). Camels in the rock art of Arabia. In D. Alexander (ed.), *The Camel*. Riyadh: King Abdulaziz Public Library.

Searight A. 1983. The Rock-Art Survey 1982. In M.C.A. Macdonald & A. Searight, Inscriptions and rock-art of the Jawa Area 1982: A preliminary report. *Annual of the Department of Antiquities of Jordan* 27: 575–576.

Winnett F.V. 1957. *Safaitic inscriptions from Jordan*. (Near and Middle East Series, 2). Toronto: University of Toronto Press.

Author's address

Ali Al-Manaser, Khalili Research Centre, University of Oxford, 3 St John Street, Oxford, OX1 2LG, UK.
e-mail ali.al-manaser@orinst.ox.ac.uk

M.C.A. Macdonald (ed.), *Languages, scripts and their uses in ancient North Arabia.* (Supplement to volume 48 of the Proceedings of the Seminar for Arabian Studies). Oxford: Archaeopress, 2018: 111–119

The earliest attestation of *laysa* and the implications for its etymology

Ahmad Al-Jallad

Summary
This paper edits a Safaitic inscription containing the negator *laysa*, its earliest attestation in Arabic. Based on its form, I revisit the origins of *laysa* in Arabic as a whole and suggest a few possible scenarios to account for its source and shape.

Keywords: Arabic grammar, Safaitic inscription, Semitic linguistics, negative copula, *laysa*

Introduction

The negative copula *laysa* is unique to Arabic. Unlike its affirmative counterpart *kāna*, it conjugates only in the suffix conjugation as a medial weak verb and belongs to a class entirely of its own: in the long-vowel grade, it has a diphthong rather than a true long vowel, and in the short-vowel grade, its theme vowel is an /a/ rather than a high vowel, as in all other verbs of this class (Fig. 1).

	lys neg. cop.	qwm 'to stand'	nwm 'to sleep'
3ms (long-vowel grade)	*laysa*	*qāma*	*nāma*
3fs (long-vowel grade)	*laysat*	*qāmat*	*nāmat*
1cs (short-vowel grade)	*lastu*	*qumtu*	*nimtu*
2mp (short-vowel grade)	*lastum*	*qumtum*	*nimtum*

Figure 1. *The conjugation of* laysa.

The isolated morphological nature of *laysa* has attracted much attention in the scholarship. The main opinion seems to be that it reflects the combination of the negator *lā and an existential particle cognate with North-West Semitic *ʾiṯ (Lipiński 2001: §47.10), grammaticalized into a quasi-verb. Considering this word together with the rarer form *lāta*, Lipiński suggested that they were borrowed into Arabic, but does not go on to specify a source. Lipiński's reconstruction was discussed in detail by Măcelaru (2003), who supported the etymology of *laysa* as explained above but contests the plausibility of borrowing, mainly because there would be no source language from which Arabic could have taken over the word with an [s].[1] Instead, Măcelaru proposes that the construction, along with its alleged affirmative counterpart *ʾays*,[2] are inherited from a Proto-Semitic construction containing a reflex of the existential particle, which he reconstructs as *yṯ. This is despite the fact that Arabic [s] = *s^1 is not the regular reflex of Proto-Semitic *ṯ.[3] The supposed irregular correspondences in the reflex of the existential particle are the subject of his 2003 essay, but it is only the Arabic form that exhibits

[1] Aramaic has a *t*/*ṯ* and Akkadian and Canaanite have *š* [ʃ]. While Măcelaru expects North-West Semitic š to be loaned into Arabic with *šīn* [ʃ], this is in fact not what is attested. Early loans containing š are almost always rendered with Arabic *sīn* [s], probably because this was the only pure voiceless sibilant in early Arabic, the *šīn* originally being a lateral, see the discussion in Al-Jallad 2017: 138–140. This pattern is clearly illustrated in Classical Arabic words like *yasūʿ* 'Jesus' < yēšūʿ, and in Safaitic *s^{1}bṭ* [sabāṭ] 'January-February' < Aramaic šbāṭ (Al-Jallad 2016: 96–97).

[2] I have doubts that *ʾays* is an authentic word: firstly because it occurs only in dictionaries, and always in the same phrase *ʾaysa wa laysa*, and never in authentic early texts. It is likely that writers such as al-Kindī based their use of the term on such lexicographical works. Its absence in earlier sources makes its existence highly suspicious, and I therefore think it is safer to regard it as a back-formation rather than a truly productive existential particle (Al-Jallad 2015a: 42), agreeing with Murtonen (1989: Section Bb, 223).

[3] Other attempts at explaining the problematic sound correspondences exist. Blau (1998: 224–225) proposes a Proto-Semitic doublet for 'being', *ʾīṯay and *yis (yiš in Blau's transcription), the latter giving rise to the Arabic negative form *laysa* and the Akkadian forms. This attempt simply recasts the problem as an explanation, and moreover does not address the problematic morphology of the form in Arabic. Bauer (1926: 8–10) proposed a more creative solution: he suggests that *laysa* was the result of taboo deformation to avoid confusion with 'lion' *layṯ*. Blau (1998: 224–225) considers this explanation absurd.

an irregular reflex.[4] The North-West Semitic forms can easily be derived from an original *ʾiṯ/*yiṯ.[5]

Măcelaru goes on to discuss the problems of finding a suitable cognate in East Semitic. He provides examples of the verb 'to have' written with the *s*-sign, thought to represent a sibilant, and *š*-sign, thought to represent an interdental, claiming this undermines a straightforward identification of the final consonant of the existential particle (2003: 234).There is, however, no reason to assume a direct connection between the existential particle and the Akkadian verb *išu/iši* 'to have'.[6] One should also mention that the orthographic practice of spelling the etymological interdental with *š* is not stable in Old Akkadian and there is certainly a trend towards the merger of the interdental and the voiceless sibilant (Hasselbach 2005: 143). Nevertheless, the true existential verb is spelled with the *š*-signs, *ba-ša-um* /baṯāʾum/, indicating that it contained an interdental, although its connection with North-West Semitic *ʾiṯ, if any, is unclear. The ṯ-final reconstruction is supported by Eblaite, which attests *i-ša-wu* as an existential verb (Lipiński 2001: 478; Măcelaru 2003: 234), although just how it relates to North-West Semitic *ʾiṯ/*yiṯ is not explained. Thus, the only problematic form is the Arabic and therefore, rather than reshuffling the sound correspondences as we know them to suit the Arabic situation, it seems, despite Măcelaru's protests, that the Arabic form is either wholly unrelated to the *ʾiṯ/*yiṯ of North-West and possibly East Semitic, or it is a loan.

The negative copula *laššu* [lassu], *lāšu* [lāsu] is attested in Assyrian[7] and *lašu* [lāṯu] and *laišu* [lāiṯū] are found in Old Akkadian. The Old Akkadian spelling la-ì-šu$_4$,[8] suggests an original lā-(y)i/īṯu(w), similar to the Ebliate *i-ša-wu* (yṯw) but negated.

While one gets the general impression that many scholars regard *laysa* as a loan, it is rather difficult to find this opinion explicitly argued for. Like Lipiński (2001: §47.10), Gevirtz (1957: 126, n. 22) suggests that Arabic *laysa* is a 'West Semitic' loan but does not propose an exact source. Jeffery (1938: 253) discussed the Aramaic origin of *lāta* but does not mention *laysa*. Healey seems to imply a connection between *laysa* and *layta*, the latter being a loan from Aramaic, but does not go into detail (2011: 649). Brockelmann (1908–1913, i: 501, §253Bc) pointed out the similarity between Arabic *laysa* and Neo-Assyrian *laššu* [lassu] and *lāšu* [lāsu] (see also Hämeen-Anttila 2000: 108; Soden 1959–1981: 339) but stops short of suggesting borrowing. Măcelaru (2003: 234) dismisses the possibility of borrowing into Arabic from Neo-Assyrian because the latter lacks the glide *y*, but with the attestation of Old Akkadian *lāiṯu*, possibilities of later spoken Assyrian dialects containing a glide in this position can be entertained.

One may doubt the possibility of contact between Arabic and Neo-Assyrian, especially to the degree to which a negative existential particle could be borrowed. The earliest attestation of *laysa* until now was the Quranic Consonantal Text (QCT), where it conjugates fully in the suffix conjugation. *Laysa* is common in Middle Arabic texts, where it does not inflect, in Andalusi Arabic as *las*, and many modern dialects of south-west Arabia, exhibit a variety of reflexes including *lays*, *lēs*, *las*, and *lis*.[9] Thus, if we regard it as a loan and take the QCT as our starting point, the most plausible source would be Aramaic; indeed, the form *lāta* is quite transparently a borrowing of Aramaic *layt*.[10] Yet, here Măcelaru's objections resonate. From which variety of Aramaic should Arabic have taken over *lays*? In 2015, I wrote a defence of the Aramaic source, arguing that we should not view borrowing necessarily into a form of Classical Arabic, but that it was possible that a construction *lāʾ-iṯ* was loaned into a dialect of Arabic without interdentals, providing evidence for such dialects in the pre-Islamic period. In such a dialect, it is conceivable that /ṯ/ could have been rendered as [s] (Al-Jallad 2015a: 43–44). The Safaitic inscription that I will study in the

[4] Măcelaru (2003: 234) has also included the Modern South Arabian *śi* [ɬi] into his group of problematic etyma, but there is no reason, besides its function, to consider the Modern South Arabian form a reflex of a putative Proto-Semitic **yiṯ* or **yis* since it has absolutely nothing in common phonologically with this reconstructed form. Wilmsen (2014) picked up this connection and produced a monograph arguing for it, but his arguments have failed to convince most specialists, e.g. Al-Jallad (2015a); Souag (2016); Pat-El (2016). Since the problems with this assumption have been fully fleshed out in the aforementioned works and alternative interpretations provided, I will not discuss Modern South Arabian *śi* in this essay.

[5] These are Ugaritic *ʾiṯ*, Official Aramaic *ʾyty*, Old Aramaic *yš* /yiṯ/ (= *lyšh* in the Bar Rakib inscription), Hebrew *yēš*.

[6] See Testen (2000) on reservations regarding this connection.

[7] The form is attested once with stative suffixes in Old Assyrian lá-šu-a-tí-ni /lassuātīni/ 'you were/are (?) absent' but is in all other cases not conjugated. This would seem to reflect the sporadic extension of these suffixes to the form.

[8] See Milano & Westenholz 2015; I owe this reference and the discussion of the Assyrian material to Mr Ø. Bjøru. Errors in its presentation and interpretation are my own.

[9] For a good overview of *laysa* in all of its forms in Arabic, see Wilmsen (2016) and the references there.

[10] Following Jeffery 1938; recently, Grande (2016) has offered a creative Arabic-internal etymology, namely a combination of *lā* and *ta*, which he calls a deictic modifier. He does not explain why *lāta* should not be understood as a loan from Aramaic, and his construing of the second syllable of this construction as a deictic modifier, connected to the feminine ending (!), fails to convince me. One may also regard the Arabic *layta* as a related particle, both ultimately deriving from Aramaic.

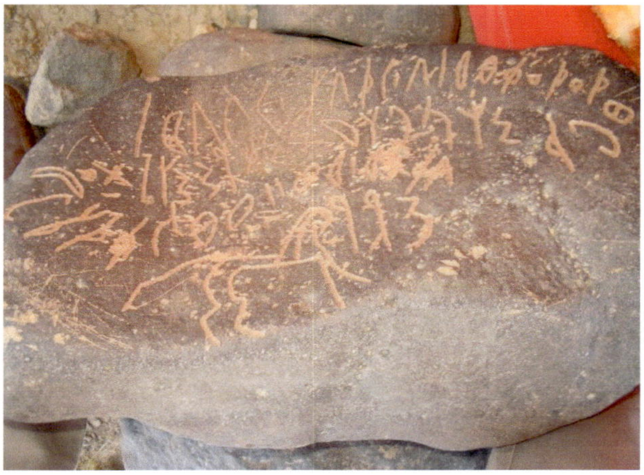

Figure 2. *AMSI 41 (photograph ʿAli Al-Manaser, courtesy of OCIANA).*

Figure 3. *A tracing of AMSI 41 (by the author).*

following section, I believe, renders this scenario rather unlikely. At the same time, it pushes back the date of *laysa* at least half a millennium,[11] suggesting that its source may not be Aramaic at all. In the following section, I will provide an edition of the inscription containing *laysa* and in part three revisit the etymology of this word in light of the Safaitic evidence.

The inscription

The inscription AMSI 41 was discovered by Ali Al-Manaser in 2004 in Wādī al-Ḥašād in the Mafraq Governorate, north-eastern Jordan.[12] It was published in OCIANA in 2017 with a reading of the glyphs but without an interpretation or commentary. The reading given by the *editio princeps* (*ed. princ.*) is thus:

l ms^{1}k bn ˀs^{1}d bn s^{1}lm w qʿd ʿd wrd f ḏkr h-mt f qṣf f h lt ʿmr ṣdq-k w gnn gmn m{t} {d}s^1 fṣy

After a close examination of the photographs (Figs 2 & 3), I have concluded that the reading of the last two clauses is incorrect. My new reading of the text and translation is as follows:

l ms^{1}k bn ˀs^{1}d bn s^{1}lm w qʿd<ʿd> w rd f ḏkr h-mt f qṣf f h lt ʿmr ṣdq-k w gnn w mn mt ls^1 fṣy

'By Ms^{1}k son of ˀs^{1}d son of S^{1}lm and he halted again, while going to water, and remembered the dead and grieved so, O Lt, give long life to your righteous [servant] and protect [him] but from death there is no deliverance.'

The personal names

The genealogy *ms^{1}k bn ˀs^{1}d bn s^{1}lm* occurs only one more time in the OCIANA corpus, in the inscription AAEK 322. The text is written in the same script style, the so-called fine-letter forms (Clark 1979: 70), so it is possible that this text was produced by the same individual. Nevertheless, all three names are extremely common in Safaitic and one cannot therefore rule out a coincidence.

Narrative

qʿd <ʿd> wrd

The first clause of the narrative poses several difficulties in its interpretation. The verb *qʿd* is clearly connected to Classical Arabic (CAr) *qaʿada* 'to sit' and is attested only six times in the corpus. It is used three times in conjunction with verbs of grieving or remembering; in these contexts, I would suggest that the verb means 'to halt':[13]

[11] The dating of the Safaitic inscriptions is notoriously difficult. Conventionally, the entire corpus is placed between the first century BC and the fourth century AD, but this is only a guess. The present inscription, however, is carved in the so-called 'fine script' (Clark 1979: 70). Texts produced in this hand tend to refer to events within this time frame, when they refer to recognizable events at all.

[12] Precise coordinates are: *Lat.* 32.510104, *Long.* 37.320623. I thank K. Jaworska for bringing this unique text to my attention during our work on the Safaitic dictionary.

[13] The custom of stopping to weep for loved ones is well attested in the Classical Arabic poetic tradition and a number of scholars have remarked upon this similarity, e.g. Eksell (2002; 2005).

ASWS 70: *qᶜd f bky ᶜl-ʾḫt-h mtt*

'he halted and wept for his sister who died'

WR.A 19: *qᶜd f ḏkr h-mt f bʾs m ẓll*

'he halted and remembered the dead, for those who remain (alive) despair'

KRS 863: *f qᶜ[d]t f bkt*

'so she {halted} and wept'

The interpretation of the following five letters is open to several possibilities. We can take the following *ᶜd* as dittography, and simply omit it from the interpretation. This would produce the translation:

qᶜd <ᶜd> wrd 'he halted while going to water' or 'while going to the lowlands (= descending)'.[14]

It is also possible to interpret the *w* as a conjunction, producing *qᶜd w rd* 'he paused and then returned'.

qᶜd ᶜd wrd

The second interpretation takes the second *ᶜd* as intentional. One may suggest that it is a preposition *ᶜad*, cognate with, for example, Aramaic *ᶜad* 'until'. In my view, however, this fails to produce a meaningful sentence: 'he paused until going for water' or 'until descending'. It is better, I think, to take *ᶜd* as a variant of the adverb *ᶜwd* 'again',[15] meaning: 'he halted while going to water/the lowlands yet again'. The sense of halting yet again to weep, emphasizing the tragedies the author has experienced, seems very appropriate for this genre of text. This is my preferred interpretation.

f ḏkr h-mt f qṣf

The exact phrase following *qᶜd* is attested in WR.A 19. The substantive *mt* is probably the equivalent of CAr *mawtā*, the plural of *mayyit* 'dead' (Lane, 2724b).[16] The verb *qṣf* is one of the many verbs of grieving in Safaitic (Abbadi & al-Manaser 2016: 48) and suits the present context well.

f h lt ᶜmr ṣdq-k w gnn

This is the first attestation of such a prayer and it is worth discussing each of its words individually.

Figure 4. *The negative of* ls^1 *in AMSI 41.*

ᶜmr: the word *ᶜmr* here is best understood as a denominal imperative, probably a D-stem, of the noun *ᶜmr* 'long life'. The noun is attested, for example, in the following prayer:

SIJ 688:[17]

wgd ʾṯr hnʾḫyr f ql l-ʾl-h h-ᶜmr

'he found the traces of Hnʾḫyr and said: may his people have long life'

ṣdq: the term *ṣdq* is frequently attested in Safaitic as a 'friend' or 'confidant' (e.g. KRS 1287; Al-Jallad 2015b: 346). Such a meaning is plausible here, in the light of epithets such as Abraham being called the 'friend of God'.[18] On the other hand, it is possible to take it as a nominalized adjective 'righteous one' or better yet, 'righteous worshipper/servant'.[19]

[14] On the meaning of *wrd*, see Al-Jallad & Jaworska, forthcoming.

[15] For example, SIJ 1008: *w dṯʾ w qyẓ w* s^2*ty h-rḥbt ᶜwd* 'while he spent the season of the later rains, the dry season, and the winter at this *raḥabah* again'; Al-Jallad (2015b: 305); Aramaic *ᶜōd.*

[16] The spelling *mt* can reflect a pronunciation *mawtay*; see Al-Jallad & al-Manaser 2016 on the orthography of diphthongs.

[17] This is my reading and interpretation. The *ed. princ.* reads this part as *wgd ʾṯr hn-ʾḫyr f qll ʾl-h h-ᶜ{m}r* 'He found the traces of the excellent (people) and he examined them. Verily he is the builder'; this is the translation currently on OCIANA but it will be corrected during phase 3.

[18] For example, Isaiah 41: 8; I thank Prof. H. Gzella for this suggestion.

[19] Note the phrase *ts*^{2}*wq l-kll ᶜ*s^2*r ṣdq* 'he longed for every righteous kinsman' (HCH 191). Consider also Aramaic *ṣdq* 'to be guiltless' and *ṣdqw* 'righteousness' (CAL).

Figure 5. *The damage to the glyphs encircled.*

gnn**:** the term is attested for the first time here, although other derivatives are known.[20] In the context of a prayer, it seems likely that the meaning of this word is 'to protect' or 'to conceal' rather than 'to drive or go insane'.[21] In terms of its morphological identity, it is probably an infinitive of command rather than an imperative where one would more often than not expect a pronominal object (Al-Jallad 2015b: 184).

{w} mn mt ls^1 *fṣy*[22]

The *ed. princ.* took the tenth letter from the end as a *g*, but there is damage in its centre and it appears to me that the damage covers a medial crossbar. Therefore, the glyph is more likely to represent a *w*. This reading is further supported by the syntactic context. Our interpretation up to this point would suggest that this letter marks the beginning of a new clause, which would suggest that, since this letter is damaged, the reading *{w}* is the safest option.

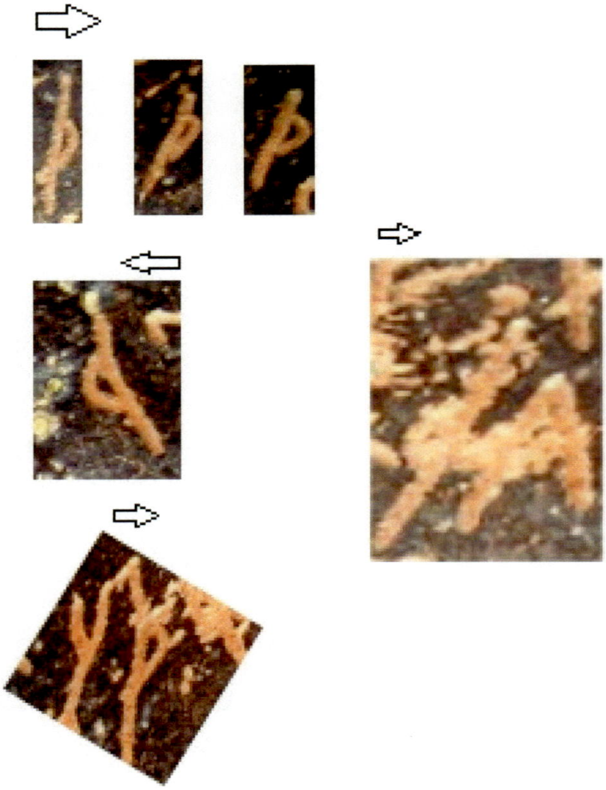

Figure 6. *A comparison of the forms of* d *in the inscription.*

[20] For example *ngn* 'to go mad (from grief)' (MAHB 2 and see Al-Jallad 2015b: 315); and *ˀtgnn*, a T2-stem, with the same meaning (BS 880). Both interpretations are my own. On the morphology of *ˀtgnn*, see the discussion of the verb in a forthcoming grammar and dictionary of Safaitic, Al-Jallad & Jaworska, forthcoming.

[21] CAr *janna-hu* 'it veiled, concealed, hid, or protected, him' (Lane, 462a).

[22] I am currently preparing an essay on the concept of fate in the Safaitic inscriptions, where this prayer and others like it will be discussed in their broader religious context. For now, only its linguistic features concern us.

The following *m n m* are clear but the *t* is rather damaged. Its arms are, nevertheless, visible from under the damage and the letter can hardly be anything else. The topic of the present paper is encountered in the following two letters. The *ed. princ.* reads the pair as *d s¹*. The loop of the alleged *d* is, I think, the result of damage. The negative of the photograph makes it clear that the apparent loop is of a different texture and patina to the shaft, and similar to the damage on the *s¹* (Figs 4 and 5).

Moreover, the apparent loop faces in the opposite direction to all the other examples of *d* in the inscription and is distinctly different in shape. The other examples of *d* have a large, open loop while this supposed *d* has a small half-circle, filled in. While it is true that letter shapes can experience variation even within a single inscription, the consistency in shape of the confirmed examples of *d* combined with the analysis of the damage to this area of the rock strongly support excluding the loop as part of the inscription and reading the glyph as *l* (Fig. 6).

This gives us the reading *ls¹* from these two glyphs, and the reading of the final word *fṣy* 'to deliver, deliverance' is clear (Al-Jallad 2015b: 314).

The spelling *ls¹* permits many possible vocalizations: it can reflect a form similar to Andalusi or Yemeni *las* or *lis* or may reflect the full form *laysa,* as internal diphthongs are not represented in Safaitic orthography.[23] What the Safaitic cannot represent is a tri-syllabic form *layVsa,* presumably the antecedent of Classical Arabic *laysa.* This ambiguity naturally obscures its syntax. With these facts in hand, let us return to the etymological discussion.

The source of *laysa* revisited

The Safaitic form *ls¹*, I believe, rules out any possible derivation from Aramaic. Safaitic retains the interdentals (Al-Jallad 2015b: 42) and, moreover, it does not seem that spirantization was a feature of the Aramaic dialect(s) with which Safaitic was in contact.[24]

At the beginning of this paper, I noted a few irregularities regarding the shape of *laysa* that place it in a category of its own: the /a/ vowel in the short vowel grade and the diphthong in the long vowel grade. Both of these features suggest that in Classical Arabic and in Quranic Arabic, *laysa* is a loan.

Proto-Form	Expected form	Attested form	Comparative evidence
*layisa	***lāsa*	*laysa*	Gəʿəz: *qoma* < **qawma* < **qawəma* (Huehnergard 1995: 178, n.78)
*layista	***lista*	*lasta*	Hebrew: *qámtā* (Suchard 2016)

Figure 7. *A table showing the collapse of triphthongs to produce* laysa.

The medial-weak verbs can be reconstructed with a consonantal medial radical for Proto-Arabic in the long vowel grade and behaved in all ways like strong verbs. The single exception is that this root class only had roots of the intransitive pattern in the suffix conjugation, that is CaCiCa and CaCuCa; thus, we would have forms like *qawuma 'he stood' and *śayima 'he put away' (Van Putten 2017: 69–70), a situation partially preserved in Safaitic (Al-Jallad 2015b: 119–120). Both Quranic Arabic and Classical Arabic collapsed the medial triphthong of such verbs according to the following rules:[25]

Long-vowel grade:	áGv > ā	:	*máwita > māta
Short-vowel grade:	aGí > i	:	*mawíttu > mittu
Short-vowel grade:	aGú > u	:	*qawúmtu > qumtu

Since medial weak verbs only belonged to CaCiCa and CaCuCa patterns, no a-theme vowels in the short-vowel grade occur. Thus, the form *laysa* cannot be native to either variety in which it occurs as it reflects a completely different line of development. It seems to stem from a language that, on the one hand like Gəʿəz, elided the vowel of the medial radical in the long-vowel grade but on the other, like Hebrew and Aramaic, had an a-vowel in the short-vowel grade (Fig. 7).

Since the above situation strongly indicates that we are dealing with a loan,[26] we now come to the more speculative part of our investigation: finding the source of *laysa*. If we wish to maintain a connection between *laysa* and the existential particle *ʾiṯ, then I think it is better to appeal to a loan from another Semitic language rather than an unattested dialect of Arabic. Here I will discuss

[23] This point is discussed in detail in Al-Jallad and al-Manaser (2016: 59–60), where in a bilingual inscription Safaitic *ġṯ* is rendered as Γαυτος <gautos> in Greek, clearly illustrating this orthographic practice.

[24] The same seems to be true of Quranic Arabic; I have made this point already in Al-Jallad 2017: 119–120, n. 65.

[25] These rules were first suggested by Bauer (1912: 111), and discussed again by Voigt (1988: 142–148), Huehnergard (1995: 176–178), Al-Jallad (2015b: 119), and Van Putten (2017: 70). 'G' stands for glide (= y/w).

[26] While negators are not easily borrowed, borrowing is attested in the world's languages, see e.g. Kossmann 2013: 336 and Matras 2009: 208–209; I thank Prof. M. Kossmann for these references.

both possibilities: either *laysa* is a loan and reanalysis of Assyrian *laššu/laišu* or it comes from another unattested or poorly attested Semitic language of Arabia.

***laššu* [lassu]:** if we argue for a Mesopotamian source, I believe it is best to see the indeclinable forms of *laysa* as original, as the particle is indeclinable in its source. The Safaitic form certainly permits such an interpretation. One would then argue on the basis of its semantics, perhaps in analogy with *kāna*, and the *u*-termination on the Assyrian form which is similar to the masculine plural of the perfect, that it was attracted to the suffix conjugation. Thus, the innovative quasi-verb *laysa-lastu* would have developed in a dialect that followed a different route in the collapse of its medial triphthongs, described above. This form then would have diffused to Quranic Arabic and ultimately Classical Arabic, while its source dialect would have become extinct. The context for borrowing between ancient forms of Arabic and Neo-Assyrian would probably have been in the early to mid-first millennium BC in Mesopotamia: people whom the Assyrians and Babylonians called Arabs settled along the upper and lower Euphrates throughout the first millennium BC and texts in the South Semitic script have been found in southern Mesopotamia.[27] Nevertheless, the most intense locus of interaction seems to have been Babylonia, where the negative existential was *yānu* (Woodington 1982: 194).

***laysa*:** the source of *laysa* may be sought in a more obvious place but one with much poorer linguistic documentation — North Arabia. In the middle of the first millennium BC, the oasis of Taymāʾ had its own script and language, conventionally called Taymanitic. While the textual witnesses to this language are sparse, Kootstra (2016: 104–107) has very skilfully argued from what little evidence we have, that Taymanitic should be excluded from the Arabic category. Instead, it shares some affinities with North-West Semitic and may reflect a southern peripheral North-West Semitic language. Only future discoveries can confirm this hypothesis, but as it stands, the exclusion from the Arabic category seems secure.

Unlike Arabic, Taymanitic does not merge *s^1 (Proto-Semitic [s]) and *s^3 (Proto-Semitic [ts]); instead, it merges *s^3[ts] and **ṯ* [ž] (Kootstra 2016: 75). While the phonetic realization of both of these phonemes is unclear, it is very likely they were realized as [s], based on the spelling of foreign names. So, if a negative existential construction consisting of *lā* and the existential particle *ʾiṯ, *yiṯ existed in Taymanitic, it would have been realized as [lāʾis] or [lāyis].[28] The phonological similarity it had to medial-weak suffix conjugated verbs could have attracted it to that morphological category, producing *layisa* and ultimately *laysa,* if the phonological developments discussed above occurred in Taymanitic.[29] This scenario would then posit that Proto-Arabic, or perhaps some varieties of an early Arabic dialect continuum, borrowed the construction from Taymanitic and from there it was either inherited or diffused to other varieties of Arabic, including Safaitic, Quranic, and Classical Arabic.

A final option, related in a way to the one discussed in the previous paragraph, is simply to argue that **lā-ʾiṯ* was a Proto-Arabic construction, and that the form *laysa* developed in an unattested variety of Arabic that merged *s^1 and **ṯ* to [s]. This dialect would have also collapsed medial diphthongs, as shown in Figure 7. This option is the least attractive as we have *no* evidence for a variety of Arabic that merged sibilants and interdentals in the pre-Islamic period and such a merger is extremely rare even in the modern dialects. Moreover, there is no trace of *yiṯ* or *ʾiṯ* in any form of Arabic; this is especially remarkable if we posit that the particle was productive at the Proto-Arabic stage.

Concluding remarks

Considering all three options, I believe we can make the following statements, ranging from most certain to speculative: 1) *laysa* is a loan in its Quranic and Classical Arabic context; 2) its attestation in Safaitic rules out an Aramaic source and suggests its origins to be much earlier than the Quranic linguistic milieu; 3) it is possible that *laysa* was loaned and eventually reanalysed as a verb from Assyrian, where a related form exists although the evidence for intense contact is weak, or from a North Arabian language like Taymanitic, where the sound correspondences work but for which we have no attestations of a negative existential construction.

[27] These sources are well known and discussed extensively in Ephʿal (1974; 1982: 20–54). On the South Semitic texts from Mesopotamia, see Sass (1991: 58–65). With regard to the Safaitic inscriptions, evidence for contact with Mesopotamian civilization is attested in the names of the zodiac constellations (Al-Jallad 2016: §5), which mostly reflect calques of the Babylonian names rather than Aramaic or Greek.

[28] The negative adverb *l* */lā/, however, is attested (Kootstra 2016: 96).

[29] Medial weak verbs have not yet been attested in Taymanitic, with the exception of Kootstra's interpretation of *ḥll* as a *polel* of *ḥwl* (Kootstra 2016: 94).

Acknowledgments

I thank Øyvind Bjøru, Benjamin Suchard, and Na'ama Pat-El for commenting on a draft of this paper on Academia.edu. All errors are my own.

Sigla

AAEK	Safaitic inscriptions in Al-Manaser 2008, see OCIANA.
ASWS	Safaitic inscriptions in Awad 1999, see OCIANA.
BS	Safaitic inscriptions from the Badia Epigraphic Survey and published in OCIANA.
CAL	Comprehensive Aramaic Lexicon (http://cal.huc.edu/).
HCH	Safaitic inscriptions in Harding 1953.
KRS	Inscriptions recorded by Geraldine King on the Basalt Desert Rescue Survey in north-eastern Jordan in 1989 and published in OCIANA.
Lane	Lane 1863–1893.
MAHB	Safaitic inscriptions published in Ababneh 2007, see OCIANA.
OCIANA	*Online Corpus of the Inscriptions of Ancient North Arabia* http://krc2.orient.ox.ac.uk/ociana/
SIJ	Safaitic inscriptions in Winnett 1957, see OCIANA.
WR.A	Safaitic inscriptions from the promontory at the confluence of Wādī Rushaydah and an unnamed wadi, recorded by the Safaitic Epigraphic Survey Programme (SESP) and published in OCIANA.

References

ᶜAbābneh M.I. 2007. Safaitische Inschriften aus el-Hseniyyat/jordanisches Badiyah. *Journal of Epigraphy and Rock Drawings* 1: 19–28.

Abbadi Ṣ. & Al-Manaser ᶜA. 2016. Remarks on the etymon *trḥ* in the Safaitic inscriptions. *Arabian Epigraphic Notes* 2: 45–54.

Awad ᶜA. 1999. Dirāsat nuqūsh safawiyyah min janūb wādī sārah al-bādiyah al-ᵓurdunniyyah al-shamāliyyah. MA thesis, Institute of Archaeology and Anthropology, Yarmouk University. [Unpublished].

Bauer H. 1912. Mitteilungen zur semitischen Grammatik. *Zeitschrift der Deutschen Morgenländischen Gesellschaft* 66: 103–114.

Bauer H. 1926. Einige Fälleabsichtlicher Umgestaltung von Wörten im Semitischen. *Islamica* 2: 5–10.

Blau J. 1998. Marginalia Semitica II. Pages 222–246 in J. Blau, *Topics in Hebrew and Semitic Linguistics*. Jerusalem: Magnes/Hebrew University.

Brockelmann C. 1908–1913. *Grundriss der vergleichenden Grammatik der semitischen Sprachen*. Berlin: Reuter & Reichard. [Reprint, Hildesheim: Olms, 1961.]

Clark V.A. 1979. A Study of New Safaitic Inscriptions from Jordan. PhD thesis, University of Melbourne. Ann Arbor, MI: University Microfilms International.

Diem W. 2014. *Negation in Arabic. A study in linguistic history*. Wiesbaden: Harrassowitz.

Eksell K. 2002. *Meaning in Ancient North Arabian carvings*. (Stockholm Oriental Studies, 17). Stockholm: Almqvist.

Eksell K. 2005. The verb *wgm* in Safaitic Inscriptions. Pages 163–171 in T. Bauer & U. Stehli-Werbeck (eds), *Alltagsleben und materielle Kultur in der arabischen Sprache und Literatur: Festschrift für Heinz Grotzfeld zum 70. Geburtstag*. Wiesbaden: Harrassowitz.

Ephᶜal I. 1974. 'Arabs' in Babylonia in the 8th Century B.C. *Journal of the American Oriental Society* 94: 108–115. Available at https://doi.org/10.2307/599734.

Ephᶜal I. 1982. *The Ancient Arabs: Nomads on the borders of the Fertile Crescent, 9th–5th centuries B.C.* Jerusalem: Magnes.

Gevirtz S. 1957. On the etymology of the Phoenician particle אש. *Journal of Near Eastern Studies* 16: 124–127.

Grande F. 2016. From word to construction: A syntactic etymology of the Qurᵓānic Arabic *lāta*. *Jerusalem Studies in Arabic and Islam* 43: 101–140.

Hämeen-Anttila J. 2000. *A sketch of Neo-Assyrian grammar*. (State Archives of Assyrian Studies, 13). Helsinki: Neo-Assyrian Text Corpus Project.

Harding G.L. 1953. The Cairn of Haniᵓ. *Annual of the Department of Antiquities of Jordan* 2: 8–56.

Hasselbach R. 2005. *Sargonic Akkadian: A historical and comparative study of the syllabic texts*. Wiesbaden: Harrassowitz.

Healey J. 2011. Syriac. Pages 637–652 in S. Weninger, G. Khan, M. Streck & J.C.E. Watson (eds), *The Semitic languages: An international handbook*. Boston/Berlin: De Gruyter.

Huehnergard J. 1995. Features of Central Semitic. Pages 55–203 in A. Gianto (ed.), *Biblical and oriental essays in memory of William L. Moran*. i. Rome: Pontificio Istituto Biblico.

Al-Jallad A. 2015a. What's a caron between friends? A review article of Wilmsen 2014, with special focus on the etymology of Modern Arabic ši. *Bibliotheca Orientalis* 72: 34–46.

Al-Jallad A. 2015b. *An outline of the grammar of the Safaitic inscriptions*. (Studies in Semitic Languages and Linguistics, 80). Leiden: Brill.

Al-Jallad A. 2016. An ancient Arabian zodiac. The constellations in the Safaitic inscriptions, Part II. *Arabian Archaeology and Epigraphy* 27: 84–106.

Al-Jallad A. 2017. Graeco-Arabica I: The southern Levant. Pages 99–186 in A. Al-Jallad (ed.), *Arabic in context: Celebrating 400 years of Arabic at Leiden University*. (Studies in Semitic Languages and Linguistics, 89). Leiden: Brill.

Al-Jallad A. & Jaworska K. (forthcoming). *A Dictionary and Grammar of Safaitic*. (2 volumes). Leiden: Brill.

Al-Jallad A. & Al-Manaser ʿA. 2016. New epigraphica from Jordan II: Three Safaitic-Greek partial bilingual inscriptions. *Arabian Epigraphic Notes* 2: 55–66.

Jeffery A. 1938. *The Foreign vocabulary of the Qurʾān*. Baroda: Oriental Institute.

Kootstra F. 2016. The language of the Taymanitic inscriptions and its classification. *Arabian Epigraphic Notes* 2: 67–140.

Kossmann M. 2013. *The Arabic influence on northern Berber*. Leiden: Brill.

Lane E.W. 1863–1893. *An Arabic-English lexicon, derived from the best and most copious Eastern sources*. London: Williams & Norgate.

Lipiński E. 2001. *Semitic languages: Outline of a comparative grammar*. Leuven/Sterling, VA: Peeters.

Măcelaru A. 2003. Proto-Semitic *YŠ: Problems and possible solutions. Pages 233–240 in M.L. Bender, D. Appleyard & G. Takács (eds), *Afrasian: Selected comparative-historical linguistic studies in memory of Igor M. Diakonoff*. Munich: Lincom Europa.

Al-Manaser ʿA.Y.Kh. 2008. *Ein Korpus neuer safaitischer Inschriften aus Jordanien*. (Semitica et Semitohamitica Berolinensia, 10). Aachen: Shaker.

Matras Y. 2009. *Language contact*. Cambridge: Cambridge University Press.

Milano L. & Westenholz A. 2015. *The Suilisu archive and other Sargonic texts in Akkadian*. (Cornell University Studies in Assyriology and Sumerology, 27). Bethesda, MD: CDL.

Murtonen A. 1989. *Hebrew in its West Semitic setting: A comparative survey of non-Masoretic Hebrew dialects and traditions* (3 volumes in 4 parts). (Studies in Semitic Languages and Linguistics, 13, 16). Leiden: Brill.

Pat-El N. 2016. Review of Wilmsen 2014. *Journal of Semitic Studies* 61: 292–295.

Sass B. 1991. *Studia Alphabetica: On the origin and early history of the Northwest Semitic, South Semitic and Greek Alphabets*. Freiburg, Switzerland: Universitätsverlag/Göttingen: Vandenhoeck & Ruprecht.

Soden W. von. 1959–1981. *Akkadisches Handwörterbuch*. Wiesbaden: Harrassowitz.

Souag L. 2016. Review of Diem 2014 and of Wilmsen 2014. *Linguistics* 54: 223–229.

Suchard B. 2016. The Hebrew verbal paradigm of hollow roots: A triconsonantal account. *Zeitschrift der Deutschen Morgenländischen Gesellschaft* 166: 317–322.

Testen D. 2000. Conjugating the 'prefixed stative' verbs of Akkadian. *Journal of Near Eastern Studies* 59: 81–92.

Van Putten M. 2017. The development of the triphthongs in Quranic and Classical Arabic. *Arabian Epigraphic Notes* 3: 47–74.

Voigt R.M. 1988. *Die infermen Verbal typen des Arabischen und das Biradikalismus-Problem*. Stuttgart: Steiner.

Wilmsen D. 2014. *Arabic indefinites, interrogatives, and negators: A linguistic history of Western Dialects*. (Oxford Studies in Diachronic and Historical Linguistics). Oxford/New York: Oxford University Press.

Wilmsen D. 2016. Another croft cycle in Arabic: The *laysa* negative existential cycle. *Folia Orientalia* 53: 327–367.

Winnett F.V. 1957. *Safaitic inscriptions from Jordan*. (Near and Middle East Series, 2). Toronto: University of Toronto Press.

Woodington N.R. 1982. A grammar of the Neo-Babylonian Letters of the Kuyunjik collection. PhD thesis, Yale University. [Unpublished.]

Author's address

Ahmad Al-Jallad, Centre for Linguistics and Leiden Institute for Area Studies, Postbus 9515, NL-2300 RA Leiden, 2313 NL Leiden, The Netherlands.
e-mail: a.m.al-jallad@hum.leidenuniv.nl

Papers read at the Special Session:

Ahmad Al-Jallad	*The Proto-South Semitic script: a reconstruction of its glyphs and phonemic repertoire*
Chiara della Puppa	*On the 'Safaitic square script': a reassessment of the evidence*
Ali Al-Manaser	*Between place and inscription: a new understanding of the Safaitic inscriptions*
Hani Hayajneh	*The identity of the Ancient North Arabian Madabite language based on new epigraphical evidence from Wādī al-Thamad — central Jordan: an appraisal*
Sulayman Al-Theeb	*The development and the evolution of the Ḥāʾil Thamudic inscriptions*
Jérôme Norris	*The Ancient North Arabian inscriptions from the Dūmat al-Jandal area (Saudi Arabia) and their archaeological significance*
Alessia Prioletta	*New research on the Thamudic graffiti from the region of Ḥimā (Najrān, Saudi Arabia)*
Christian J. Robin	*Who wrote the South Arabian and Thamudic inscriptions of Ḥimā (southern Saudi Arabia)?*
Fokelien Kootstra	*Scribal practices in contact: the case of Dadan*
John F. Healey	*'Literacy in literate societies': the scribe in Nabataean and other Aramaic contexts*
Peter Stein	*The role of Aramaic on the Arabian Peninsula in the second half of the first millennium BC*
Läila Nehmé	*The script of the Nabataeao-Arabic inscriptions from north-west and south Arabia: a re-examination based on new evidence*
Ahmad Al-Jallad & Fokelien Kootstra	*New horizons in digital epigraphy*